WORLD RELIGIONS

WORLD

Fortress Press

RELIGIONS

Our Quest for Meaning

David A. Rausch
Carl Hermann Voss

Minneapolis

WORLD RELIGIONS
Our Quest for Meaning

Cover design: Jim Gerhard
Illustrations: Lynne Stevenson Rausch

Library of Congress Cataloging-in-Publication Data
Rausch, David A.
    World religions: our quest for meaning / by David A. Rausch and Carl Hermann Voss.
    p.   cm.
    Bibliography: p.
    Includes index.
    ISBN 0-8006-2331-2
1. Religions.   I. Voss, Carl Hermann.   II. Title.
BL80.2.R35   1989
291—dc20   89-34198
                                                                    CIP

The paper used in this publication meets the minimum requirements of American National Standard for Information Sciences—Permanence of Paper for Printed Library Materials, ANSI Z329.48-1984.   ∞ ™

Manufactured in the U.S.A.   AF 1-2331
93   92   91   90   89   1   2   3   4   5   6   7   8   9   10

To Jim and Mary Jo Stevenson

To Christina Elisabeth Gierlotka Wynings
and Russell Park Wynings

CONTENTS

FOREWORD

World Religions: Our Quest for Meaning is fourth in this series of volumes on major religious faiths. The first volume, *Judaism—An Eternal Covenant* by Howard R. Greenstein, was followed by *A Catholic Vision* by Stephen Happel and David Tracy and then by *Protestantism—Its Modern Meaning* by David A. Rausch and Carl Hermann Voss.

World Religions begins with an introduction to the vast and amazing religious impulse in humankind, noting the global religious landscape and our approach to the study. A chapter on ancient traditions follows, which also discusses current tribal practices and shamanism. Subsequently, separate chapters delve into the fascinating worlds of Hinduism, Jainism, Buddhism, Confucianism, Taoism, Shinto, Judaism, Christianity, and Islam. Finally, the conclusion draws from our decades of experience in the history and culture of world religions, both in teaching the subject and in traveling the globe to experience the religious landscape of the world firsthand. We count it a privilege to have close friends who are adherents of many of the religious faiths related in this text.

While it is inevitable that, in a volume of this small size and large scope important doctrines and cultures be summarized, we have attempted to add significant theological and historical detail in places that may benefit the student as well as the layperson. Nevertheless, this is a survey and will not exhaust every facet of every religious tradition. We have explored, however, the basic belief structure of each of the world's major religious traditions, the historical circumstances that modified and adapted that tradition to its present status, and a perception of the personal practices of the adherents. Most importantly, we have sought to study world religions without prejudgment or bias, accepting them on their own terms in an effort to hear accurately what they are saying. Our desire to make reading this work an interesting and enjoyable as well as enlightening experience is, we hope, evident in the following pages.

Our detailed index will help locate specific topics, while our Suggested Reading section at the end of this volume will lead to more detailed studies and in-depth bibliographies. The reader may find additional material from the religious texts and documents that have served as the basis for our translations and quotations in this work by consulting the Suggested Reading section as well. The authors' biblical quotations are taken from the King James Version with modifications from the Greek and Hebrew by the authors. We are aware that centuries of scholars have preceded us in this endeavor of illuminating the religious experience of humankind. May your own particular faith experience be strengthened through this journey.

David A. Rausch   Carl Hermann Voss
Ashland, Ohio   *Jacksonville, Florida*

INTRODUCTION

Religion—the awe one feels in the perceived presence of a higher power, the communion with that which is greater than one's self, the concern for ultimate reality and destiny. Foremost among the beliefs, sentiments, and values of humankind, religion arouses intense feelings for that which is considered sacred, binding together members of a group and setting them apart from others. From monotheism (one god) to animism (spirits in all), from monism (reality is one) to magic (extraordinary powers), religion forms a way of life around doctrines and beliefs about the sacred. That way usually includes a set of complex rituals through which piety is expressed, a set of beliefs, and a code of ethics, all directed by a hierarchy of religious functionaries who set standards for the community.

Although religious literature and folklore abounds, the student of religion finds motifs and meanings common to most faiths. "There is only one religion," declared George Bernard Shaw, "though there are a hundred versions of it." These "versions" must be studied because the peoples of the world are so dominated by their particular religious traditions that they are sometimes willing to kill or, more often, be killed in defense of their religious beliefs.

Studying world religions and the human quest for meaning is among the most important of pursuits because religion has interacted with political, economic, and cultural factors to produce the social order in which we live. Religion continues to affect the most secularized and scientific of contemporary societies, so it is often difficult to determine where the religious aspect of an ideology ends and the secular begins. It was the pacifist Hindu, Mohandas Gandhi, who perceptively asserted: "Those who say that religion has nothing to do with politics, do not know what religion means."

Today, as we move toward the twenty-first century, grievous political conflicts trouble the earth, conflicts mostly rooted in and fueled by religious differences. No one can understand the human race without having encountered the faiths of humanity. Nevertheless, throughout history, religion has been able to bind diverse peoples together, uniting them in a spirit of love and loyalty. Cleansing ourselves of stereotypes and caricatures of other religions fosters a worldview that clears away Western biases that may hinder our own relationship with God. Ironically, a true understanding of the beliefs and practices of our religious neighbors broadens and deepens our own religious commitment.

THE GLOBAL RELIGIOUS LANDSCAPE

The major religions of the world originated in remarkably small areas, Judaism and Christianity in the area of modern-day Israel, Islam around Mecca in western Arabia, Hinduism in the Indus Valley of northwestern India, and Buddhism in the kingdom of Prince Siddharta in northeastern India. Judaism, Hinduism, Shinto, and the Chinese moral-philosophical systems are basically *ethnic religions,* that is, they share a set of beliefs and practices as members of a particular nation or civilization; tribal religions also fall into this category.

In contrast, Buddhism, Christianity, and Islam are *universalizing religions.* They aim at worldwide acceptance, above and beyond national or communal ethnic traditions. Actively evangelizing and proselytizing, the universal religious traditions have developed a message and creed for all humankind. Newcomers are accepted into a fellowship spread throughout the world by committing themselves to the tenets of the particular faith.

Hinduism and Buddhism are, however, highly localized. Over 650 million Hindus are confined largely to the peninsula of India, while 300 million Buddhists are found mainly in East Asia. Christianity's one and one-half billion adherents are located predominantly in Europe, the Near East, the Americas, and Australasia, but are now spreading throughout the Third World. Islam has diffused from its birthplace in western Arabia in the seventh century C.E. to the west through the northern half of Africa, and to the east through central Asia, India, and Indonesia. Over 800 million Muslims face Mecca five times daily. Each universal religion has at one time been part of an ethnic religion before reaching out to the world at large. Likewise, each universal religion has developed many subgroups that have adapted and modified the universalizing traditions to their own particular needs and culture.

While culture and environment have had an important influence on world religions, a common faith can unite peoples from radically different backgrounds, crossing vast barriers of culture, environment, geography, politics, and economics. The human landscape has been traversed by religious missionary fervor and modified by historical circumstance. At times religion has encouraged standardization and strongly influenced social institutions and law. The caste system in India is closely associated with religion, and marriage customs throughout the world are part of religious rituals. Religion dictates both yearly cycles and life cycles, and it has not only spread languages but has also kept them alive. Judaism's Hebrew, Christianity's *koine* Greek, and Islam's Arabic are actively studied in the modern world. Devout pilgrims return to the land of their religious origins, linking tradition with territorial concern.

APPROACHING OUR STUDY

Because religion may engender intense passions, the student of world religions may have difficulty in *hearing* what the adherents of another religious tradition have to say. A committed Christian, for example, may find it difficult to perceive the deepest convictions of a Buddhist and comprehend the beliefs and worldview of the Eastern mind. An agnostic may be just as subjective as the most committed adherent of any set of religious beliefs, encountering an obstacle in ascribing value to "religion" and, consequently, struggling to maintain objectivity and sensitivity. A Muslim may consider the eclectic nature of Hinduism so incomprehensible that he or she must conquer revulsion even to attempt a personal understanding of Indian traditions. In like manner, the imperative and impassioned claims of some traditions may appall others. One soon finds, however, that commitment to one's own religious tradition or philosophical belief does not preclude appreciation of other faiths. The more one listens, the more one learns; the more one

learns, the more one understands. Although one may never be totally objective in this learning process, one can be balanced, just,
and honest in approaching the religion of another.

It is also important not to try to fit another religion into one's own
particular system of faith. Other religions must be accepted on their
own terms and through their own explanations. They must be studied to the extent possible without bias or prejudgment. Thus each
religious tradition may portray itself as it sees itself, providing an
accurate portrayal of the belief structure and a basis for comparing
it with other traditions. Viewing a religion from its own perspective
not only captures the mystery and convictions of its believers; it
also helps us to analyze our own principles of faith and the quality of
our own persuasion—to appreciate the better *who we are.*

Studying religion from this perspective will broaden and en-
lighten. In the following pages we will discuss life and death, peace
and conflict, joy and suffering, forgiveness and harmony. The
world's living religions will be seen as growing organisms, dynamic
and vibrant. Rival organisms and philosophical systems will also be
investigated. We will find that each great religious tradition is mul-
tidimensional.

The first dimension is the *basic belief structure,* that is, its pre-
eminent concerns. What does it teach about itself? What did its
founder or early teachers say?

A second dimension is how *historical circumstance* has worked
to adapt or modify that religious tradition. Centuries of belief have
brought both change and innovation.

Third, we consider the *personal practices* of the adherents. How
do individual believers apply their religion in their everyday lives?
What is the reality of their experience? Although such dimensions
are difficult to investigate and evaluate totally and conclusively, the
following chapters will relate to these different expressions of the
religious phenomenon.

Through such study we may perceive our own religious tradition
through the eyes of another. A Christian Westerner, for example,
may be able to view the Western mode of burial from the perspective of a Hindu of India. To the Hindu, some Christian Westerners
may appear to deny the death of a human being, attempting to create the illusion of a living being in the casket, through cosmetics,

fine clothing, and embalming. In America, this almost living being "receives" his or her friends one last time in a flower-laden parlor, with soft music playing in the background. Sadness appears to be banished from the farewell ceremony as much as possible, and often a parklike cemetery becomes the "home" of the departed. A memorial stone marks the spot.

To the Hindu—whose funerary customs include the washing of the body by relatives, no embalming, wrapping the dead in a shroud, and carrying the body amid loud, expressive wailing to a common cremation ground—some Christian Westerners seem engaged in an attempt to spatialize the body that is surpassed in grandeur only by the ancient Egyptians. Their behavior is in sharp contrast to the Hindu practice, where no physical trace of the dead person is left behind.

Much wisdom may be learned from the ways in which other religious traditions deal with death. Psychologists know that a grieving process is extremely important to the emotional health of every human being who has suffered a great loss, and religious rituals incorporate such wisdom. A specified period of grieving, for example, is traditionally practiced in Judaism, the parent faith of Christianity.

Our study of world religions should provoke insight as well as knowledge, introspection as well as explication. We begin with ancient traditions, in which some facets of the religious psyche of humankind are manifestly evident, and aspects of which appear even in our modern world. As we embark on this journey of understanding and sensitivity, absorbing the human quest for meaning, perhaps the old saying should be kept in mind: "Religion has two purposes: to comfort the afflicted and to afflict the comfortable."

ANCIENT TRADITIONS

Across a Void of Mystery and Dread

Long before sagas of historic tribes were recorded, religions arose all over the world. Sages and poets, seers and soothsayers, healers and dispensers of magic, chieftains and kings sought answers to perplexing questions. They tried to solve the mysteries of life and death. The religious rites and beliefs they created reflected a desire for knowledge about their own origins and their destinies. Ancient peoples yearned for assurance that life had purpose and that death was not the end. As they confronted human existence they experienced awe, sometimes fear, often exultation.

Environment tended to dominate their religious beliefs. Physical surroundings often determined representations of gods and ideas of another world. In areas of seasonal or unpredictable precipitation, the rain god was commonly worshipped. Tribes dependent upon fishing often acknowledged a god of the sea. In deserts, the afterlife was thought a place of fountains and cool, sparkling streams, while tribes in the polar north viewed "heaven" as a place of warmth. Ancient peoples were like modern humans in that religion might dictate their mode of dress, eating habits, folklore, rituals, and seasonal cycles.

Ancient tribes found their physical surrounding to be, for the most part, puzzling and unpredictable, sometimes hostile and even destructive. Yet it might also be full of beauty and joy; it might bring a measure of comfort and, in certain seasons and places, an amazing abundance. Life could be cruel and hard, frequently brief; but above all else it was uncertain. Humans could not control the elements of sea and sky, forest and field. They might kill wild beasts, catch huge fish, vanquish old enemies, conquer a nearby tribe; but in the world about them and in the life they lived so precariously, disasters came swiftly and without warning. Forces and powers over which they had no sway triumphed and seemed always to be victorious.

THE SHAMAN

In the effort to be in harmony with nature and to control the environment, *shamanism* became one of the most universal of institutions. The shaman was a religious practitioner recognized by the tribe or community as having supernatural powers. He or she had the gift of ecstasy, appeared to have the ability to move out of the body and mediate with the world of spirits. Deriving power directly from the gods, the shaman discerned the will of the spirits and foretold the future. The shaman sometimes used magic, often went into trances or seizures, sometimes spoke in other tongues, and often dealt in the mysterious lore of the tribe. Conjuring spirits in and out of individuals, the shaman was both healer and exorcist. The shaman constantly interpreted the uncertain environment, giving some semblance of predictability and control, a path of action. Through myth and storytelling this ancient specialist was often a key influence in forming the community's worldview. From creation legends to an account of the tracking of a soul or a spirit, this charismatic individual was entertaining yet convincing, invoking both fear and emotional release.

In the study of religions, "myth" does not mean fiction or fabrication, but often has basis in history and fact. Historians, for example, have learned the value of folklore in their quest to separate legendary embroideries from authentic foundations and in their search for historical truth. No less applies to the world's great sagas and myths. A myth hearkens back to the origins of the religious tradition and past events that may be long forgotten. Myth gives rise to ritual and yet additional myths may evolve as ritual is performed. The myths of a group are often the fabric that ties together the political, social, religious, intellectual, and economic strands in a community's worldview, and myth in many cultures has mediated between the beliefs a group holds and the rituals it performs. The importance of storytelling in tribal societies and the impact of oral tradition on the life of the community cannot be underestimated. Conveying deep truth through such mechanisms as myth and legend, storytelling and tradition, religious practitioners through the ages have provided the overarching story as well as the significant detail of a community's reason for being and the mystery of existence. Through myth, the stories and legends that convey deep truth and knowledge, are fashioned the community's notions of nature, ultimate reality, society, and self, into an interconnected pattern of group life and individual purpose. Myth validates, preserves, and justifies tribal traditions and community values.

Throughout history the functions of the shaman have varied from one society to another, yet some characteristics appear consistently. Each tribe had its own means of finding young candidates, male or female, and each candidate underwent comprehensive initiatory rites and ordeals as well as training in the traditions. In many tribes the candidate experienced symbolic ritual death and resurrection, traveling, it seemed, to the abode of the gods.

In Siberia, whence came the word *shaman,* the initiatory rite included apparent transportation to the spirit world, symbolic dismembering of the candidate's body, and resurrection of a reconstituted body. Upon returning to life, the shaman was able to move at will between the physical realm and that of the spirit. Thus, through testing, divine ordeal, remaking by the gods, and vividly relating the whole episode to the tribe, the shaman took a place of spiritual leadership in the community.

Sometimes, instead of the shaman's traveling to the realm of the gods, the spirit came to the shaman and, through traditional rites, was believed to possess the initiate. In Japan, for example, after intense training in the art of trance and divination, shaman initiates were thought to have been possessed by one of the 800,000 *kami* spirits of the Shinto religion. Shamanism appears to have dominated the folk religion of the villages of Japan, and in contrast to

Siberia where the shamans were mainly male, Japanese shamans were female. Even in this century in the northeastern part of the island of Honshu, Japanese shamans continued an initiation rite for mostly blind young girls, giving a glimpse of religious traditions dating back millennia. After three to five years of training in communication techniques and shamanist traditions, the initiate, clothed in a white funerary robe and sitting face to face with her teacher, went through a symbolic death and resurrection, which culminated in possession by a spirit. Naming the spirit that possessed her, the initiate donned the Japanese wedding garment and was linked to the spirit from that time forward.

The more we learn of shamanism and its many facets, the more we perceive its influence on religious traditions and religious practitioners throughout history. Even in the major world religions today, some facets of shamanism appear to be present in segments of the population. Among Hindus in the Himalaya Mountains, for example, villagers seek out the local shaman to contact the spirit world and reverse their misfortunes. Among the peoples of Tibet, some local Buddhist monks dabble in a form of shamanism. Among the Chinese, Taoist priests sometimes go beyond their technical ritual function to embrace the domain of the shaman. Nevertheless, it is among the modern tribal societies with oral traditions that the ancient religious phenomena are most visible.

TRIBAL RELIGIONS

Before the advent of writing, groups of families or clans descended from a common ancestor flourished throughout the world. These *tribes*, composed of preliterate peoples, embraced religion as a way of life, believing that spirits were in all things and in control of every aspect of their being. While these tribal societies are sometimes called "primitive," this value-laden term was actually coined by a technological and highly organized society. Hunting, gathering, and fishing tribes have always required special skills to subsist in a hostile environment. Such intelligence, sensitivity to nature, and foresight needed to survive on marginal land have been lost in our scientifically oriented, automated world. Western technological societies have cultivated not only a different orientation but also a different set of values. Ironically and tragically, modernity's excessive interest in wealth and self, widespread pollution, and misuse of natural resources have shown the mindset of Westerners to be at times simple, rough, and "uncivilized," consonant with the common association with the word *primitive*. Because of this failure, the respect of tribal religion for nature and the centrality of conservation in the society of oral peoples have something to teach modern citizens in a highly technological community.

The American Indian, for example, had no concept of private ownership of land. No one could "own" that which the primary holy force held together. Nature was permeated with divinity, and a variety of spirits worked both good and evil, sustaining all things that had been created and protecting the interests of nature itself. Shamans worked particularly well in such an *animistic* culture (the belief that spirits are in all things), and harmony with nature and with the willful, human-like spirits was sought through traditional ceremonies. Some tribes believed that nature would cease to exist if they did not practice their religion.

The American Indian is thought to have crossed from Siberia to Alaska through a land bridge across the Bering Strait more than ten thousand years ago. The similarities between even the modern Native Americans and their Russian relatives is remarkable. For the American Indian, as with so many tribal societies around the world, the primary goal was to be in harmony with nature, and the native shaman functioned as mediator in this supernatural drama. White settlers called him a "medicine man," because they were struck with his function in healing. But his powers also included divination and prophetic interpretation. Many tribes taught that a boy entering maturity must seek the control of a guiding spirit, often in his *vision quest* ceremony. This rite of passage provided harmony in the present life, a harmony that was the seat of joy and happiness. A harmonious relationship with departed ancestors, reverence for the land, and traditional practice of religious ceremonies were instinctively engendered by a close-knit community. Disharmony with nature and the spirits led to disaster, and misfortune was often blamed on witchcraft. These attitudes of harmony are in distinct contrast to modern urban concepts of power through possessions and status, and a decimated Native American population currently struggles against total annihilation by a technological society with other values.

Important in the vision quest of some tribes and in the psyche of Native American religion today is the revelatory nature of dreams and visions. A child was sent to encounter such a vision by leaving the tribe for a period of days and seeking a guiding spirit through fasting and ritual. Throughout life, such visions were important on the eve of great decisions and great battles, and they contribute to the very personal character of the religion of the Native American. Although the ancient specialists in spirit manipulation were often called upon, each member of the tribe was expected to dance, sing, perform rituals, and through visions and dreams contact the spirit world.

Among the Australian aboriginal tribes, the concept of *dream-time* expands the Native American visions into a religious worldview. Aborigines believe the world always existed but had no shape. At the beginning of the dream-time, a time when humans could change into animals and animals into humans, creator beings gave shape to the land through their travels. Various animals represented the creator beings, whose travels and adventures constituted the lore of the tribe. The creator beings at will could turn into stone and thus became part and parcel of the landscape surrounding the tribe. A mountain, valley, or large rock would be viewed as the embodiment of a particular creator being, and that inanimate object would become the focus of the life force. Tribal religious ceremonies not only ensured unity with the life force by reenacting great deeds and complying with ancient laws; they also initiated the members of the tribe progressively into the dream-time of their eternal ancestors. As they aged, members of the tribe actually became more dreamlike and detached from the physical world. Tribal shamans led the ceremonies and dances so that the vaguely defined life force would endure in beauty, protection, and bounty. The shaman could tap into the power of the dream-time to heal an illness or to guide a deceased member of the tribe to join the creator beings. Burial rites were complex, and only the initiated members of the tribe could pass on the oral knowledge to the next generation.

In the last two centuries, the arrival of white explorers and settlers has changed the complexion of a dream-time-oriented Australia, so that only a few tribal groups remain on small parcels of tribal lands. Disease and disruption have taken their toll on these tribal societies of oral peoples, and one by one the ancient traditions are being lost.

Disease and breakdown in family values have also taken a heavy toll on the Inuit (the "real people"), whom Westerners refer to as Eskimos ("people over there"). These tribes, which stretched from Alaska across Canada to Greenland, viewed their whole world as being alive. Even sleep was "alive," although humans and animals were the only beings to have souls. Souls were miniature shadows or apparitions of the human or animal, and like breath they could be implanted into similar beings after death. Spirits abounded; but the Great Spirit controlled the fury, as well as the bounteous potential, of natural phenomena.

The belief in a harsh nether world corresponded to the severity of life for the Inuit, and the shaman once again mediated between the tribe and the forces of the spirit world. Because men and women could exist only by "consuming souls," that is by eating fish, caribou, etc., a respectful peace and placation with all life had constantly to be maintained. Culture was intrinsically linked with the environment, and the preservation of selfless group participation was the key to survival. So successful were the tribes of Inuit that they had a wide linear expansion from their roots in Siberia all the way east to Greenland—roving peoples in the midst of the rigors of the Arctic. The marginal existence of these fishing and hunting communities in delicate balance with nature was permanently disrupted by invading exploiters from industrialized nations. Modern societies progressively swallowed up these smaller tribal societies to such an extent that today it is increasingly difficult to understand the nature of original Inuit religion.

Traditional religion among African tribes is also difficult to recover because universal religions, such as Christianity in the south and Islam in the north, have permeated the continent. Nevertheless, ancient traditions and practices have intermingled with newly adopted major religions, adapting them to the African way of life. African tribes are deeply involved in religion. Traveling, eating, sleeping entail religious rites and consultation of the gods and lesser spirits. Creation stories abound, often involving a Creator Spirit, a supreme being who, once intimately involved in the affairs of the world, later withdrew from close personal activity in the world. Lesser gods, spirits, and ancestors are much more active in everyday life in the polytheistic orientation of African tribal society. When evil befalls, it is either because one has offended the gods or because one has been "bewitched." Yet many Africans dispute the Western use of such terms as "animism," "paganism," and "ancestor worship" to define tribal religion. Most agree with the Yoruba tribal saying from southwestern Nigeria: "A foreigner has eyes but cannot see."

Ancestors, for example, are not worshipped but rather approached as mediums to reach the spirit world. They are often responsible for enforcing social and moral codes among their relatives, more so than the spirits that enliven the African world. Most tribes have a concept of "recent dead" and "dead dead" among ancestors, which enables the shaman, or even the head of the household, to appeal to the departed ancestor on behalf of the family. In contrast to the other tribal shamans we have mentioned, African shamans today mainly function as priests and prophets, rarely traveling out of their own bodies. Yet they are intensely interested in the spirit world, steeped in tribal lore and spiritual experience that can transcend "magical" devices, perform the needed rituals, speak to the spirit world, and hear the commands of the gods. While witches are usually female and viewed as defiantly wicked, "witch-doctors" are male "doctors to the bewitched," good in both intention and demeanor, striving to provide the best for individual tribal members. Thus, the witch-doctor functions as a benevolent shaman even in modern African society.

It is perhaps the eclectic African tribal religious system that points most directly to the ancient religious practices of the Near Eastern civilizations. While appreciating the modern tribal religions and their respect for nature and ecological balance, we must also note that intense fear and unwarranted superstition could infect such practitioners to the detriment of their societies. Initiations could be brutal, sacrifices could involve the death of human beings, shamans and rulers could exert malevolent power and cruel authority, perceived vindictive forces could create a society of emotional and psychological cripples, and unreasonable taboos could create misery and despair in the midst of natural beauty. However, *every* world religion has had to cope with such aberrations.

THE FERTILE CRESCENT

Foremost among the regions from which the earliest religions appear to have emerged was the fertile crescent, the semicircular area of arable soil that stretches northwest from the Persian Gulf, around the valley of the Tigris and Euphrates rivers, then southwest down along the Levant into Syria, Lebanon, Jordan, Israel, and the Nile Valley of Egypt. It is here that nomadic tribes with oral traditions give way to literate, urban civilizations with highly structured religious systems and temple complexes.

An agricultural revolution between 9000 and 8000 B.C.E. had made this possible. Tribes began to cultivate crops such as wheat, barley, and other cereals, and to domesticate animals. They began to settle in one place, forming the bottom layers of the archeologist's mounds (or "tels") of the Ancient Near East. Tel-es-Sultan, better known as Jericho, reveals the earliest known city in the world, a town that was settled about 7500 B.C.E. By 6800 B.C.E. Jericho had a population of more than 2000, and the urban area covered nearly ten acres. The early inhabitants of Jericho buried their dead under the floors of their homes. The skulls of the dead, however, were removed from the bodies, covered with plaster, and probably were kept above ground. Canaanite religion would develop here, vying for the loyalties of the ancient Hebrews for centuries after Joshua crossed the Jordan and conquered Jericho.

In Mesopotamia, between the Tigris and Euphrates rivers, cultures arose among settlements that led to the first great civilization on earth. The Hassuna culture (c. 5000-4700 B.C.E.), west of the Tigris near Nimrud, developed oriental homes with rooms grouped around a central courtyard, a style still found in Iraq. The doors in these homes pivoted on stone sockets and hinges. A fertility cult surrounding a Mother Goddess is clearly evident, and these peoples buried infants in jars used for foundation sacrifices for buildings. Vessels containing food and water seem to have been buried with the dead for the afterlife. Both the Samarra culture (c. 4700-4500 B.C.E.), north of Eshunna on the Tigris, and the Halaf culture

(c. 4500-4000 B.C.E.), northeast of Nineveh, demonstrate the wide influence of a fertility cult with a dominant Mother Goddess represented by clay statuettes of pregnant, seated women. Although other statuettes exist, the Mother Goddess figure is the most common, symbolizing the fertility of the earth and the progressive religious worship of the goddess throughout the Ancient Near East. During the Halaf period, wheeled vehicles became commonplace, and the towns had cobbled streets.

These cultures to the north were finally supplanted by the Ubaid culture (4300-3500 B.C.E.) in the south. Their elaborate temples developed into the religious specialization of the first civilization, i.e., Sumerian civilization during the Uruk period (c. 3500-3100 B.C.E.). The Uruk period is named after the city in which the attributes of the first civilization on earth were found. Genesis 10:10 refers to the city of Uruk as *Erech*, and today it is Warka in Iraq.

To historians and archeologists, writing constitutes the advancement that combines with cities, government, mathematics, law, art, metallurgy, religion, specialization of tasks, and economic advancement in trade to form a full-fledged civilization. An oral culture may contain some of these same elements but lacks a written language. In the area of Sumer in southern Mesopotamia between the Tigris and Euphrates rivers and near the Persian Gulf, the first human civilization was born. The Sumerian language was written in a cuneiform (wedge-shaped) script. Characters representing syllables were incised on clay tablets with a stylus. Although it died out as a spoken language after 1800 B.C.E., giving way to Akkadian (the main cuneiform language of the world of the Bible), Sumerian remained the classical language of the Ancient Near East well into the first century of the Christian Era. Sumerian civilization predated even that of Egypt, and the Sumerians built sophisticated cities at a time when the Egyptians were still fishermen living in huts.

Religion was central to Sumerian civilization. Houses within city limits were clustered about a towering temple complex. These immense man-made mountains, known as *ziggurats*, contained a sanctuary, workshops, storehouses, and rooms for the scribes. The earliest ziggurat found at Uruk was forty feet high and covered an acre of land. Ascending stairs and ramps led the worshippers around many corners and up the four or five stories, until they arrived at the white, glistening temple shrine. There sacrifices were offered before the statue of the local god. In Sumerian religion, the god was landlord of the city-state as well as "owner" of the ziggurat and all agricultural fields. Temple priests became quite powerful, and at least 25 percent of the harvest was stored in the temple, a sacrifice to the god. In return, the god pleaded the cause of the people to the other deities.

The Sumerian pantheon was complex and far-reaching. The god of heaven, Anu, was the highest of the gods, dominating the visible universe. The region between heaven and earth was the domain of Enlil, the god of the wind and storm. Enki was the god of the earth and sea, but Inanna was portrayed as Mother Earth in a fertility cult that reached back into the precivilization period. She became the morning star, Venus, the goddess of love. The sun god was Utu, while the god of the moon was Nannar. Many other gods represented other aspects of the natural forces of the universe, and myths abound linking them in relationship and parentage. Below the gods were numerous good and evil demons, who could wreak havoc in a Sumerian's life. Sumerian religion developed a sacred calendar of feasts and festivals, and prayer was always linked with ritual.

Fertility was very important, and consorts to the gods and goddesses would perform sexual acts in "sacred marriage." In hope of better harvests, temple prostitutes of both sexes provided fertility action for worshippers, as a reminder and model to the gods and goddesses. This fertility cult and temple complex infiltrated every aspect of Sumerian society. Choirs provided an appropriate atmosphere; sorcerers and magicians provided the special effects. Sacrifice was a central part of the ceremonies, and included animals and vegetables as well as gifts of jewels, perfume, and clothing. Ziggurats became larger and more elaborate as the *ensi* and his family administered the temple estates for the city deity. Soon most of the land in Mesopotamia's city-states was held by the temples, and temple serfs and sharecroppers were told that they were "fortunate" to live their lives in service to the gods. Even craftsmen had to finish the god's "tasks" before doing their own work. This virtual religious enslavement was much like the medieval Christian manor. And, like the medieval Christian monasteries that were to arise four thousand years later, the temples of Sumer were centers of education, training young people to be scribes. The sole life-purpose of men and woman in Sumer was to serve the gods as best they could.

The historical sources of Mesopotamia are in agreement that a natural catastrophe occurred that threatened the very existence of life between the two great rivers. This flood came about, the traditions hold, because the gods were displeased with the actions of humankind, yet all sources maintain that a worthy remnant was spared. In their earliest forms, these traditions mention the king of Shuruppak, who used a boat to ride out the flood. In one ancient Sumerian fragment, the counterpart to the biblical Noah is Ziusudra, a god-fearing and pious ruler who was commanded to build a giant boat to save himself. Although fragmented throughout, some of the lines of the tablet read:

> All the windstorms, exceedingly powerful, attacked as one,
> At the same time, the flood sweeps over the cult centers.
> After, for seven days and seven nights,
> The flood had swept over the land,
> And the huge boat had been tossed about by the windstorms
> on the great waters,
> Utu [the sun god] came forth, who sheds light on heaven and
> earth,
> Ziusudra opened a window on the huge boat,
> The hero Utu brought his rays into the giant boat.
> Ziusudra, the king,
> Prostrated himself before Utu,
> The king kills an ox, slaughters a sheep.

Later, Ziusudra prostrated himself before the gods Anu and Enlil, and he was given "life like a god . . . breath eternal like a god they bring down for him." Ziusudra thus moved into the paradise reserved only for the immortal gods. The text relates: "Then, Ziusudra the king, the preserver of the name of vegetation and of the seed of mankind, in the land of crossing, the land of Dilmun, the place where the sun rises, they caused to dwell."

The Sumerian King List states that kingship was "lowered from heaven" to Eridu, one of five cities mentioned as existing before the flood, passing on from that city-state to the others. After the flood, kingship was "lowered from heaven" once again. This time divine rule passed to the cities of Kish in the north and Erech (Uruk) in the south. Such power from the gods led both to benevolent kings and arrogant tyrants, depending on the moral fiber of the ruler of the city-state. Priestly governors gave way to kings by divine right, with a cadre of priests. Urukagina, the king of Lagash in the third millennium B.C.E., claimed to have protected "the mother that is in distress" and made sure "the mighty man shall not oppress the naked and the widow." He also limited the power of the priests to "pick all the fruit" in the orchard and prevented the gentry from "taking away fish in the poor man's fishpond." Others, such as the legendary Gilgamesh, king of Erech (Uruk) and a Sumerian counterpart to Hercules, were selfish and arrogant toward their people, greedily fulfilling every base desire at the expense of the populace.

That the Sumerians believed the gods were interested in justice is amply revealed in the greatest epic poem from Mesopotamia, *The Epic of Gilgamesh*. Praising the magnificent walls, fine brickwork, pure sanctuary, and efficient city planning of Erech, the poem contrasts the tyrant Gilgamesh's sensual injustices. The people of the city cried out to the gods to rescue them, and the gods fashioned a creature from clay, Enkidu, a bull from the waist down and a human from the waist up. After a stalemate in battle, Gilgamesh and Enkidu join together to fight others in mighty missions. The death of Enkidu, however, sets Gilgamesh on the quest for immortality. In this epic, a divine barmaid tries to talk Gilgamesh out of his quest to find Ziusudra (here called Utnapishtim), the legendary Noah of the Sumerians who had obtained eternal life. Her advice reflects a theme in Sumerian religion, that the gods prevent humans from obtaining immortality and that one should accept and enjoy life on earth while it is at hand. She advises:

> Gilgamesh, whither runnest thou?
> The life which thou seekest thou wilt not find.
> When the gods created mankind,
> They allotted death to mankind;
> Life they retained in their own keeping.
> O Gilgamesh, let thy belly be full,

Day and night be thou merry!
Make every day one of rejoicing,
Day and night, dance and play!
Let thy clothes be clean,
Thy head washed
And thy self bathed in water.
Cherish the little one holding thy hand
Let thy wife rejoice in thy bosom.
This is the lot of humans.

Gilgamesh is thwarted in his endeavor, becoming an example for the Mesopotamians. To the Sumerians, the gods had instituted laws that dictated existence and ensured order. Men and women lived to execute the divine commands, ensuring the seasons and the fertility of their world. Sumerian religion put great emphasis on structured worship on earth but, unlike Egypt, little importance was attached to the tomb. The underworld was a realm of shadows, terrible judges, and sadness. It was "the land of no return."

As Semites migrated into Mesopotamia between 3000 and 2500 B.C.E., they adopted and adapted their pantheon of gods and goddesses to the religion of the Sumerians. Under Sargon of Akkad (to the north of Sumer), the Semites came to power for the first time around 2300 B.C.E. Sargon forged the first great Mesopotamian empire out of the fiercely independent and squabbling city-states. Uniting Mesopotamia under his sole rule, he pushed deep into Anatolia in the west and conquered Elam in the east. A brilliant political strategist, he assured his kingship over the key city-states of Ur and Uruk by appointing his daughter, Enheduanna, as high priestess of the moon-god Nannar at Ur and of the sky-god Anu at Uruk. For centuries rulers would use this religious ploy to consolidate their power.

While the Sumerians would rise to dominance once again in the Third Dynasty of Ur (c. 2100-2000 B.C.E.), the "Golden Age of Sumerian Civilization," the destiny of Mesopotamia was to be in the hands of the Semites. In fact, the Akkadian language that became the *lingua franca* of the Ancient Near East is alternatively known as Babylonian or Assyrian, spoken by both groups. The Semites introduced a world perspective of conquest, the idea that the conqueror could become "king of the four quarters [of the world]." While incorporating the culture, gods, and myths of the Sumerians, the Semites added their own innovations, including a concept of land tenure. Instead of the city-state's lands belonging to a god, the Semites believed that land could be owned by the clan, by a king, or by a private citizen. Under the Semites, Babylon would remain one of the most famous cities in Mesopotamia for nearly 2000 years.

It was the renowned King Hammurabi (reigned 1792-1750 B.C.E.) whose military and political activities converted the city-state of Babylon, a flourishing urban complex, into a considerable empire. In Babylonian society, the king mediated between the gods and the people. The gods regulated the affairs of state through the king, and his word was law. By the time of Hammurabi, the Semitic storm-god Marduk, whose symbol was the thunderbolt, had become the undisputed master of heaven and earth to the Babylonians. Although the old Sumerian pantheon was allowed to exist, Marduk became the international supreme being as the Babylonian empire expanded. With one imperial king and one imperial god that spoke through that king, the Babylonian monarch was undisputed ruler. All peoples and nations were to serve and obey him.

This fusion of religion and state is clearly evident in Hammurabi's famous Code of Laws. Following the Sumerian custom of a prologue and epilogue, the Semitic king declared before elaborating the laws in his code:

> When lofty Anu, king of Anunnaki [divine beings in the service
> of Anu]
> And Enlil, lord of heaven and earth,
> The determiner of the destinies of the land,
> Determined for Marduk, the first-born of Enki,
> Dominion over all mankind . . .
> Then did Anu and Enlil name me,
> Hammurabi, the devout, god-fearing prince,
> To make justice rule in the land,
> To destroy the wicked and unjust,
> That the strong might not oppress the weak;
> To rise like Shamash [sun-god] over the Mesopotamian people
> And to light up the land,
> To promote the well-being of the people.

Hammurabi's epilogue tells of the peaceful empire he had fashioned, underscoring once again that "the great gods called me." "I took to my bosom the peoples of Sumer and Akkad," he related later, insisting that under his leadership "the strong might not oppress the weak" and "justice might be done to the orphan and the widow."

The second millennium before the Common Era was a period of rampant superstition, both in organized urban religion and on the family level. While the Sumerian pantheon of gods was accepted with some name changes and some additions, the national gods were not as easily transferred. Babylonians exalting Marduk as creator and orderer of the universe were quite a contrast to the Assyrians, who exalted Assur, a deity as warlike, cruel, and savage as the fierce people who worshipped him at Nineveh. The Assyrian ruler was actually viewed as the high priest of the god Assur, performing sacrifices and newly crowned each year while the Assyrians cried, "Assur is king!" Certainly, conquest only could determine who was more powerful. Nevertheless, other conquering peoples, such as the Hittites and Hurrians, who appear to have been more eclectic and ameliorating in their adoption and adaptation of Mesopotamian religion, helped to curb the narrow, vindictive national Semitic gods. Hittites and Hurrians allowed the practice of numerous religious systems in their federalistic empires.

In the complex religious system of the Mesopotamian peoples were also a multitude of lesser deities and demons. Over the centuries a large cadre of priests and priestesses were employed both to exorcise the deities' spell and foretell their next devilish attack. Idols flourished, often carved from a piece of wood and ornamented with metals and precious stones. For the Babylonians, there was a definite point in the manufacture of the idol at which the deity indwelt the idol. A ritual known as "opening the mouth" facilitated this event. In one rite to provide an idol for a temple, two pots of holy water were provided in the idol maker's shop, and a preliminary ritual occurred in which the mouth of the idol was "washed." Incantations were recited, informing the idol that "from this time forth you shall go before your father." The idol was led by torchlight to the river bank at night and seated on a reed mat, facing east.

More offerings to the god, incantations, and washings were conducted. Turning the idol to the west, the ritual was repeated. In the morning, a ram was sacrificed, the priest declaring: "Holy image that is perfected by a great ritual." Touching the eyes of the idol with a twig of the magical tamarisk, the eyes of the god were "opened" and the god was led to the temple. With more sacrifices and incantations, the god was placed on a throne, and insignias of divinity were placed on the deity that night. Now the god and the priests had power over a segment of the populace.

For much of the time, the men and women of Mesopotamia appear to be strangers to laughter, never really learning to enjoy life. Their gods were relentless in their demands, and demons and demagogues were swift to plague them throughout their life on earth. While Mesopotamian religion had little concept of a day of judgment after death, neither did it have much hope of paradise. King and peasant alike dropped through a spiritual trapdoor to the underworld, a well-guarded "land of no return," lacking food and drink (except for funerary offerings from one's friends and relatives). This airless, dark, and dusty region was a fearful and pitiable existence, quite a contrast with the religious worldview of the Egyptians. For to the common peoples of Mesopotamia, death played the final cruel joke on them—a cruelty that surpassed their marginal life on earth.

THE ANCIENT EGYPTIANS

The ancient Egyptians had an enduring civilization. They called their land *Kemet* ("the black land"), because of the dark silt that was deposited on the soil by the annual flooding of the Nile River. The Nile rose in summer, cresting in September or October. The silt it deposited was rich and fertile, and planting could begin soon after the Nile receded. Crops would be harvested in April or May. The failure of the Nile to flood would produce instant famine, because the delta area ("Lower Egypt," north of Memphis) received only ten inches and Upper Egypt (south of Memphis) less than a fifth of an inch of rain each year. Since the Nile is the only river to flow north across the Sahara Desert, it indeed provided life-giving substance on its banks.

17

The Red Land, the instant desert that soon surrounded the narrow Black Land, served as a protective barrier from intruding peoples and cultures. Little wonder that *ma'at*, the endurance of the accepted order in religion, society, and government, was a central Egyptian concept. The ancient Egyptians strove to *perpetuate* their world, and for 3000 years maintained the *status quo.*

The first farming culture uncovered in Egypt dates from c. 4300-4000 B.C.E. These Badarians are best known for their cemeteries, and burial rites became a standard feature of Egyptian culture. The Badarians buried their dead, knees flexed, in roughly circular graves about three feet deep and four feet across. The shallow grave in dry sand quickly dehydrated the corpse, thus preserving it. The body was wrapped in skins, matting, or wickerwork, and was buried with a number of possessions including pots of food and—with the men—ivory statues of women. Animals were buried in the same cemeteries with humans. The Badarians appear to have believed that life after death was little different from life on earth. In the subsequent Naqada culture (c. 4000-3100 B.C.E.), there seems to have been some contact with ancient Mesopotamian civilization. For example, writing appears full-blown, with no decipherable antecedents, near the end of the fourth millennium B.C.E. It arrives in time to document the consolidation of Upper and Lower Egypt around 3100 B.C.E.

During the Archaic Period (c. 3100-2700 B.C.E.) of the early dynasties, Egyptian kings were believed to be the incarnation of the falcon god, Horus. As the god of the sky, Horus commanded a pantheon of gods and goddesses, until he was joined by the sun-god Re in the second dynasty (c. 2890 B.C.E.). The god Set joined them later in association with the king, neither god diminishing the power of Horus in the eyes of the Egyptians. Thus began two facets of ancient Egyptian religion that are evident over three millennia: (1) religious syncretism, which seems puzzling to the Westerner in light of the numerous religious contradictions, but which posed little problem for the Egyptian, and (2) the king himself as "god."

God-kings of a united Egypt divided the land into districts called *nomes.* Upper Egypt was divided into twenty-two districts, Lower Egypt into twenty. Each nome had a principal town and a local deity worshipped in a main temple complex. Religion and administration were intricately woven together, as society was divided into the king, the nobles, and the lower classes. Royal tombs progressed from large pits with several rooms covered with rubble, to complex rectangular mastabas with stairways and large stone slabs. One king, Wadji (Djet), had 355 servants buried with him, a practice uncommon in later Egyptian history but paralleled in the great "death-pits" of Sumerian civilization. The Egyptians' love of life led to their determination that there was an even better life beyond the grave. They were intent on providing for greater pleasure and satisfaction in their future existence.

During the Old Kingdom (c. 2700-2200 B.C.E.) Egypt became a major world civilization. This "Pyramid Age" was perhaps rivalled only by Sargon's kingdom in Mesopotamia, and at that time the concept of the god-king developed fully. The *pharaoh* was a perfect god, who administered the world on his *own* behalf, rather than on the behalf of his people or even the gods. The son of Re, he was also considered the incarnation of Horus and, because of *ma'at*, the pharaoh could not be evil nor could he err. In Mesopotamia, the king was the god's representative, and intense dialogue occurred between the king and his god, the people and their gods. In ancient Egypt, the pharaoh *was* god, and therefore it was no longer necessary to seek the will of heaven but only to obey the pharaoh's every command. His word was law, and the magnificent pyramids of this age, staircases to heaven for the king's spirit, are ample reminders of the infinite might and splendor of the god-king. As a god, the Egyptian king prepared for an afterlife different from his subjects. He would join the other gods who accompanied the sun-god Re in his daily boat journey across the sky.

While a vast religious organization with priests and bureaucrats functioned at the base of the Egyptian pyramid-tower, the priesthood in the Old Kingdom did not have the power of the priesthood in Mesopotamia. The physical edifices that were built, however, soon rivalled the marvelous ziggurats of Sumer. Djoser's Step Pyramid, the oldest stone monument in the world (ziggurats were constructed of mud-brick), was built by the master-builder, Imhotep, and its rectangular enclosure was laid out like a small city. A mile in perimeter, the complex included shrines, altars, storehouses, and courtyards, in addition to the commanding pyramid. Large building stones were cut with great precision, cased in fine white limestone. Djoser was the second king in the third dynasty (c. 2686-2613 B.C.E.), and it appears that mummification was established around the time of his reign.

During the Old Kingdom, pharaoh Khufu ("Cheops" in Greek) built the renowned Great Pyramid at Giza. He was the second god-king of the fourth dynasty (c. 2613-2494 B.C.E.) and ruled at a time when Egypt was rich, stable, and secure. Caravans brought gold from Nubia, copper and turquoise from the Sinai, and wood from Lebanon's great cedars. All life centered around the pharaoh, and the Great Pyramid has been called the single most amazing work of ancient Egypt. Built seventy years after Djoser's Step Pyramid, it represents a spectacular advance in size and use of materials. The Great Pyramid covers thirteen acres and is 481 feet tall. From nearby quarries, 2,250,000 limestone blocks averaging two and one-half tons apiece (some core blocks weighed 200 tons!) were cut, floated close to the site by barges during the Nile floods, and maneuvered into place by the use of levers, ropes, and sheer human effort alone. The Nile River flows north into the Mediterranean, carrying barges and boats with its current. The winds often blow south, moving sailing vessels with ease. Such excellent navigation and travel throughout the Black Land not only facilitated trade and communication, but contributed significantly to such feats of construction as the pyramids. Some of the granite facing blocks, weighing more than thirty tons, were brought north from Aswan by boat, 500 miles.

The gods of the Egyptians represented the strong forces that controlled their world. They included cosmic forces such as the sun, wind, storm, harvest, and the Nile. Numerous animal cults also arose, including the falcon, lion, beetle, crocodile, and even domestic animals, such as the cow, that were encouraged to proliferate. The Egyptians looked upon the animal as possessing remarkable power and conveying wisdom, fertility, and strength to humans. Temples were built to these gods, and many of the principal deities were worshipped in various towns. The gods of the animal cults had human bodies with animal heads, allowing the priest to don an animal mask to perform daily rituals. Re of Heliopolis, the sun-god who had as his symbols the pyramid and the winged sun disk, was particularly popular during the Old Kingdom with its capital at Memphis. Local loyalty to a particular god seems to have rarely worked divisiveness among the Egyptians, and in their religious syncretism and tolerance favorite personal gods could be easily overshadowed by another god who was thought to be more effective at a certain occasion or place. Religion was a powerful force in Egyptian society, both for political stability and personal satisfaction, and a large number of amulets and charms were coveted among the populace.

The basis for mummification and the pharaoh's preparation to travel with Re on his daily boat journey was in the Osiris cult and was conveyed by the many myths that surrounded this god of the Nile. According to one version, Osiris was a kind ruler of the Nile Delta area. He was murdered by his jealous brother, Set, by being tricked into entering a box that was thrown into the Nile. Osiris' body was washed up on shore near Byblos and was recovered by his wife, Isis. However, Set stole the body and cut it up into pieces, scattering parts throughout Egypt. Isis patiently collected every part of Osiris' dismembered body and, with the help of Thoth, the ibis-headed god of writing and wisdom, completely bandaged the body back together (hence, mummification). Isis then conceived a child, Horus, fathered by the resurrected Osiris; and Horus avenged his father's death, while Osiris became ruler of the afterworld and a symbol of resurrection. The many variations of this theme that permeates Egyptian history were all acceptable to the Egyptians in their all-encompassing religious syncretism.

At first, mummification was reserved only for the pharaoh as god-king. Later it would pass on to the nobles and, in less elaborate forms, to the populace at large. The ancient Egyptians believed that a human being was born with an invisible, shadowy twin, the *Ka*, that lived with the person throughout life. As long as one was linked to one's *Ka*, one was alive. When the *Ka* was lost, death occurred. The *Ka* itself, however, never died, but waited for the deceased in the afterworld, where the two would live forever. Humans were also believed to possess a *Ba*, a soul, that left the body after death and returned to it after the funeral. It was for the *Ba* that mummification was necessary, so that the soul could recognize the body that it used as a base of operations and cosmic travel. The *Ba* would return to the mummy at night. Again, religious syncretism permeated Egyptian belief, as they believed that the deceased went to a blessed afterworld in a distant place and also believed that the deceased lived in the tomb. Such apparent contradiction did not disturb the ancient Egyptians. They simply provided for both!

Religious ceremony permeated the preparation of the corpse, and incantations and rites were performed at every stage. In the embalmer's shop, the contents of the abdomen were removed through an incision on the left side. Toward the end of the Old Kingdom, jars for this viscera were provided and stored with the corpse. The liver, the stomach, the lungs, and the intestines were stored in separate jars, each protected by a different god whose head adorned the lid. The heart, which the Egyptians believed to be weighed on the Great Scales and balanced against the feather of righteous truth in the presence of Osiris, remained in the body. The brain was removed through the nostrils with long instruments that resembled metal hooks.

Preservation of the body itself was much like that of drying meat. Natron, a hydrated sodium carbonate containing salt, was wrapped in linen and placed in the corpse. Packed in this salt, the body slowly dried for over a month, depending on the wealth and status of the deceased. Once dried, the body was given a sponge bath, and the skin was embalmed with oils and resins. Then, linen soaked in the same coniferous resins was stuffed into the empty abdomen, and the body was wrapped. The most expensive embalming process, including rituals, took seventy days. By 1600 B.C.E., the embalmers began inserting pads in the muscles and cheeks to make the corpse look more lifelike. While the corpse was being carefully prepared, funerary equipment, supplies, coffins, and masks were being constructed. At last, an elaborate funeral took place, and at the close of the funeral procession during the final rituals at the tomb, the ceremonial "opening of the mouth" occurred—the mummy regained the ability to talk, to eat, and to move. The senses were believed to be restored to permit a satisfactory life in the afterworld.

During the fifth dynasty (c. 2494-2345 B.C.E.), the spectacular pyramid construction waned, and the priesthood of Re began to assert its authority, but impressive religious temples continued to be erected. The dynasties of the god-kings continued as well, but a class of nobles became very powerful. Their quarrels finally broke up the Old Kingdom into a cadre of semi-feudal territories. What has been called the First Intermediate Period (c. 2200-2040 B.C.E.), nearly two centuries of chaos, anarchy, and civil war, intruded into the social milieu of Egyptian *ma'at*. A period of philosophical and religious reflection occurred during this time, a process in which the ancient Egyptians were forced to assess their ethics, values, gods, and themselves.

When the Middle Kingdom (c. 2040-1800 B.C.E.) was finally established by a revived leadership centered in the city of Thebes, this new dynasty of kings chose to view themselves as "good shepherds" of a united Egypt. They promoted public works projects and irrigated thousands of acres of land. They seemed to be concerned with all Egyptians, even the common people, and a democratization in the realm of religion occurred as the immortal god-king turned into the benevolent, good shepherd, god-king. For example, one king combined his pride in social accomplishment with ancient religious practice by having his mummy placed in a tomb forty feet below his personal irrigation project to help struggling farmers.

Rulers of the Middle Kingdom appear in portraits with "character lines," wrinkles that convey kings responsible to the gods for the good of their people, rather than the self-sufficient god-king of the Old Kingdom. Although these kings conquered territory outside Egypt, one of them advised his son: "Learn eloquence, for power is in the tongue; and speech is mightier than fighting." Patriotism was linked to religion during the Middle Kingdom, a strong love of country that is found in a literary masterpiece from the period, "The Story of Sinuhe."

No one is certain of what brought an end to the Middle Kingdom. After a Second Intermediate Period (c. 1800-1550 B.C.E.), in which Egypt was controlled by foreigners (Hyksos), the New Kingdom (c. 1550-1150 B.C.E.) arose. Humiliated by foreign domination, stimulated by a shattered isolation, the New Kingdom pharaohs determined to create an empire. Insisting that they would never again be dominated by foreigners, pharaohs such as Thutmose III (c. 1490-1436 B.C.E.), the "Napoleon of Egypt," penetrated deep into the Near East. In his hymn of victory, Thutmose III insisted that the great god had said to him: "I am come to make thee trample on the great ones of Syria . . . I am come to make thee trample on the Asiatics." Nevertheless, Egyptian rule appears to have been mild compared to the brutality of the Assyrians, and it included no mass deportation of entire populations, as was common with Mesopotamian victors.

The priests of the New Kingdom gained immense power and wealth as most of the spoils of war went to the temple complexes. Thebes' supreme god, Amun, was linked with Re as part of the compounded god, Amun-Re. Amun-Re was believed to be the god responsible for the victories over the peoples of the Near East, the god who had blessed the Egyptians with an empire that stretched to the Euphrates River. Gold and slaves flooded into Egypt, producing an opulent, urban society of splendor and culture. This was the Golden Age of Egyptian architecture and painting, the age that produced King Tut's tomb. Amun-Re as "king of the gods" provided for a very religious, yet sensual, populace. The plethora of gods and goddesses, demigods and guardian spirits, temples and animal cults, amulets and magical potions, combined in a *ma'at* that spanned back centuries to the early dynastic cultures. Even after the New Kingdom and centuries of decline and defeat, a dynamism infused the religion of Egypt to such an extent that the Greek historian, Herodotus (484?-424?), wrote of the Egyptians that they were *more* religious than the rest of humankind.

The famed *Book of the Dead* (actually entitled *Incantations for Going Forth by Day)* from the New Kingdom indicates that the Egyptians were concerned with judgment after death and were chagrined over personal acts that could bring a negative afterlife. Even in the Second Intermediate Period, it was customary to place an amulet on the breast of a mummy, a heart scarab on which were written instructions from the *Book of the Dead*, pleading with the heart not to make trouble while being weighed on the Great Scales. Similar treatises, such as *The Book of Gates* and *What Is in the Afterworld*, also tried to give the living some help in the judgment. These were buried with the dead owner, portions being inscribed on his coffin as well. The Egyptians appear to have had faith that a wonderful eternal life awaited them.

The perpetuation of Egyptian religious syncretism was tested during the Amarna Revolution and the reign of Amunhotep IV (c.

1363-1347 B.C.E.). Much has been written about him and his reign by scholars of repute, yet there are numerous disputes over facts. He appears to have taken up the worship of the god Aten, a god of the sun represented by a solar disk. Early in his reign, Amunhotep IV changed his name, which represented the god Amun (*Amun*hotep), to Akhenaten ("he who is devoted to Aten"). He also built a new capital named Akhetaten ("the horizon of Aten"), and spent his days with his wife Nefertiti and his daughters worshipping Aten. As a minor sun cult god, Aten had been tolerated as one of the gods of Egypt. Akhenaten appears, however, to have claimed that Aten was to be worshipped exclusively. Scholars of religion have debated whether this represented monotheism on Akhenaten's part or a controversy engendered by the powerful priests of Amun-Re, who were soon to eclipse the power of the pharaoh. In any case, the religious syncretism of the Egyptians and the power of the priesthood led the majority of the populace to oppose Akhenaten and his reforms.

There is debate, too, about what happened to Akhenaten and his lovely wife. That his ten-year-old younger brother changed his name from Tutankhaten ("Pleasant is the life of Aten") to Tutankhamun ("Pleasant is the life of Amun") and moved the capital back to Thebes in subordination to the powerful priesthood underscores the fact that Egyptian society was not ready for such a striking religious revolution. The new city of Akhetaten was finally destroyed, the "sun hymn" engraved amid the rubble:

> Thy dawning, O living Aten, is beautiful
> on the horizon. . . . O Beginning of
> Life, Thou art all, and Thy rays encompass
> all. . . . Thou art the Life of life;
> through Thee men live.

The failure of Akhenaten in ancient Egypt is evident in the fact that when the Nubians conquered Egypt in 720 B.C.E., the son of the reigning king was the high priest of Amun-Re. Even Alexander the Great, after wresting Egypt from Persia in 332 B.C.E., felt it necessary to go to a desert oasis to "consult" an oracle of Amun-Re. Hailed by the Egyptian people as a deliverer, Alexander was informed he was a divine son, was installed as pharaoh, and was assured by the religious authorities that he would conquer the world.

GREEKS AND ROMANS

During the two millennia or more that the Mesopotamians and Egyptians waxed and waned in their power and influence, developments in religion were under way in the Hellenic Peninsula and islands that would make themselves felt throughout the world and down to this very day. The ancient Greeks refined beliefs and rites in the centuries from about 1000 B.C.E. to almost the beginnings of the Common Era and with their signal contributions in thought and conduct had an incalculable effect on the Western world.

When the Indo-Europeans poured down from Central Europe to fuse their destiny with the Minoan and Aegean civilizations around 2000 B.C.E., they helped to create a host of native deities. The Indo-Europeans, of obscure origins, had practiced tribal forms of religion and had the usual array of gods and goddesses; these invaders from the northern regions brought to the people of the Greek plains and valleys a newer set of gods, some fresh terms to describe godly attributes and failings, and a hearty gusto in celebrating both the virtues and the vices of the gods and goddesses.

Confusion reigned. The Minoans and Aegeans had revered sea-gods and river-gods, fertility-gods and goddesses. Now there prevailed a bewildering complexity, a melange of old deities and new deities merging, then proliferating, vanishing and later re-emerging. More order and more unity began to develop, but "pagan" ("country dweller") habits were hard to cure; polytheism and magic, recourse to superstitions and oracles were still strong and unrestrained.

All the gods resembled human beings. The only difference between gods and humans lay in the superior strength and greater beauty of gods; these endowments entitled them to their immortality. Even here there was discrimination: Only the most heroic of humans and the most favored among the gods were chosen for the Elysian fields, Greek mythology's paradise for the virtuous after their death. The vast majority of people, joined by some of the gods, went on to a spirit world that was dreary, dank, and dark. Life after death, it should be noted, did not assume as much importance among the Greeks as it had, for example, among the Egyptians.

During the long centuries that Greek mythology prevailed, Mount Olympus was the home of the gods; and in the pantheon of the Olympic gods, Zeus stood supreme as the father of all humankind. He was the god who reigned over humanity and, at the same time, over all the gods and goddesses, among whom were the twelve great gods: Zeus himself, Hera, Poseidon, Demeter, Apollo, Artemis, Ares, Aphrodite, Hermes, Athena, Hephaestus, and Hestias.

Zeus was not, however, the All Supreme, for even he had to bow before destiny or fate. The gods might be suprahuman but they "lived and moved and had their being," as did humans, within the framework of history and nature. Such forces as death and strife and terror, humor and error and folly, operated with fate to spell people's—and the gods'—joy and woe, success and failure.

Religion in Greece took a new turn in the eighth and seventh centuries B.C.E. with the Athenian festivals and the mystery religions. In the mystery religions the Greeks sought personal salvation and the assurance of immortality by means of an emotional religion. The gods on Mount Olympus were remote, and the rites to honor and propitiate them, too formal and unemotional.

The most notable contribution of Hellenic civilization, however, was that of the philosophers. Many of them were profoundly religious in their thinking as they sought a unifying principle behind all phenomena. As a study of ultimate reality and the causes and principles that underlie all thinking and all being, Greek philosophy differs from theology by eschewing dogma and by dealing with speculation, not faith. The pre-Socratics—venturesome thinkers like Thales, Anaximander, Heraclitus, Parmenides, Anaxagoras, and Democritus—tried to find the one natural element common to all being and all nature. Many of the more daring and courageous scorned the older, more conventional explanations of life and its origins; they scoffed at the gods and their frailties. Some endured expulsion from the city of Athens. The high-minded Socrates, though he stood in reverence before the gods, suffered death as his penalty for being both rational and skeptical.

Eventually, and almost inevitably, most of them (notable exceptions: Democritus and Protagoras) arrived at a belief in one God;

Aristotle refers to Xenophanes as having been the first to believe in a unity of everything: "There is one God who is greatest among gods and men and is not like mortals either in form or in thought." Plato and Aristotle influenced religious thought profoundly through the next 2500 years, Plato probably more so than his pupil, Aristotle: both emphasized the goodness and greatness of God. In spite of the philosophers, however, the popular religions continued with scarcely any change.

The persuasive power of works by such dramatists and poets as Aeschylus and Sophocles, Aristophanes and Pindar in the fifth century B.C.E. caused a literal, unthinking, uncritical belief in the gods to begin to give way. The effort of poets and philosophers to envision a universe wherein the supreme problem was the moral struggle had a far-reaching effect. The Greek dramatists, focusing on good and evil, revenge and retribution, guilt and punishment, also upheld the objective of the good life: "Know thyself! Never exceed. The middle way is best."

In the closing years of the fourth century B.C.E., the Greeks in Asia Minor and, later, in Athens were attracted by the teaching of a philosopher named Epicurus. To him philosophy was more than its literal definition ("the love of wisdom"), it was the subordination of metaphysics to ethics so that pleasure might be the highest good. Although intent on making life happy, Epicurus did not counsel a careless indulgence: he advocated serenity and the avoidance of pain, intellectual rather than bodily pleasures, and a prudential social code of strict honesty and justice.

A more rigorous, somewhat sterner, but no less attractive school of philosophy was Stoicism. Led by Zeno of Citium and instructed by him in the *stoa poecile* ("the painted porch"), the young men of these same decades adhered to Zeno's interpretations of Socrates' ideals of self-sufficiency and virtue, Heraclitus' explanation of the physical universe, and Aristotle's logic.

After a century, Stoicism was introduced in Rome. In later decades, it included among its ardent adherents the dramatist-philosopher-statesman Seneca (c. 4 B.C.E.-65 C.E.) and the philosopher-emperor Marcus Aurelius (reigned 161-180 C.E.). The Stoics' ethical creed, "to live consistently with nature," called on them to subdue their passions, curb unjust thoughts, restrain all indulgence, and do their duty. Although mystery religions still attracted the Romans, many of them found Stoicism more in accord with their way of thinking and their mode of life. They preferred the Stoic outlook to any other school of Greek philosophy, for this approach to life, imported from Greece, had all the grace, logic, and power that a vital religion was expected to inculcate in a person.

In their later centuries the religions of Greece and Rome were similar to each other and appeared to call for the worship of the same gods. But in the earlier period the religion of Rome was uniquely its own, quite different from that of the Greeks. The Greeks may have thought of their gods as persons, but Roman religious observances were much more animistic and were used to propitiate innumerable spirits for the purpose of safeguarding the worshippers' lives. The mysterious Etruscans, who ruled Rome in the sixth century B.C.E., were a vigorous and sensuous people. Yet they were very concerned about life and death and foretelling the future from animal entrails. They loved athletic contests, and staged duels to the death at funeral services (the forerunner of later Roman gladiatorial contests). Fond of grotesque demons and temple ornaments, the Etruscans revelled in Greek mythology and stocked their tombs with jewels and possessions for the afterlife. Their complicated religious ceremonies, elaborate stone sarcophagi, and painted tombs affected later Roman religious practices.

Primarily, the Romans concerned themselves with the spirits of their houses and fields, their professions, ambitions, and ancestors. Holding these spirits in awe, they placated them with prayers and offerings. To them religion was like the fulfillment of a contract; the gods not only were to be appeased but even could be controlled by invoking the right words and using the proper rituals. To perpetuate his family the farmer gave offerings to his guardian spirit Genius for virility in men and to the goddess Juno for the power in women to conceive. To maintain his household's safety, the Roman worshipped Vesta, guardian spirit of the hearth fire; the *lares*, deified spirits of ancestors who watched over their descendants and guarded the fields; the *penates*, guardians of the entire household; and Janus, god of the beginnings and the guardian of the door.

Eventually a hierarchy of priests developed. The priests, looked upon as public officials, practiced divination, borrowing from the Babylonians the art—or the pretense—of determining the will of the gods by studying the constellations, observing flights of birds, and examining entrails of sacrificed animals. Often they were tempted to use their powers for purely political ends; public offices in Rome were secured as political spoils and civic morality was brought to a low level. Even during the *pax romana* (the Peace of Rome, 30 B.C.E.-180 C.E.) under the imperial emperors, there was no political rule without religious rule.

ANCIENT AMERICA

In the Western hemisphere arose the religions of the Aztecs in Mexico, the Mayas in Yucatan and other parts of Central America, and the Incas on fertile plateaus high in the Andes Mountains of Bolivia and Peru. Although these religions are more recent (some of the rites developed to their highest forms in the twelfth to sixteenth centuries C.E.), the observances and beliefs have remained vague to us. Our ignorance about them is due partly to our limited ability to decipher their hieroglyphics and interpret their codices, and partly to the Spanish conquistadors of only four centuries ago, who thought they were serving their Christian God by effacing such records as existed and thus obliterating almost all traces of these well-developed religions.

Of these religions, that of the Aztecs seems to have been the most advanced. An elaborate priesthood in the temples conducted the rituals with rigor and regularity, performed the sacrifices, led the people in regular classes of instruction, interpreted the concepts of life after death, held confessionals, and granted absolution. Despite rituals that were bloody and fertility ceremonies that were unrestrained, the Aztecs had a distinctive, highly developed religion of rare beauty and meaning, with powerful psalms and beautiful hymns, monasteries and convents of priests and priestesses. Some of their leaders in later centuries held views that bordered on the belief in one God; in one place a temple was built to the "unknown god," not pictured in material or physical fashion and possessing spiritual attributes of a high level.

The Mayas, farther to the south, constructed a complex civilization graced with artistry, culture, and beauty. Many clues about

Mayan religion survive, but specific information on names and meanings is lacking. Their gods were many and bizarre; their followers reflected awe before the mysterious, fear before the unpredictable and unknown. Lovely temples, daringly designed and tastefully executed, reflect a high level of aspiration and imagination among these Native Americans.

The religion of the Incas, parallel in many ways to those of the Aztecs and the Mayas, had elaborate ritual and complex organization, at the heart of which was the worship of *huacas* ("holy places or things"). In this state religion, the sun was the center of veneration; but above Ynti, the sun, was the supreme being, Viracocha. Human sacrifice did not prevail as among the Aztecs, but it did exist. The Incas had no written language but recorded history in *quipus* (colored strings with knots) and in this way distinguished themselves from the Aztecs and Mayas, who used hieroglyphics.

ANCIENT TRADITIONS

Such were some of the precursors of today's prevailing religions, ancient traditions groping, sometimes feebly but often courageously, toward the light of reason and more creative "revelations." Still others might be mentioned, the religions of the Celts, the Slavs, and the Teutons, the Polynesians, and many another; each reveals faltering, often crude, yet noble and admirable attempts of the ancients to seek clues to the mystery of existence. Most of these faiths from long ago are now dead, but each in its era was a striking example of humankind's ceaseless quest for meaning.

Nineteen centuries ago Plutarch, Greek essayist and biographer, ascribed to the goddess Athena the saying: "I am all that has been, is, and will be, and no mortal has yet lifted My veil." These words were inscribed by a priest to his deity Neith (whom the Hellenes identified with their Athena) on the wall of an ancient temple at Sais in the northwest delta of the Nile. Many years later, according to tradition, a pilgrim of another era visited the sacred site and wrote on the opposite wall: "Veil after veil we lifted and ever the Face is more wonderful."

2

HINDUISM

The Vision Inward

Shiva—one of the most popular gods in Hinduism—is a link with the ancient Indic past that spans four millennia. Often depicted as Lord of the Dance, with flying hair and poised step within the arc of the eternal cycle of the universe, this god of death, destruction, and disease is known as the Destroyer. Yet, to the Hindu, death is but a door to another life, and Shiva also represents human reproduction and sexuality. Shiva's drum determines the tempo of the universe, and he crushes evil demons with his ankleted foot. Portrayed with his constant companion, the bull Nandi, Shiva is absorbed in contemplation of future lives and future worlds. That a prototype of Shiva was among the archeological finds of the Indus Valley civilization (c. 2300-1800 B.C.E.) as a part of the ancient fertility cult of the inhabitants of the impressive cities of Mohenjo-Daro and Harappa underscores the enduring roots of religion in India.

Hinduism defies the systemization that is often associated with the living religions of the world. It has no centralized structure of hierarchy, no uniform body of doctrine or orthodoxy, and no specific founder. In fact, Hinduism represents almost every belief and religious expression found in the world today. As it has evolved over the centuries, it has absorbed most religions that have penetrated the borders of India, sometimes modifying them greatly in the vast practice of Hinduism. Because it is made up of the cultures and worship of many peoples, and despite its impressive contributions to religious thought and philosophy, Hinduism is for most Indians the way things are—it is simply their way of life—nontheological, nonanalytical, nontheoretical, and non-comparative.

THE ARYANS

Although nomadic bands of Indo-Europeans from the shores of the Black and Caspian seas may have infiltrated the Indus Valley civilization in the third millennium B.C.E., a massive assault appears to have taken place around 1500 B.C.E. These tall, fair-skinned Aryans (from *arya*, the Sanskrit word for "noble" or "lord"), with elongated heads and pointed noses conquered the Dravidians, the short, dark, snub-nosed inhabitants. It has been suggested that these invaders, who traveled by horse and herded cattle, may have used the war chariot and that their kinsfolk were responsible for conquering Egypt in the Second Intermediate Period. They were of the same stock as the forebears of most European peoples, including the Celtic peoples of the British Isles. Eating and drinking freely, the Aryan tribes were ruled by a *rajah*. Unaccustomed to living in cities, they passed on their traditions orally through enthusiastic singing and storytelling, and their rural tribal life was much like life in Indian villages today.

From around 900 to 500 B.C.E., small territorial states were created by the all-powerful rajahs, who built palaces in the midst of cities encompassed with moats and walls. Theoretically the rajah "owned" the land in his state, but he rarely interfered with a village in his domain if it paid its taxes. The oldest father was in control of each family in the village, and the family unit was made up of descendants of a common ancestor. When the patriarch died, authority was transferred to his oldest son. Because property belonged to the family as a whole, serious matters went to the entire group of males. Marriages were arranged and had to strengthen the family unit. Thus two pillars of Indian society were established: the autonomous villages and the joint family.

As the center of power and culture shifted from the upper Indus Valley eastward to the Ganges region, the Aryans were concerned about intermarriage and the threat of being absorbed racially by the Dravidians. They instituted class divisions to separate themselves from the Dravidians; but in time this caste system, the third pillar of traditional Indian society, involved the social stratification of the Aryans themselves. They evolved into three distinct classes: the Brahmans or priests; the Kshatriyas or warriors, among whom were the kings, nobles, and most government officials; and the Vaisyas, or artisans and peasants, men of mercantile status. A fourth caste with many gradations, the Sudras (the vanquished people) served these three higher castes and undertook all kinds of work considered too menial for the upper castes. Then a fifth group, the Pancamas (known also as Pariahs or Asprishyas, i.e., "Untouchables"), had the most lowly of occupations. Strictly speaking, however, the Untouchables were outside the caste system. The non-Aryan population consisted of either Sudras or Untouchables.

The Aryans merged their religious beliefs with the concepts of *karma*, reincarnation, asceticism, fertility, and methods of yoga that had been practiced for centuries in the Indus Valley civilization. The gods of the Aryans were active in the affairs of humankind, dwelling on the earth, in the atmosphere, and in the sky. In this three-level division of the cosmos, the gods of the atmosphere were the most dynamic, Indra emerging as the favorite of the Aryans. Indra, the god of war and storm, led his band of warriors across the sky in chariots, wielding thunderbolts, slaying monsters, eating cattle, and drinking the magical *soma*. Defeating the powers of darkness, Indra's victory was apparent in every morning sunrise.

VEDAISM

The mixture of Aryan and Indic religion is known as Vedaism, because when the resultant oral traditions were finally written down, they were called the *Vedas* (Sanskrit for "knowledge"). Four compilations make up the Vedas, and three additional literary collections have been added to these traditional Vedic scriptures. The compilations are: (1) the *Rig-Veda* ("knowledge of praise"), the largest compilation; (2) the *Yajur-Veda* ("knowledge of rites"), instructions for sacrifice to the gods; (3) the *Sama-Veda* ("knowledge of the chants"), basic verses recited by priests during the sacrifices; and

(4) *Atharva-Veda* ("knowledge given by the sage Atharva"), popular prayers and incantations to ward off evil. Later commentaries include the *Brahmanas*, books of priestly ritual; the *Aranyakas*, books of theology concerning sacrifices; and the *Upanishads*, philosophical speculations on the ultimate order of the universe.

The oldest and most important of these sacred books of India was the Rig-Veda, a collection of over one thousand *suktas* (hymns, prayers, magical poems, legends, and riddles) to exalt various gods: the mother goddess (Prithivi-Matar), the father-sky (Dyaus Pitar), the sun god (Mitra), and such nature deities as the storm god and war god (Indra), the mountain god (Rudra), the god of the skies (Varuna), the god of the dawn (Ushas), the god of fire (Agni), the god of the dead, of heaven and hell (Yama), and the spirit of the drink god (Soma), the brew that strengthened Indra for his incredible feats.

In one typical hymn from the Rig-Veda, the poet describes a sunrise, invoking Indra as god of the bright day, who takes as his companions the Maruts (troops of the storm) and rides the sun as his steed. Sacrifice is performed to Indra, the worshipper concluding:

> From yonder, O traveller [Indra], come hither
> or from the light of heaven;
> the singers all yearn for it.
>
> Or we ask Indra for help from here,
> or from heaven, or from above the earth,
> or from the great sky.

Whether Indra comes from the regions of the earth, or heaven itself, or even the atmosphere, the worshipper has fully recited his or her praises and expects the supplications to be answered. In a later hymn invoking the Maruts the worshipper cries out: "Speak forth forever with thy voice to praise the Lord of prayer, Agni (god of fire), who is like a friend, the bright one." "Fashion a hymn in thy mouth!" the supplicant continues, "Sing a song of praise." The Rig-Veda is filled with such Sanskrit hymns, each addressed to singular deities, gods, and goddesses who number in the dozens throughout the collection.

One of the *suktas* of the Rig-Veda (10:129) relates the creation of the world but questions whether any person can know for certain what occurred, since it transpired before the birth of the gods.

Then was not non-existent nor existent: there was no realm of air,
no sky beyond it.
What covered in, and where? And what gave shelter? Was water
there, unfathomed depth of water?

Death was not then, nor was there anything immortal: no sign
was there, the day's and night's divider.
That one thing, breathless, breathed by its own nature: apart
from it was nothing whatsoever.

Darkness there was: at first concealed in darkness, this All was
indiscriminated chaos.
All that existed then was void and formless: by the great power
of warmth was born that unit.

Thereafter rose desire in the beginning, Desire, the primal seed
and germ of spirit.
Sages who searched with their heart's thought discovered the
existent's kinship in the non-existent. . . .

Who verily knows and who can here declare it, whence it was
born, and whence came this creation?
The gods are later than this world's production. Who knows,
then, whence it first came into being?

He, the first origin of this creation, whether he formed it all or
did not form it,
Whose eye controls this world in highest heaven, he verily
knows it, or perhaps he knows not.

Such philosophical questioning, however, is unusual, for the
Rig-Veda usually praises a god and then asks for help. For example,
over 450 hymns of the Rig-Veda are addressed to Indra or Agni.
This particular *sukta*, however, foreshadows the development of
the Upanishads ("confidential sessions" or "intimate sittings with a
teacher"), commentaries on the wisdom of the universe for the ma-
ture Hindu student. The Upanishads (c. 800-400 B.C.E.) are considered the final section of the Indian Vedic Scriptures. They
represent an internal cry of the Hindu spirit to be released from the
developing complexity of priestly ritual.

In fact, it is the reaction to the increasing power of the priesthood
and the religious enterprise that ultimately changed Vedaism into

the Hindu religion we recognize today. As in many ancient empires, the priesthood grew in power as sacrifices became more elaborate. Soon only the priests understood the complicated rituals, and the people of India were heavily burdened by their religious dictates. The priest became a technician of the occult, as the formulae of the Brahmanas had to be pronounced precisely for divine efficacy. Magical rituals consumed nearly every hour of the day, and both intellectuals and the illiterate yearned for a more personal, satisfying, internal religious experience. Both Jainism and Buddhism (see chapters 3 and 4) would develop in reaction to the all-encompassing sacrificial cult of the Vedic priests. Since Brahmans were intrinsically involved in the process, scholars often refer to this phenomenon as Brahmanism.

The Horse Sacrifice, which took a year to perform, is indicative of the problems the Indian populace faced from an incessantly chanting and developing priesthood. A young white stallion was ritually bathed, fed, and consecrated for days before being set free in the company of 100 other stallions and a cadre of mounted soldiers. The ruler for whom the consecration was performed had his armies follow the young stallion as it roamed throughout neighboring territories, trying to capture all lands through which the horse traveled. The rulers of these territories tried to kill or capture the stallion in order to bring divine retribution on the priests and ruler initiating the sacrifice or to reap blessings for themselves.

After a year the horse was brought back. As the populace and priests joined in the rites of sacred fire, sacrifices of over 600 animals (from elephants to insects) were offered. Some accounts imply that at times a human was sacrificed as well. Bedecked in jewels, the white stallion was then sacrificed. Covered with a blanket, the dead horse was joined by the queen, who was supposed to have "sexual intercourse" with him while priests shouted risqué encouragement. The symbolized fertility of the stallion was thus ritually passed on to the queen. The horse was then eaten by the participants, the priests assuring the king of prosperity and health throughout the kingdom. In like manner but on a smaller scale thousands of other sacrifices were performed for Indian householders who could pay the priest-magicians for their services.

CLASSICAL HINDUISM

Hinduism would be indebted to the Vedas, as well as to the art of ritual and sacrifice, even as it sought to reform and refine the excesses involved in Vedaism. From the henotheism (worshipping one god, such as Indra, without denying the existence of other gods) and the polytheism of Vedaism, the Upanishads became the basis for a Hindu philosophy characterized by monism (one ultimate in which all share). The old gods, so many and varied, dropped into the background. In their place stood Brahman, the World-Soul, who was the One, the Creator, the Self-Existent, the sum of all that was and is, the It, the That. This Hindu philosophical system is popularly known as Vedantism ("the end of the Vedas").

The Upanishads taught that a man's life had four stages or *ashramas:* the student, who concentrated on the Vedas for a number of years; the householder, who married, raised a family, and was a responsible citizen; the forest dweller or hermit, who gave up his home to meditate in isolation from life; and the ascetic, alone and aloof from all family life, who became a mendicant intent solely on meditation. As one aged, one was to be drawn by an urge to flee from life, reject its joys, renounce its comforts, and withdraw from the world. Only thus could a man become holy, seek to elicit reverence, and merit respect.

Philosophic Hinduism introduced the doctrine of a universal soul with which the individual soul could be reunited after it had overcome *maya,* the illusion of time and space. Only dimly had the Rig-Veda hinted at these two new ideas of *samsara,* a rebirth by the transmigration of souls or reincarnation, and *karma.* The thinkers of India considered themselves to be on a wheel of rebirth, whirling ceaselessly; to them religion's basic purpose was to learn how one might find release from that wheel, freedom from the necessity of coming back to live on earth in an endless cycle of reincarnation.

Tied to this idea of rebirth was the law of *karma,* an Indian version of the belief common to every culture that "whatsoever a man soweth, that shall he also reap." In India this "law of the deed" kept people on the wheel of life and therefore the perplexing question arose: how could one overcome karma to be released from the wheel? The Upanishads (often called the Vedanta, "conclusion of the Vedas") focused now on something other than the techniques of the sacrifices. The emphasis centered instead on salvation through contemplation.

The goal of Vedantic Hinduism was the union of the soul (*Atman*) with the World-Soul (*Brahman*). But only through insight could this be achieved. Knowledge derived from insight—the illumination that came from contemplation—held the secret for release from karma. If one realized that life was sheer illusion (i.e., *maya*), that person would know suffering no more. If one saw that nothing in life was real, that all was illusory, one could escape and identify with the World-Soul, Brahman, ultimate reality.

The system of yoga arose from this desire to secure the requisite knowledge to bring release. Yoga prescribed specific directions for meditation: suspend all physical functions, including breathing; suppress all mental activities until pure peace of mind and body are attained. It calls for both physical and mental control, but it is not a denial of action; action is to be performed without involvement or attachment.

Philosophic Hinduism did not meet the needs of all Indians. Though modified, Vedaism with many gods and involved ritual continued. Devotional movements (*bhakti*) added to the growing complexity of Hinduism. Additional facets of Hinduism grew in response to challenges by materialists, Jainists, and Buddhists. In fact, both Jainism and Buddhism flourished from about 600 or 500 B.C.E. to about 400 or 500 C.E. and made a frontal attack on the elaborate ideas and rituals of the Hinduism of those ten to eleven centuries. The Brahmanism of the time, adopting some features of those religions, created the *Laws of Manu*, a book of its own rituals. To the *Sruti* (revelation of the Vedas) it provided commentary to make the Vedic literature more comprehensible and practical. The resulting works formed Smriti, an authoritative tradition.

The *Code of Manu*, written between 300 B.C.E. and 300 C.E. and representing the best-known ancient lawgivers of India, defined the ethical and social system of classical Hinduism. It is only one of a great number of law codes and commentaries from this period, a vast literature developed by a half dozen schools of Hindu philosophy. The *Code of Manu* declared:

For that man who obeys the law prescribed in the revealed texts
and in the sacred tradition, gains fame in this [world] and after
death unsurpassable bliss.

By the *Sruti* [revelation] is meant the Veda, and by *Smriti*
[tradition] the Institutes of the sacred law: those two must not
be called into question in any matter, since from those two the
sacred law shone forth.

Every twice-born man who, relying on the Institutes of
dialectics, treats with contempt those two sources [of the
law], must be cast out by the virtuous as an atheist and a
scorner of the Veda.

The Veda, the sacred tradition, the customs of virtuous men,
and one's own pleasure, they declare to be visibly the fourfold
means of defining the sacred law. (2:9-12)

Hinduism, biding its time, soon was absorbing its competitive religions in India. It indeed proved itself an umbrella religion, en-
compassing all challengers.

The *Smriti* (tradition) created a Hindu trinity, the Trimurti, of
central gods. Brahma, a male manifestation of Brahman, became
an impersonal Creator god, the All-Father. Vishnu became the
popular Preserver, a gracious god who sends help to humans. As
we have seen, Shiva is the Destroyer and became the third member of the Trimurti. To Hindus in many centuries the Brahma-
Vishnu-Shiva trinity has represented the spectrum of divinity.

After the reform movements of the Jainists and the Buddhists
had emerged and slowly moved under way during the sixth century
B.C.E., Hinduism began to encourage the use of images and the
construction of temples. Now images abounded; temples were
built in such numbers and to such an extent in the next fourteen
centuries that India now has more images and temples than any
other country in the world. The sacred city of Benares has the greatest number of temples in all India; millions of pilgrims go there
every year to bathe in the Ganges because they consider it to be
holy and capable of bestowing special blessings upon them.

GOALS AND WAYS

As Hinduism adapted itself to changed conditions in India during and after the sixth century B.C.E., it formulated four permissi-

ble goals in living and approved of three ways to salvation, all seven of which meant new directions for the pilgrims and devotees. Of the four goals in life, two went along the path of desire and two, the way of renunciation:

1. The first was pleasure *(kama)*, particularly through love, physical exercise, and intellectual pursuits. For the uninitiate, Vatsyayana's *Kamasutra* instructed in the art of love; and the *Natyasastras* provided a knowledge of drama, poetry, and storytelling. One was to realize, however, that something more durable and satisfying lay beyond pleasure-seeking.

2. The second goal was power and possessions *(artha)*, which would lead to social standing and material success. *Artha*, signifying both wealth and influence and based upon relentless competition and an admitted quest for affluence, was not to be condemned; but the seeker would learn that *artha* was not a high objective. Ultimately it would give way to a third—and later a fourth—along the paths of renunciation.

3. The religious and moral law, *dharma*, opened a more worthwhile and satisfying life, for the *dharma*-follower served family and caste, community, and country. Instructed by the *Laws of Manu* and the *Dharmasastras* (the law books), a person could serve the good of everyone and forswear an ego-centered striving for social advancement and financial gain, for sensual joys and personal delights. Yet the great happiness one knew in loyalty to a high ethic was only partial. There was really but one genuine satisfaction, *moksha*, which meant authentic liberation or salvation.

4. *Moksha* was the highest goal, the Hindu ideal of final redemption; but it could be attained only by being released from the endless cycle of rebirths and all the problems of life.

Hinduism then pointed to the three ways of salvation: the Way of Works *(Karma Marga)*, the Way of Knowledge *(Jnana Marga)*, and the Way of Devotion *(Bhakti Marga)*.

1. The Way of Works *(Karma Marga)*, time-honored method of observing duties, especially within one's own caste as outlined in Hindu scriptures, was designed to earn merit for a person and, in accord with the law of *karma*, to guarantee to that individual who performed more good deeds than bad that he or she would have the highest form of reincarnation in the next life. The Way

of Works required sacrifices and rites at all important stages of life, from birth to death, and honor of the spirits of departed ones in the family.

2. The Way of Knowledge (*Jnana Marga*) had its foundation in the thought of the Upanishads, which taught that ignorance (*avidya*) caused all evil and misery. Right thinking and abolition of ignorance were the cures for mental mistakes and counterforces to wrongdoing. If one knew Brahman, one had begun to understand and apprehend that which is "real," for only Brahman was true reality. If one studied all of the sacred writings, practiced the disciplines of yoga, and meditated intensively on Brahman, one would be spared both "suffering and evil." If one considered oneself to be a separate self apart from the All-Soul and remained ignorant of Brahman, one was doomed to the unchanged, unchanging fate of the ceaseless cycle of the law of *karma*. Only life-long, disciplined preparation could bring the knowledge, lightning-like within an instant of illumination, that salvation was at hand: the pilgrim along the Way of Knowledge would be conscious that the law of *karma* was no longer effective and repeated rebirths were at an end.

It was at this point that the Way of Works and the Way of Knowledge merged for the observant Brahman, and the four stages (*ashramas*) could become goals to be sought: as the student of religion, as the married man and householder, as the hermit or recluse, and as the holy man-mendicant.

3. The Way of Devotion (*Bhakti Marga*) filled a need that could not be met by the Way of Works, so practical and so legalistic, or by the Way of Knowledge, so philosophical and so intellectual. The Brahmans realized that the common people were unmoved by the intellectualism of the higher classes but were attracted, especially in later centuries, by temple worship and by temple priests, as well as by piety in their private lives. The average person's awe before unseen powers and unknown mysteries led to *bhakti*, the dependence on an impassioned worship of dieties, both gods and goddesses. *Bhakti* did not deny the worth of the Way of Works or the Way of Knowledge; on the contrary, those two ways were heightened in their importance. The Way of Devotion contended, however, that it was only one of the real ways, true and tested, to

achieve salvation, not distinct from the other two Ways, but perhaps in conjunction with them.

From the growing popularity and seeming efficacy of the Way of Devotion *(Bhakti Marga)* as a means to assured salvation came the great religious classic *Bhagavad-Gita* ("Song of the Blessed Lord"). It told of the Kshatriyas, but in particular of the god-hero Krishna, as he led the Pandavas in their successful war against their blood relations, the Kaurava princes (the War of the Bharats three thousand years ago). The great Pandava warrior Arjuna must lead his brothers and their fellow soldiers against his cousins, the princes of the Kaurava clans; but he hesitates. The call to battle brings both sides into furious, thunderous combat, but still Arjuna falters, confessing to Krishna his horror at the internecine strife and the senseless slaughter. Not so, says Krishna; and in a long discourse urges Arjuna to the battle, justifying its purpose and its carnage in terms of promised salvation through higher knowledge, good works, and unselfish devotion. Krishna then reveals himself as Vishnu, the Preserver god, the Eternal Brahman. Arjuna is almost overcome at the supernal sight. At Arjuna's pleading that he resume human form, for the vision has been too dazzling and awesome, Vishnu becomes the charioteer, Krishna, again. But Krishna's point is clear: unconditional surrender in devotion, the unreserved *bhakti*, is the message of the "Song of the Blessed Lord." Its influence on Hinduism was so profound that about 100 C.E. it was melded into the great epic of over 100,000 couplets, the saga of the Kshatriya caste, *Mahabharata;* and even today this unique poem, as a vivid, powerful part of the *Mahabharata*, has extraordinary prestige. It has satisfied the intellectual and the devotional needs of Hindus more than has any other writing in Hinduism, probably because it succeeded so well in interweaving the three Ways of release: Works, Knowledge, and Devotion, and perhaps because it so dramatically illustrates the meaning of the word *avatar.* Just as Rama, the hero of the folk epic *Ramayana*, was an *avatar* or embodiment of Vishnu, so was Krishna.

The Way of Devotion demanded self-dedication in loving devotion to one or another god or goddess, for each reflected Brahman and tended to instill some specific aspect. One might rid oneself of evil and merit reincarnation if one were devoted to the deities, especially the Preserver-god Vishnu and his helper-gods, or the Destroyer-god Shiva and his cohorts among the lesser gods. Vishnu, linked with Brahman and assuming a physical body by which he can overcome evil, is divinely reincarnated in the god Krishna who had urged his followers:

> . . . Cling thou to Me!
> Clasp Me with heart and mind! So shalt thou dwell
> Surely with Me on high. But if thy thought
> Droops from such height; if thou be'st weak to set
> Body and soul upon Me constantly,
> Despair not! Give Me lower services! Seek
> To read Me, worshipping with steadfast will;
> And, if thou canst not worship steadfastly,
> Work for Me, toil in works, pleasing to Me!
> For he that laboreth right for love of Me
> Shall finally attain! But, if in this
> Thy faint heart fails, bring Me thy failure! Find
> Refuge in Me!

These three Ways led then to a fourth Way, the Way of Concentration, which enabled an individual to be freed of both conscious and unconscious thought, thus to uncover the real self that is identical with the All-Soul, Brahman. Only by strict and careful discipline of the self can this be attained. The simple things come first: do not lie, do not cheat, do not steal, remain controlled, stay clean, study regularly. But one thing more is important, all important: avoid distractions, sit in a cross-legged position like the lotus, control the breath, and subdue all sensation. In that manner, a human being can lose consciousness of both time and self, and be absorbed into Brahman.

HINDUISM TODAY

The goals and ways of Hinduism have interacted with historical events to produce a plethora of orders and sects within modern Hinduism. Since the vast majority of the 650 million Hindus live in India, the whole spectrum of this complex religion may be found interacting in that nation. In its struggle against the British for independence between the two World Wars, nationalism burned within the psyche of Hindus. Under such charismatic leadership as that of the famed Mohandas K. Gandhi (1869-1948) India gained its independence on August 15, 1947. Gandhi ("Mahatma" or Great Soul) favored nonviolent disobedience against British imperialism. He also attempted, though in vain, to reconcile the bitterly antagonistic Hindus and Muslims.

Devotees of Islam had lived in India since their first invasion in the 700s and had established a sultanate in Delhi that lasted from 1206 to 1526. Hinduism finally dominated the Muslim presence, but the Muslims were not absorbed in the broad Hindu sea as other religious groups had been. Muslim nationalism resulted in the formation of the Muslim League in 1906, and Hindu-Muslim conflict became increasingly acute. Muhammad Ali Jinnah (1876-1948), leader of the Muslim League, negotiated for, and later demanded that, a Muslim state be established in areas where Muslims were in the majority. Muslim Pakistan ("Land of the Pure") was founded out of Indian territory a day before India gained independence in 1947, and a bloody transfer of populations took place amidst massacres and pogroms initiated on both sides. Gandhi was assassinated by a fanatical and demented member of a high Hindu caste because the great leader had pleaded for friendship with Muslims. All India mourned, and a close associate of Gandhi, Jawaharlal Nehru (1889-1964), served as India's first prime minister. India, however, had been partitioned, and the Indus Valley, which gave birth to ancient Indian civilization, now lay in West Pakistan.

A graduate of Cambridge University, Nehru declared that religion had brought only misery and slavery; and he fought against child marriage, enforced widowhood, *suttee* (the "voluntary" cremation of a widow on the funeral pyre of her husband), and the caste system. In 1950 the constitution of the independent democratic republic and subsequent government policy sought to establish human rights, eliminate the segregation of the Untouchable class, introduce land reform, raise living standards, and expand industry. Few practitioners within Hinduism have not been affected to some degree by these changes. Nevertheless, Hinduism is woven into the fabric of Indian society to such an extent that it would be impossible to eradicate or even reduce the hold of this religion on the nation. Of pressing concern to modern India is the debate over caste, the role of women, Sikhism (a devotional movement founded in the early 1500s in the Punjab by Guru Nanak that never totally identified with Hindu tradition and has some apparent indebtedness to Islam), and India's entrance into the technological world. Each of these will be briefly considered after discussing religious practice in modern Hinduism.

Religious Observance

There is little congregational worship among Hindus, and worship in the home is more widely practiced than worship in the thousands of temples that dot the landscape of India. Hindus often declare that their deities number 330 million, but the particular deities that a Hindu chooses to worship are often determined by family or village traditions. The large majority of Hindus live in rural villages, where the center of attention is focused on local spirits and village shrines. In both rural and urban Hindu homes, however, a worship area displays the images of the favorite deities, and many families observe a morning ritual of prayers, songs, washings, and sacrifices. Hindus insist that they do not worship objects, idols, or natural shrines, but treat them as symbols or manifestations of the divine. In numerous cases one deity is chosen as a personal deity to guide and help a person throughout life. As Absolute Reality (Brahman) is revealed in Vishnu and Shiva so, too, Hindus believe that Vishnu and Shiva may be incarnated in various forms. In fact, there are at least ten popular incarnations of Vishnu, and these *avatars* "save" the Hindus and their world from catastrophe.

Throughout India are large public temples where priests attend huge statues of gods and goddesses. These elaborate sculptures are treated as though they were living beings and are clothed, fed, and bathed by a devoted religious hierarchy. During special festivals the statues are paraded through the village or city. Every Hindu realizes the inner spiritual significance of these ancient external rituals. Pilgrimages include visits to the temples, and Hindu devotees who come to the city of Benares to purify their bodies in the sacred waters of the Ganges River will often seek a temple specializing in their particular requests. They believe that their ills are caused by evil spirits; and they pray that the deity of the temple will protect them, initiating a spiritual warfare on their behalf. Many Hindus believe that if they die in the sacred city of Benares, they will achieve *moksha* ("liberation"), and cremation sites abound along the Ganges River.

The family priest is significant in the life-cycle rituals of the observant Hindu family. Soon after a child is born, friends and relatives gather in the home for the ritual naming of the child and purification rites to ward off evil. The name whispered into the baby's ear by the father is secret and is used only during important life-cycle rituals. A formal rite attends a child's first feeding of solid food, first hair cutting, second birth (the three highest castes are known as "twice-born," although the thread investiture ceremony in which a young Hindu boy is given his sacred thread by his uncles, a thread which he should wear for life as a symbol of his second birth, is becoming rarer), marriage, and death. Almost all Hindu rituals include the elements of earth, air, water, and fire, and are accompanied by music and dancing. In every ceremony, the Hindu is obligated to follow the path of *dharma*, the "duty" required by one's village, family, or caste.

One of the duties that is baffling to most Westerners is Hinduism's veneration of the cow. Killing of cows is forbidden, and even the accidental killing of this animal necessitates some form of "cow-death expiation ceremony." Whenever a Hindu has become greatly "unclean," the five "holy substances" of the cow (milk, curds, clarified butter, urine, and dung) are mixed by priests into a concoction for cleansing. Cows are adorned with garlands around their necks and anointed with oil on their foreheads. These gentle, hump-backed, white cows appear as a national symbol of maternalism, a counterpart to the mother goddess who is greatly venerated in Indian villages today. Gandhi defended the protection of the cow as a "central fact of Hinduism, the one concrete belief common to all Hindus . . . one of the most wonderful phenomena in human evolution." He considered such reverence to signify "protection of the whole dumb creation of God." In almost all the small villages of India, cow dung is used for purposes ranging from medicine and disinfectant to fuel. It even serves as an ingredient in mixing plaster or mortar, and modern scholars are convinced that milk and dung from such cows contribute far more to Indian society than butchering the scrawny beasts would accomplish.

Hindu priests may minister at the local shrines; but they are aided—and sometimes hindered too—by the *yogin*, the *swami*, and *guru* that pass through the modern villages. The yogin or yogi renounces worldly life and, by methods of yoga, seeks to attain reunion with Brahman as he extinguishes or "blows out" the flame of life. A swami received this Hindu title of respect because, as a member of a religious order and as a religious teacher, he vows poverty, chastity, and obedience. A guru is a preceptor who gives general guidance on religious matters, while *upadya* and *acharya* are religious teachers entrusted with the task of teaching the Vedas, usually to boys and young men but often to entire families as well. Such teachers and religious counselors add to the complexity of religious practice among Hindus today, and varieties of folk religion permeate the worship of millions of Hindus.

The yogis hope to reach the level of the *sannyasis* and the *sadhus*. The sannyasis, often devotees of Shiva, have taken vows of renunciation and have been true ascetics in their own estimation, thus attaining the fourth stage of the cycle of life, the existence of a holy man. The sadhu ("one who has renounced") has reached the goal of spiritual unity with Brahman and has experienced *samadhi* (the highest state of meditation or yoga). He is considered, therefore, genuinely holy. Sadhus are familiar to us in the West from pictures of holy men of Hinduism subjecting themselves to the ordeals of fire and, by self-mastery, overcoming pain and ignoring sensation.

Most Hindus, however, are a people of festivity and celebration. Religious festivals encompass every area of life, from the celebration of the New Year to the re-creation of ancient stories involving heroes and deities. Such festivities vary from area to area, but Divali or Dipavali ("a row or line of lights") is the most widely celebrated. It is a festival of lights that illuminates the night with thousands of lamps, torches, and, in some areas, fireworks. Some believe that the souls of departed ancestors visit at this time, while others pay homage to Lakshmi, the goddess of wealth and good fortune. Local deities are honored, and festive clothes, meals, and sweets abound. Hope replaces despair, joy obliterates misery.

Caste

Despite the effort of the government of India to outlaw caste, Hinduism reinforces its practice. So stratified is Indian society that estimates on subgroups (*jatis*—literally "births") within castes run as high as 25,000. Some small villages consist of a single caste with subgroups, while others contain several castes with many *jatis* and a dominant caste that controls the village. Based on the Hindu doctrine of ritual cleanliness, those born into the lower castes are viewed as "pollutants" to higher caste members. Barred from eating, drinking, and casual interaction with the upper castes, lower-caste people engage in menial, low-paying, inherited occupations. Villages are often divided into wards that converge on the public square—wards determined solely by caste.

Most of the poor in India today come from the low and Untouchable classes. Due to fear of upper caste reprisals, the poor often refuse to learn skilled trades and are uninterested in sending their children to government schools. In some areas, the rigidity of the *jatis* becomes so effective that fishermen who weave their nets from left to right will not speak to fishermen who weave their nets from right to left. Thus, the *jati* is an expression of intense group loyalty.

In large cities where lower castes might receive a government-sponsored education, educated young people continue to have a difficult time securing jobs in their newfound fields. While religious movements within Hinduism, such as the *bhakti* (devotional) cults, have tried to transcend the caste system, over 150 million Indians are relegated to the lowest ranks of society. Secular periodicals have urged them to give up Hinduism, while Christian missionaries have urged them to convert to a "faith of brotherhood." Nevertheless, the *jatis* represent to many the organic unity of life, and even Indian Christians, Buddhists, and Muslims have been affected by such societal norms. *Jatis* can be transcended over time; but this is usually a group phenomenon, rather than an individual accomplishment, and often takes several generations. Arun M. Gandhi, the grandson of Mohandas K. Gandhi, worked in rural community development in India and in 1988-89 was engaged in a comparative study of racial and caste discrimination in Mississippi and India. His work underscores the socioeconomic problems that confront Indian society today. There seems to be no indication that the caste system will be eliminated in the near future.

Women

The plight of women in Hindu society has been well documented. In a traditional ritual still practiced today a married couple invites friends and relatives to their home to pray that the pregnant wife will have a son. Religious duty stipulated that the woman should always be subordinate to the man and that her virtue lay in how well she functioned as a devoted servant. Generally, a woman could not obtain *moksha*, although in rare cases she might attain the future state her husband would obtain; and her only hope was to be reborn as a man. Her *dharma* is to be an obedient woman.

In her childhood, her father and the males of the family controlled her life. Married at a young age and receiving no education, she submitted to the authority of her husband and his family. Even in her maturity, she was subject to her eldest son, who determined her destiny. A woman's main function was to have sons, and if she was unfortunate enough to be widowed, her plight was compounded. So that she would not become a burden to the family unit, a widow was often expected to commit *sati (suttee)*, to climb on her husband's funeral pyre and burn with his corpse. Ironically, Hindu law decreed that a widow must do this out of adoration and love for her departed husband, not from personal despair. Despite laws prohibiting *suttee*, the custom continues in modern India. Most alarmingly, women's organizations in India claimed in 1989 that there had been an increase in the past few years of widows being burned in their husband's homes in fires that had been labelled "kitchen accidents" or "suicides." The organizations claimed that these were actually murders, and the Indian government vowed to investigate the suspicious deaths.

In some areas of Indian social strata, education and laws against child marriage have alleviated the plight of women. Nevertheless, social taboos and strong religious traditions have continued to inhibit the liberty of most women in the culture of India, and a strong disdain for women continues as a current in the male-dominated society. Even in Tantrist sects, which claimed to admit women as equals and had little regard for caste, women were used by males in sexual rites so that the men could gain *moksha*. For most women of India, their *karma* from a previous life has dictated their current situation as surely as the Untouchables have been relegated to theirs.

Sikhism

One of the crucial religious conflicts in India today is between the Hindu government and the Sikhs of the Punjab. Located in northern India and on the Pakistan border, the Punjab, home to the vast majority of the world's 8 million Sikhs, houses the holy city, Amritsar, in which their Golden Temple is located. Although apparently a majority in the Punjab, the Sikhs have, however, been weakened in political oversight of their own affairs. Some radical factions have been insisting that Punjab become an independent Sikh nation, an action the Indian government opposes. An unfavorable press in the 1980s and the assassination of Prime Minister Indira Gandhi by Sikh bodyguards in 1984 have unfortunately overshadowed the values of Sikhism. The governmental attack on the sacred Golden Temple and the use of anti-Sikh prejudice to gain political victories in national elections have infuriated the Sikhs of the Punjab.

This is ironic because Sikhism was founded by those who believed that Hindus and Muslims did not have to live in an atmosphere of violence and hostility. The traditional founder, Guru Nanak (1469-1538), was born into a Hindu Punjabi family and educated by a Muslim teacher. Receiving a vision from God at the age of thirty, Nanak was given the message: "There is no Muslim and there is no Hindu." God was the Supreme Being, who was universal, all powerful and truthful. Preaching the unity of all peoples under God, the True Name, who requires compassion and good deeds instead of ceremonies, pilgrimages, and respect for shrines, Nanak declared:

> There is but one God,
> His Name is true,
> He is the Creator,

Devoid of fear and enmity,
He is omnipresent,
He is immortal, unborn,
Nor does He die to be born again.
He was true in the beginning,
The true one was when time began to run its course.
He was the truth,
He is true now,
And truth shall ever prevail.

It is said that Nanak wore a combination of Hindu and Muslim clothing as he preached his message throughout India. His followers were called Sikhs (Punjabi for "disciples"), and they organized communities of the faithful. Like Nanak, they accepted reincarnation and *karma*, insisting that one lives again and again by the fruit of one's deeds until one is freed from the cycle by the "True Name." They also believed that since human beings were God's greatest creation, humans were allowed to eat animals.

Today, one becomes a Sikh by baptism, and congregational worship is the norm. Men and women worship together, as do members of different castes. Although there are no priests, and worship is led by lay leaders, the authorities of the Sikh world do make decisions on worship at the Golden Temple complex. In stark contrast to Nanak's pacifism, Guru Gobind Singh (1675-1708), the last of the Sikh gurus, introduced the five *K*'s to his elite society of warriors, in order to preserve the Sikh faith against the Muslim Mongul onslaught: *kesha*, the long hair wrapped in a turban and accompanied by long beards; *kangha*, the wooden or ivory comb; *kachha*, military knee breeches; *kara*, a steel bracelet; and *kirpan*, a sword, that in modern apparel is usually a facsimile inset in the comb. The order of warriors are part of the Khalsa, the society of the guru's own, and take the surname Singh ("lion"). Sikhism also maintains a sect of holy men *(Udasis)*, who resemble the ascetics of Asian religions, and a pacifist sect *(Sahajdharis)*, who are clean-shaven devotees of Nanak. Tragically, Sikhism, the religion that sought to ameliorate the struggles of two great world religions, Hinduism and Islam, seems destined to be embroiled in conflict well into the twenty-first century.

Technological Challenges

While political conflict with the Sikhs and the persistence of caste constitute significant challenges to India and Hinduism as a new century approaches, the Hindu village itself faces crisis. There is an inequitable distribution of land and wealth. As the population of India grows, the scarcity of land becomes acute. Increasing job scarcities and the effects of natural disasters compound the problems. In 1961, landless households in India comprised 15 million. By 1981, the figure had risen to 26 million, and it is projected that, by the year 2000, the number of landless rural households will reach 44 million. Villagers are paying interest rates well over 30 percent on loans to provide food. Hundreds of thousands of transients migrate to the overburdened cities each year. The resultant squalor and human misery are beyond belief.

The Indian government's zealous effort to slow population growth in the 1970s led to charges of coercive sterilizations. The religious outcry and resultant public pressure dealt 'a blow to the general family-planning program. A new Five-Year Plan is aiming at two-child families and hopes to achieve replacement-level fertility by the year 2000. India has endorsed goals of 31 million sterilizations, 21 million prescriptions of intrauterine devices, and 62 million users of contraceptives by 1990. With an annual population growth of 2.3 percent, Hindu society is gravely threatened by food and water shortages, soil erosion, deforestation, and desertification. From 1972 to 1982, Delhi lost 60 percent of its surrounding forest area. With only 24 percent of India's population of nearly 800 million people in cities, the growth of Delhi, Bombay, Calcutta, and other metropolitan centers will certainly increase through rural migrations caused by economic distress.

Although the government and secularism challenge the organized temple structure, Hinduism in the villages appears to be neither secularizing under modern influences nor converting to new religions. As its people adapt in the face of increasing technology, Hinduism may continue to reform and revitalize as it has done in past centuries, both in rural and urban areas.

THE VISION INWARD

Within Hinduism over the centuries there have been strong re-form movements. One of the most effective reformers was Sankara (788-820 C.E.). A philosopher and Vedanta commentator of astute-ness and originality, he is revered to this day as one of India's great-est spiritual leaders. It was Sankara who composed one of the Hindus' favorite prayers:

> O Lord, pardon my three sins:
> I have in contemplation clothed in form Thee who are
>   formless!
> I have in praise described Thee who are ineffable!
> And in visiting shrines I have ignored Thine omnipresence.

In a similar fashion millions of Hindus utter each day the anony-mous prayer: "As different streams having different sources and with wanderings crooked or straight, all reach the sea, so, Lord, the different paths which men take, guided by their different tenden-cies, all lead to Thee."

If it be objected that too many gods and goddesses impede spir-itual progress in Hinduism and blind Hindus to one God, India's former president, Sarvepalli Radhakrishnan, insists:

> Those who live in God do not care to define. They have a peculiar
>   confidence in the universe, a profound and peaceful acceptance
>   of life in all its sides. Their response to Ultimate Reality is not
>   capable of a clear-cut, easily intelligible formulation. The
>   mystery of God's being cannot be rationally determined. It
>   remains outside the scope of logical concepts. Its form does not
>   lie in the field of vision, none can see it with the eye. There is no
>   equal to it. An austere silence is more adequate to the
>   experience of God than elaborate descriptions.

It is just such a spirit that enables Hindus to tolerate and absorb the beliefs of others and to grant freedom of operation even to religions remote from and alien to their own beliefs. This stands in stark con-trast to the rigidity of their own caste system.

Sometimes the tolerance of other religious groups shown by the Hindus is mere indifference; but on other occasions Hinduism has had a tendency to adopt what is best in another faith. This conviction caused the great reformer, Ramakrishna (1836-1886), to declare: "Different creeds are but different paths to reach the Almighty. As with one gold various ornaments are made, having different forms and names, so one God is worshipped in different countries and ages, has different forms and names."

The vision inward—perhaps that is why Mohandas Gandhi was influenced by the reform movement of Jainism and *ahimsa,* the theory of nonviolence, while remaining a devout Hindu. When Gandhi urged his followers to "turn the spotlight inward," he was only emphasizing the essence of the Upanishads 2500 years earlier: "The senses turn outward. Man, therefore, looks towards what is outside and sees not the inward being. Rare is the wise man who . . . shuts his eyes to outward things and so beholds the glory of the *Atman* [the inner self or soul] within." Thus, Gandhi interpreted afresh the insight that, in poetic form, served as a basic theme of the *Bhagavad-Gita* almost 2000 years ago:

> Only that yogi
> Whose joy is inward,
> Inward his peace,
> And his vision inward
> Shall come to Brahman [the Ultimate Reality]
> And know Nirvana [absorption in the One].

Hinduism, which has worshipped God as Many, and as Three, and as One, will not vanish in the modern world. Its resources, spiritual and intellectual, traditional and cultural, remain undiminished.

3

JAINISM

The Three Jewels

"No person can achieve salvation," say the teachings of Jainism, "unless his life is enhanced by the Three Jewels: right faith (true insight), right knowledge, and right conduct." These are the real means of final liberation for 4 million Jains.

In the sixth century B.C.E., Jainism arose as a protest against the growing power of the priests of Vedaism and the all-encompassing sacrificial cult in Hinduism. Objecting to the stifling impersonality and involved ritualism they found in Hinduism, the Jain challenged the accepted religious structure. They resisted the claims of the priestly caste, the Brahmans, that only a Brahman could master the stages culminating in *nirvana;* moreover, many among the Kshatriyas, the kings' and chieftains' warrior caste, opposed the Brahmans' insistence that the physical world was unreal.

MAHAVIRA

Amid such latent rebellion and resistance the founder of this faith, Vardhamana, universally referred to by the title of Mahavira ("great hero"), was born in the first year of the new century, 599 B.C.E. The son of a rajah, he was raised amid luxury and married a princess with whom he had a daughter.

At the age of thirty, Mahavira decided to give up his life as a prince and to become a religious ascetic; but this action he postponed until his parents had died. After his parents' death he secured his older brother's consent and then prepared to relinquish all his belongings—gold and silver, jewels and ornaments, troops and chariots. He plucked out his hair in five handfuls, as a symbol of self-renunciation, and vowed: "I shall for twelve years neglect my body and abandon the care of it." He swore to endure with equanimity any calamity that might come from divine powers, from animals, or from persons. He set out alone, discarding his robe and wandering naked across the plains and into the villages of central India in search of release from the cycle of birth, death, and rebirth.

Chronicles of Mahavira's life described for future generations his disdain for both comforts and discomforts. "He was indifferent alike to the smell of filth and of sandalwood, to straw and to jewels, to dirt and to gold, to pleasure and to pain, attached neither to this world nor to that beyond, desiring neither life nor death."

Mahavira, "the Venerable One," paid no heed to cold or heat, we are told, for he "desired nothing of the kind; strong in control, he suffered, despising all shelter." He refused to "sleep for the sake of pleasure; he waked up himself, and slept only a little. Purgatives and emetics, anointing of the body and bathing, shampooing, and cleansing of the teeth do not behoove him."

Two major convictions impelled him: a complete asceticism and an absolute pacifism. The two were as one, for the soul could not be saved from evil without practicing such intense self-denial; and the soul could not maintain its purity and integrity unless a man practiced *ahimsa*—that is, noninjury—to all living beings. "Harmlessness," Mahavira was accustomed to say, "is the only religion."

In the thirteenth year of his wandering as a naked ascetic, the traditions relate, Mahavira was "in a squatting position . . . exposing himself to the heat of the sun . . . with the knees high and the head low, in deep meditation, [when] he reached *nirvana*, the complete and full, the unobstructed, infinite Absolute."

Now that he had succeeded in gaining control over both the world and his own body, Mahavira gave up being a solitary bent on asceticism; he became instead a leader of men and the teacher of monks. The sacred texts relate that he was an *arhat* (worthy of worship) and a *kevalin* (all-knowing, omniscient). Thereafter he was called "the Conqueror" (Jina). For the following thirty years, until he died of voluntary starvation at the age of seventy-two in 527 B.C.E., Mahavira preached and taught with extraordinary success.

His followers became known as Jains, disciples of him who conquered. Had he not conquered? Had he not attained victory over his own body and its desires?

Mahavira, a disillusioned nobleman of the warrior caste (the Kshatriyas) in Hinduism, had adopted the asceticism of the Parshva order of mendicants. He was, according to Jain tradition, the last in line of twenty-four *Tirthankaras* ("crossers of the stream of sorry life," literally "builders of the ford [which leads across the ocean of suffering]"). Twenty-three Jains—"conquerors"—had preceded him, the legends related; the preceding one, Parshva, of a century or more earlier, was apparently a genuine historical person who was recorded as living 100 years. The first Tirthankara, Rsabha, was recorded as living for 8,400,000 years.

Therefore, since Jainism is older than Mahavira, considerable debate has ensued over the Jaina canon and sourcebooks. The fourteen *Purvas* are considered the oldest part of the Jain's canon, and by some accounts trace back to the first Tirthankaras. Mahavira taught them himself, but the original text has been lost. The twelve *Angas* are the oldest source-material available, listing and quoting from the *Purvas*. Jaina traditions, sermons, liturgy, parables, history, and apologetics are contained in these volumes. Among other collections, the six *Cheda-Sutras*, which deal with the conduct of monks and nuns, and the four *Mula-Sutras*, which record Mahavira's doctrines and rules of conduct, are noteworthy.

BELIEFS AND VOWS

Basic to Jain doctrine was Mahavira's belief that everything in the entire universe is eternal; to offset any views to the contrary and to dissociate himself from the Brahmans, he specifically included matter in this category. The world is without a beginning or an end, without a supreme creator or sustainer. Spirits are conscious of their identity, Mahavira insisted; and they retain that consciousness through successive incarnations by the law of *karma*. A person's conduct during each existence affects that person's spirit for good or for ill in a later incarnation, thus having a cumulative effect, the permanent deposit in the soul of that person's deeds and actions. After knowing incarnation, however, the Jain is able to attain *nirvana* and be granted release from the body; but if the soul desires, it may, even after the attainment of *nirvana*, consent to undergo additional births if such a decision helps weaker spirits in their own search for salvation.

The Jains have always believed that the Brahman-Atman, concerning which the Brahmans of Hinduism spoke, did not exist at all. There is, say they, no All-One, no basic substance holding the world and the universe in order, no highest deity. The gods, who are higher beings and exist on different levels within the celestial sphere, are really only finite; they, too, have to be reborn. They are, however, responsible for watching and controlling true discipline. The Jinas, rather than the gods, are worshipped; but since they have transcended the worldly plane, they cannot personally answer prayers.

Only by attaining liberation on one's own could *moksha*, the salvation, be achieved. Prayers without actions were of no help, priests of no avail. The Vedas could not be invoked, for they, said the Jains, were neither sacred nor unique. The best mode of worshipping was to practice the Jina's discipline. It is in these internal concepts that the modern erection of temples is justified. Nevertheless, each person must find salvation within: "Man! Thou art thine own friend. Why wishest thou for a friend beyond thyself?" Into this single pronouncement, Mahavira packed the essence of his faith. His followers and foes alike quote it often, the former in enthusiastic support of and the latter in derisive opposition to Jainism.

To attain *moksha*, the state of liberation, the Jain must practice asceticism, rigorously and earnestly. Twelve years of self-denial and austerity, Mahavira's own time for successful attainment of *moksha*, are necessary before one can reach *nirvana*. The *yati* (an ascetic) must take the "five great vows" prescribed for Jain monks: to injure no creature, to speak the truth, to abstain from stealing, to renounce all worldly goods, and to practice continence. In this manner only can one achieve self-mastery.

The first vow, dealing with the subject of *ahimsa*, noninjury to any and all living beings, remains the most important of the five: "The first great vow, Sir, runs thus: I renounce all killing of living beings, whether movable or immovable. Nor shall I myself kill living beings nor cause others to do it, nor consent to it. As long as I live, I confess, and blame, and exempt myself of these sins, in mind, speech and body."

The renunciation of any interest in or indulgence of sexual desires—the fifth vow—is almost as important, certainly in implication if not in widespread effectiveness. Mahavira was absolutely sure on one point: "The greatest temptation in the world is women. . . . Men forsooth say, 'These are the vessels of happiness.' But this leads them to pain, to delusion, to death, to hell, to birth as hell-beings or brute beasts."

For average persons the Five Great Vows usually prove to be too stiff an assignment. For them, Jains have provided a less severe regimen—namely, twelve vows prescribing strict commandments not to take human or animal life, be unfaithful to a spouse, or to lie, steal, or cheat, and including positive injunctions to give alms, practice self-denial, guard against evil, meditate regularly, avoid needless travel, and restrain greed.

Most important was the first vow: not knowingly to take the life of any sentient creature, that is, any person or thing capable of feeling or perception. The prohibition meant that one could not till the soil; nor could one engage in fishing or butchering or follow any occupation that required the taking of life. The Jains became perhaps the earliest vegetarians in India, for they even rejected the Buddhist notion that meat is acceptable if an animal has died of natural causes. Jains pointed out that meat from such an animal bred the lowest of lifeforms and, thus, consuming such dead flesh was consuming life. Some scholars have suggested that because of its strong stand, Jainism contributed to the eventual triumph of vegetarianism throughout India.

Many Jains had come from the warrior castes and now had to relinquish their profession of shedding blood and of killing. The merchants, however, had not been dislodged from their occupations by Jain teachings and were able to compete with the Brahmans successfully. For the most part Jains came from the middle classes and thus had the social position to gather wealth and to achieve distinction in both literature and architecture.

SECTS AND SIGNIFICANCE

There have always been two major sects among Jains, the Digambaras and the Svetambaras. These two factions differed on the matter of wearing clothes, for the Digambaras insisted that Mahavira did not wear clothes and any monk owning property or wearing clothes was therefore unable to reach *nirvana*. The Digambaras—the "sky-clad" or "clothed in atmosphere"—went about naked and even denied themselves food at times, but nowadays they no longer practice total nudity. Women are not allowed to join the Digambara sect, for their traditions teach that Mahavira was a bachelor. Denied salvation, women are forced to wait for some future reincarnation as males. The other sect, the Svetambaras, are clad in white and include both nuns and monks, who devote themselves to their sacred literature and to charitable acts.

During the twelfth and thirteenth centuries C.E., Jainists were attacked by militant Hindu sects as well as Muslim invaders. They lost both temples and adherents. Jaina history teaches, however, that the greatest danger was decay from within. Monks became so temple-oriented and luxury-minded that they forsook the pure teachings of the Jina. Jainism might have been absorbed into Hinduism, but its own reform movements purified and rejuvenated both sects. Today, the building of temples and the consecration and veneration of Tirthankaras images by lay Jains are a major religious practice. Nevertheless, the images are viewed as an ideal, not as a temple "deity." They are a reminder to the devoted of the goals and aspirations of all Jains.

The Jains are especially proud of the time-honored story in their writings of the six blind men who, placing their hands on different parts of the elephant, maintained that the elephant was "like a fan," "like a wall," "like a snake," "like a rope," etc. To them this parable highlights the fallacies to which all human thought falls prey, for nothing is absolutely true or false; both yes and no are proper answers to every single question. Knowledge, say the Jains, is, at best, relative and partial.

Not without reason have the Jains exerted an influence far beyond their numbers, partly by influencing philosophy, especially logic, and partly by having molded the thought of Mohandas Gandhi, for *ahimsa*, or the theory of nonviolence, helped to formulate his spiritual views and his political policies. A revered Jain layman, Raychandbhai Mehta, who corresponded with Gandhi, was credited by the great Hindu political leader with helping him through his struggles with the concept of *ahimsa*. "When I began to feel doubts about Hinduism as a religion," Gandhi related, "it was Raychandbhai who helped me to resolve them."

Inasmuch as Jains cannot engage in any occupation that endangers life, they have had to devote themselves instead to finance and commerce. This shift in vocations and professions has resulted in their attaining unusual prosperity as lawyers and bankers, moneylenders and brokers, merchants and proprietors of land. Though they renounce the world, they are unusually rich in worldly goods; and in a land of such widespread poverty and misery as India they are a paradox of affluence. The largest group of Jains, for example, reside in Calcutta, a city of extreme squalor.

For a number of reasons Jainism is important in our times. First of all, it is the oldest personally founded religion in India. Second, it was a conscious effort to reform or improve Hinduism; but it resulted in a new and separate religion, rather than in a reaffirmation of the best in Hinduism. Third, it has given the world an exquisite architecture. And, fourth, Jains have contributed greatly, through their influence on Gandhi and his formulation of nonviolence as a political technique, to the attainment of the independence of India from British imperial rule and the assurance of India's commonwealth status in the British Commonwealth of Nations.

The second point is of greatest significance, for Jainism broke clear of Hinduism when Mahavira condemned the caste system and advocated the equality of all religious ascetics; yet only partial success resulted, for the caste system was too firmly entrenched across so many centuries and among such vast numbers of people. Despite Mahavira's denunciation of the caste system, the Jains today are a closed group.

Yet Mahavira considered the world, not his own nation or region, to be his fatherland and his homeland; he scorned the idea that one's family or caste should be the center of one's interest and loyalty. In this, he challenged Indic civilization and Hindu faith. Protesting animal sacrifices, ceremonies, rituals, and even the "sacred" archaic Sanskrit language (Mahavira taught in the language of his era and region, the vernacular called Prakit), he considered his faith to be a universal religion, meant for all nations. His words resound across twenty-five centuries: "Man! Thou art thine own friend. Why wishest thou for a friend beyond thyself?"

4

BUDDHISM

The Middle Path

In the same century, the sixth B.C.E., and less than a generation after Jainism, Buddhism arose. It had many elements in common with Jainism; its central figure, Siddhartha Gautama, like Mahavira sought to liberate the true self by denying the world. He questioned the power of the Vedas, repudiated the rituals associated with them and, as a member of the Kshatriya caste, opposed the claims of the priests in the Brahman caste that only they knew the path to salvation. Gautama broadened the appeal of this new faith to include all of Indian society.

Unlike Jainism, Buddhism advocated moderation, "The Middle Path." Gautama, the Buddha, did not believe in trying to be an ascetic and he sought to avoid both extremes: asceticism and sensualism. Living in an age of social change and intellectual ferment, he calmly counseled:

> Follow the Middle Path. There is a Middle Path avoiding these two extremes . . . a path which opens the eyes and bestows understanding, which leads to peace of mind, to the higher wisdom, to full enlightenment, to Nirvana. . . . There are these four Noble Truths. . . the Noble Truth of suffering. . .the Noble Truth of the cause of suffering. . .craving, tending to rebirth, combined with delight and passion. . .the Noble Truth of the

cessation of suffering. . .the Noble Truth of the Path that leads to the cessation of suffering. . . It [the Path that leads to the cessation of suffering] is the Noble Eightfold Way, namely, right views; right aspirations; right speech; right conduct; right means of livelihood; right effort; right mindfulness; and right contemplation.

Like Mahavira, Siddhartha Gautama came from a noble family, married, and had one child; but, dissatisfied with his life of privilege, he left his home, as had Mahavira, to become a wandering monk. Gautama turned his back on the accepted Hinduism of his time and began a new religion that knew no distinctions of caste and diverged sharply from Brahman practices. There the resemblance ends, for Mahavira's and Gautama's attitudes and careers diverged, just as do their respective faiths, Jainism and Buddhism, 2500 years later.

SIDDHARTHA GAUTAMA

Born in 560 B.C.E., in a region of northern India about 100 miles from Benares, Siddhartha Gautama, as the son of King Suddhodana and Queen Maha-Maya of the Sakya clan, knew only luxury and protective care during his childhood and youth. Despite a happy marriage and the assurance of a secure, comfortable future, both as a landowner and as a ruler, he was not at ease. A lack of inner contentment disturbed him. He felt this void at the time of his marriage in his late teens but experienced it more acutely in his late twenties when he became a father. The discontent led him to the decision to leave his family—his kindly and generous father, his lovely and gracious wife, his cherished and adored child—so that he could learn of life outside the guarded walls of the palatial estates.

A familiar legend of Buddhism, "The Four Passing Sights," describes the father's efforts to shield his son from the sordid side of life. The father of Gautama had, at the time of his son's birth, been warned that the prince might someday forsake the family, become a mendicant monk begging for alms along the road, and thus lose the opportunity destiny had in store for him of becoming "a universal monarch" as India's emperor. Carefully and intently the father kept his son from knowing the sadness and the seamy aspects of normal existence. He guarded him against seeing the inroads of disease, the erosion of age, and the tragedy of death. Amid the opulence and magnificence of three palaces, the boy grew to adulthood and knew nothing of the harshness of life, never seeing the ill or the aged and remaining unaware of the pain and disorder of the natural world.

The gods decided to send one of their own, disguised as an infirm old man, to bring the prince to reality. When the prince asked his charioteer to explain what he was now seeing for the first time, he heard an explanation of age and the inevitable, inescapable end of a man's life. A second sight, a man hideously ravaged by disease, caused him to learn how debilitated and sickened a man could be his whole life long. In a third instance he saw a corpse being carried to the cremation ground. The prince now had found out about death; in later years, he related how he had reflected: "I also am subject to decay, and am not free from the power of old age, sickness and death. Is it right that I should feel horror, repulsion, and disgust when I see another in such plight? And when I reflected thus, my disciples, all the joy of life which there is in life died within me."

The king, his father, tried to bring cheer and joy to the young prince, providing entertainment and diversions but to no avail. Torn by his conflicts and racked by his lack of inner certitude, Gautama remained distraught until the fourth sight. As he sat beneath a tree, an ascetic dressed in a saffron-colored robe came to him by the side of the road. From him Gautama heard that a man might be freed from disease and old age and death. In that hour and at that moment, Gautama resolved to leave home and to wander as a monk.

This decision his father stoutly resisted and determined to distract his son from such morbid moods. He sent dancing girls to entertain Gautama, but they left the son unmoved and still brooding. As the dancing girls became exhausted and one by one fell fast asleep, Gautama waited; when they were all sleeping, he left the room, inwardly repelled by the silent sleepers on the floor. For the last time he went to the apartment of his wife, Yasodhara, looked upon the mother and son, Rahula, bade them a mute good-bye, and left the house. He mounted a large white horse and galloped far beyond the river, the charioteer by his side. Then he cut off his beard and hair—"in all the beauty of my early prime, with a wealth of coal-black hair untouched by gray"—and gave up his fine clothes to wear the rough yellow robes of a wandering mendicant monk. He ordered the charioteer to return home while he entered the forest to begin his six years of struggle to attain salvation.

First he went to the royal city of a province called Magadha—Rajagaya—and, following some of the yoga and trance-meditation methods, lived with Brahman ascetics. Their disciplines left him unsatisfied. Stages of meditation, leading to a realm of nothingness, or of neither perception nor nonperception, did not satisfy his mind and spirit.

Now that he had given Brahmanism another chance and found it would not lead him to enlightenment, he tried extreme asceticism comparable to Mahavira's Jaina tradition. For five years, in a grove at Uruvela on the banks of a river, he practiced such arduous self-discipline and asceticism that soon he was little more than a living wraith. He found that his mind was clearer as he disciplined his body; and he believed that if he forced his mind to dominate his heart, remaining free of all the pleasures of sense, he would find salvation. For days and months he practiced such self-domination, living on vile foods, including his own excrement, sitting on a couch of thorns, lying amid the crumbling bones and decaying flesh of corpses in a cemetery, subsisting on single kernels of rice or grain. Yet the punished body, painfully thin, mercilessly disciplined, cruelly mortified, brought him no enlightenment. He then asked himself whether he should not seek other paths.

Five more ascetics gathered around him and joined in the quest. When Gautama fainted, the five thought him ready to die. Soon he revived, however, and announced that the way of mortification could not bring peace of mind. Now he would eat and drink, continuing as a begging pilgrim monk but strengthening the body so that it might support his intellect. The five ascetics, disillusioned and outraged, banned him for indulging himself in luxury. Their friend, their ideal, had succumbed to the evil of self-indulgence.

THE BUDDHA

Gautama began once more, convinced that mere meditation and mortification of the body helped not at all. He started his search anew. At Buddhagaya (Bodh Gaya) he entered a sacred grove and sat beneath a tree, which in time was described as the bo tree or the bodhi tree ("the tree of knowledge"). He vowed that he would meditate until "I attain enlightenment . . . though skin, nerves, and bone shall waste away, and life-blood itself be dried up." He thought about his seeming failure and asked himself: what have my life and my search for the past six years accomplished?

Abruptly he discovered the answer. It had been *tanha*, his craving and his thirst, a too-intent desire that had impeded him—and, for that matter, the entire human race. He, and they, had sought the wrong things. He had desired in a carnal way and thus had defeated himself. If he rid himself of that desire, he would know *nirvana*, complete and utterly blissful peace. This realization, ridding him of any sensual desires, purged him of what he termed "wrong states of mind." He knew an ecstasy now that was beyond either satisfaction or dissatisfaction, an elevation that gave him the purest of motives and the deepest mood of peace. Ignorance was gone and knowledge stood in its place. Darkness had vanished and light blazed forth. He felt that he had completed his rebirth and had attained the highest life. His task was finished and he had become "the Enlightened One," the Buddha.

He had, however, to share these insights, for he could not remain a Buddha for himself alone. He must teach and share and guide. He found again the five ascetics who had left him in Uruvela. Locating them in the Deer Park near Benares, he met only scorn from them at first, but he reflected such deep conviction and convincing power that he soon began to win them over.

In his famous "Sermon in the Deer Park at Sarnath near Benares," Gautama countered their accusations that his self-indulgence and nonasceticism had robbed him of enlightenment; and the five now acknowledged him to be an *arhat*—that is, a monk who had attained *nirvana*, or enlightenment. As they consented to try his Middle Path, founding the monastic order called the Sangha, Gautama set out on his ministry through northern India.

He found many converts in his own caste of Kshatriyas, and among lower castes as well—even among the Brahmans he instructed. He trained his monks and gathered new disciples year after year. These ten precepts guided the members of the Sangha: refrain from destroying life *(ahimsa);* do not take what is not given; abstain from unchastity; do not lie or deceive; abstain from intoxicants; eat moderately and not after noon; do not look at dancing, singing, or dramatic spectacles; do not affect the use of garlands, scents, unguents, or ornaments; do not use high or broad beds; do not accept gold or silver.

The Middle Way or Path went by these ten precepts, steering an even course between self-indulgence, which was earnestly and specifically forbidden, and extreme asceticism, which had never been commanded.

The first five of these precepts could be obeyed by lay associates of the Sangha order. Buddha allowed women to form an order of nuns; but his consent was reluctant (he refused twice), and he had grave reservations. Gautama Buddha wryly remarked to his cousin, Ananda, who had to beg him three times to allow women to enter, that "if women had not received permission to enter the order, the pure religion would have lasted long, the good law would have stood fast a thousand years. But since they have received permission, it will now stand fast for only five hundred years."

Almost a half century of teaching and preaching, planning, and working marked the Buddha's active ministry; and the "three jewels" of every traditional Buddhist to this day (the Buddha, the *dharma* or teaching, and the order) were in place as a refuge to turn from the visible to the invisible. At the age of eighty, Buddha approached his life's end in a little town named Kusinara northeast of the city of Benares. At the home of the goldsmith Chunda, he ate his noonday meal; but the food he ate (possibly mushrooms) was tainted, and he became seriously ill. He tried to continue his missionary journey by mentally controlling the effects of the illness, but when he stopped to rest, it overtook him. As he lay on the ground between two sal trees, not far from Kusinara, Gautama Buddha died.

FOUR CORNERSTONES

Two major rejections and two major acceptances were the four cornerstones on which Gautama Buddha built his structure of thought, expecting his disciples to elaborate on them.

The two rejections were his denial that philosophical speculation was of any value in finding salvation, and his turning away from *bhakti*—religious piety and devotion—as a means of attaining salvation. Ironically, in later years, the most popular Buddhist movements would be founded on traditions of *bhakti*, and Buddhist philosophical speculation would abound. But Buddha was concerned with practical and human issues. He had little patience with Hindu devotionalism or with a projection of the mind into the realm of metaphysics (that branch of philosophy that deals with first principles and seeks to explain the nature of being or reality, the origin of the world, and what constitutes knowledge). He did not believe in the efficacy of prayer or the holiness of the Vedas, the worth of rituals, or the aristocratic prestige of a priestly caste like the Brahmans. He was a nontheistic humanist and, like Mahavira, he urged his followers to look to their own strength and resources for salvation. Such views were heretical to the Hindus, especially to devoutly observant followers of Hinduism.

Yet two basic tenets of Hinduism he accepted, modifying each: the law of *karma* and the doctrine of *samsara*, continual rebirths. In the case of the former, the law of *karma*, the Buddha believed that if one altered one's ways, experienced a change of heart that brought new directions and new objectives, "the state of him that is worthy," the penalty for craving and desire in an earlier existence would not be applied. This assertion created controversy among Buddha's followers for hundreds of years thereafter—and does so to this day. Those who have become steadfast of mind and therefore are rid of desire need concern themselves no longer about *karma*, he taught, for none is needed any longer; they need no rebirth and are exempt from any longing for a future life. The living process is akin to a fire burning, but the enlightened "are extinguished at death like a lamp" and will not know rebirth. Only those who are still burdened with *tanha*, the thirst to live and the craving to have, will be reborn.

Rather than to a philosophical system, Buddha pointed to a path. A buddha was simply one who had traveled the right path and reported to others what had been learned. *Nirvana* was not mere cessation, but the attainment of the eternal, the immortal. According to tradition, Gautama realized enlightenment through four stages of trance. At first he detached himself from sensual objects and calmed his passions. Then he progressed to nonreasoning and basic concentration. Thirdly, he reached "dispassionate" mindfulness and consciousness, experiencing bodily bliss. His last stage of trance was pure awareness and peace without elation, depression, or pain.

Behind all this reflection on the need for, or the exemption from, rebirth lay the Buddha's basic conviction that the world around and within us is in flux, an endless process of change and decay, of coming and going, of becoming and vanishing. In the enlightenment experience, Gautama Buddha encountered ultimate reality, an indescribable unity; but he taught that there was no Supreme Personality, no inherent Intelligence. Being is basically impersonal, and one's ego an illusion. *Nirvana*, illimitably pure and all-embracing, is the goal, for it brings peace to the self, which no longer thinks of itself as an ego.

This *dhamma*, the doctrine of the turning of the wheel, points to the never-ending becoming, rather than fulfillment, to never-ceasing change, which reveals how impermanent is the seemingly permanent. It has been symbolized by a wheel with twelve sections or a circular chain with twelve links. The first link of this "wheel of dependent co-arising" instructs that aging and dying depend on rebirth, and the last link insists that ignorance is the basic cause of *samsara* (rebirth). Each link leads those without "enlightenment" on to the next stage of an endless spin. *Dhamma* brings the pain of knowing only incompletion, partial realization, and inevitable failures to attain the whole or the perfect.

Six realms within this wheel of rebirth depict destinies that engulf living beings trapped in the cycle of craving and desire. The lowest realm shows extreme punishment in a hell of terrors, from which one enters the human realm through rebirth after paying the debt for wicked deeds. Above this first is a world of "hungry ghosts," wandering the earth in search of subsistence. The realm of animals comes next, the least severe of the "hells" that existed. The human part, where one could practice good *karma,* was above the animal realm; and the areas of the demigods and gods composed the fifth and sixth spheres respectively. Gautama Buddha felt that humans erred in clinging to the pleasures of life in the face of such an endless, hopeless existence. So painful is existence and so wearisome is this yearning to hold to the world we know and experience consciously that it is best for one to allow it to perish, to leave the cycle of *samsara.* The state of enlightenment is better than all these planes and superior to all the gods, for even the gods have to experience rebirth.

THE FOUR NOBLE TRUTHS

When Buddha preached his first sermon to the five ascetics in the Deer Park, he gave an answer to the perplexing problem: "How should one live so one might diminish pain and suffering, might destroy the deplorable 'will-to-live-and-have' *[tanha],* and thus know liberation and its joy?" He answered by describing the Four Noble Truths. They contain the essential tenets of the *dharma,* the teaching of Gautama Buddha.

The First Noble Truth underscored the reality of suffering *(dukkha).* All life is *dukkha,* painful and unpleasant. Birth, decay, sickness, despair, and death underscore this truth.

The Second Noble Truth is that *dukkha* is caused by "craving and desire" *(tanha).* "Now this, monks, is the noble truth of the cause of pain," instructed Gautama Buddha, "the craving, which tends to rebirth, combined with pleasure and lust, finding pleasure here and there, namely the craving for passion, the craving for existence, the craving for nonexistence."

The Third Noble Truth taught that renouncing desire will stop *dukkha,* while the Fourth Noble Truth was the Eightfold Way, the way that led to the cessation of *dukkha.* This Noble Eightfold Way—right views, right aspirations, right speech, right conduct, right means of livelihood, right effort, right-mindedness, and right contemplation—marked the path that Buddha developed for those who had accepted his teaching and wanted to attain *nirvana.* The first two are the wisdom portion. Right views describes knowledge of the Four Noble Truths, the fundamental *dharma* of the Buddha. Right aspirations were noble intents to attain love for others, to eradicate wrong, and to wish not to injure any living thing.

The next three aspects comprise the morality of the Way. One must earn a living, speak, think, and act in a moral and ethical manner that bends one's being toward the liberating goal of *nirvana*. The last three aspects are the meditation portion of Buddha's Way. One's consciousness can be further refined so that enlightened understanding may take control. Right-mindedness is closely connected to the intellectual alertness of right effort. Right concentration is the advanced stage of right-mindedness. Each section of the Noble Eightfold Way reinforces the others. "It is through not understanding and not grasping the Four Noble Truths," Gautama Buddha insisted, "that we have had to run so long, to wander so long in this weary path of transmigration, both you and I!"

To the average person in the Western world, the ethics of Gautama Buddha seem to be negative and pessimistic; but this is an inaccurate judgment. The Buddha may appear to have been negative in his counsels; but he had a positive objective: spiritual happiness or "blessedness." Not all existence leads to misery, not all desire is wrong. The wise person, having overcome ignorance, is able to determine what is not miserable in existence and what is admirable in desire. To avoid suffering and cause no suffering, he advised: "Let therefore no man love anything: loss of the beloved is evil. Those who love nothing and hate nothing have no fetters."

When the Buddha urged that a person break the bonds that tie one to the wheel of existence, he sought to lift "ten fetters": (1) belief in the existence of the self, (2) doubt, (3) trust in ceremonies of good works, (4) lust, (5) anger, (6) desire for rebirth in worlds of form, (7) desire for rebirth in formless worlds, (8) pride, (9) self-righteousness, and (10) ignorance.

The goal of the Noble Eightfold Path, "the path that leads to no-desire," is sainthood or the state of an *arhat*, the "worthy" one who has attained *nirvana*, a level of calm and joy, of energy and benevolence (*sambodhi*), and who is freed from desires that bring misery. Calmly and fearlessly continuing to "put out the lamp of life," he awaits *parinirvana*, the ultimate *nirvana* upon his death. There is no more transmigration then, no pain and misery in becoming or in mere being. Perfect happiness is at hand.

At the heart of Buddhism are good will, benevolence, compassion for all. "Love all mankind with a mother's love" is a central commandment. As Gautama Buddha reminded his followers, "Hatred ceases by love, this is an old rule." He admonished, "If someone curses you, you must repress all resentment."

THERAVADA AND MAHAYANA

Soon after Gautama Buddha's death, his disciples began to disagree on the nature of his teaching. Buddhism was ultimately divided into two great traditions, Theravada and Mahayana. These major divisions of Buddhism still are prevalent today.

Theravada Buddhism

Theravada Buddhism seeks to be faithful to the original teachings of Gautama Buddha as canonized in the Pali scriptures. It centers on the role of the monk and his individual search for *nirvana*. The ideal of Theravada Buddhism is *arhat*, to become an enlightened saint, worthy of worship. Gautama Buddha is the model of this ideal, because he himself became an *arhat*. The most commendable human quality to the Theravada monk is wisdom, and purity of doctrine in regard to the Pali texts is pursued. In fact, *Theravada* means "Doctrine of the Elders," and this tradition is the conservative branch of Buddhism. Philosophical metaphysics is strictly avoided, and meditation takes the place of prayer.

Theravada monks do not rely heavily on symbols or rituals; their altars are simple and their possessions are few. In Burma, for example, the monks possess only a begging bowl, three colored robes, a belt, a mending needle, a fan for modest cover of the face, a razor, and a water strainer to prevent them from swallowing small forms of animal life. In accordance with the Middle Path of Gautama Buddha, food must be eaten before noon each day. Begging for food among the populace, the monks reaffirm their separation from gainful employment, the pursuit of the Middle Path, and their dedication to the goal of *arhat*. Heads shaven, they renounce the vanities of human existence and the pride that accompanies individuality.

Much of Theravada Buddhism's influence outside India can be attributed to an ancient royal convert, Emperor Asoka (c. 304-232 B.C.E.). Bringing the Mauryan empire created by his grandfather, Chandragupta (ruled c. 322-298 B.C.E.), to the zenith of its power and prosperity, comprising two-thirds of India, Asoka was horrified by the devastating slaughter of men, women, and children during his conquest of Kalinga. Consequently, he rejected violence and converted to Buddhism. Transformed into a man of peace, Asoka propagated his newfound faith by expressing his genuine and profound regret for having killed and displaced so many hundreds of thousands of people, and by vowing to be henceforth gentle, meek, and patient. He supported the Sangha, the *dharma*, and the Buddha, the three jewels of Buddhism. He abolished the royal hunt, forbade the slaughter of animals, and urged all his people to be good Buddhists. Throughout his kingdom, Asoka built temples and schools, cultivated trees and provided water, constantly building monuments on which he inscribed the precepts of Buddhism. He sent missionaries into other lands, not only to Sri Lanka and Burma but even to the Hellenistic kingdoms in Asia, Europe, and Egypt. Asoka's grandfather, Chandragupta, had made a treaty in 304 B.C.E. with one of Alexander the Great's generals, Seleucus Nicator. In 247 B.C.E., Asoka summoned the Third Buddhist Council to eradicate heresy, achieve orthodoxy, and determine the authoritative texts.

Because of Asoka's vision of Buddhism spreading worldwide and his support of Buddhist missionaries, the Theravada Buddhist tradition is widely practiced today in Burma (recently renamed Myanma), Thailand, Sri Lanka (formerly Ceylon), Cambodia, and Laos. As a religious tradition, Theravada Buddhism has rarely developed intricate ceremonies or rites of passage. Rather, it has incorporated the festivals and customs of its host country. Yet there is unity exhibited in the culture of the diverse peoples influenced by this Buddhist tradition.

Although monasticism is central—and a small group of *bhikkuni* (Buddhist nuns) in Sri Lanka and Thailand have revived female participation in the order—Theravada Buddhism has encouraged its laity to lead a religious life of Buddhist expression. In Sri Lanka and Thailand, monks are often involved in weddings, funerals, and other ceremonies. In Burma, young Buddhist boys are taken to the monastery by their parents for a short stay as novices. Hair cut and begging bowl in hand each day, these boys are taught important lessons about the Buddha and their religious heritage. In Sri Lanka, traditional Buddhist families send their young men to the monasteries for a year.

Nevertheless, most laypersons meditate at home, and their primary merit-producing activity (outside of the traditional five precepts) is to provide food and robes for the monks. The more wealthy Theravada Buddhist laypersons build pagodas, which symbolize Buddha and may contain relics of the Buddhist faith. Such pagodas dot the landscape of Theravada countries.

Mahayana Buddhism

Mahayana means "Great Vehicle;" and Mahayana Buddhism teaches that as a large raft crosses a river, so too, multitudes may be carried to *nirvana*. It declares that Buddhism is a religion for lay people as well as for monks and explains that each person is involved with other believers, helping one another. The most commendable human quality is *karuna* (compassion), which is clearly exhibited in the life and choices of Gautama Buddha. Caricaturing Theravada Buddhism as *Hinayana* (the "Lesser Vehicle," i.e., a "small" raft for only a few monks), Mahayana Buddhists assert that each person can attain *nirvana* through assistance.

Although its precursors date back to the feuding disciples of Gautama Buddha and the sects that developed during the centuries after his death, Mahayana Buddhism became a clearly visible religious development between 100 B.C.E. and 100 C.E. Its lay orientation was freer in spirit, and it proclaimed that the Buddhist ideal was *bodhisattva*, a saint or enlightened one who compassionately holds back on the very threshold of complete Buddhahood, to help others attain *nirvana*. Gautama Buddha was only one of many buddhas and bodhisattvas that helped others to enlightenment. Mahayanists delightedly point to stories in the Pali canon of Buddha's former lives.

To the Mahayana tradition, Buddha was not only a model to follow, but also a savior who would help. Prayers and petitions to Buddha were advocated just as fervently as was meditation. While they did use portions of the Pali texts, Mahayanists created their own scriptures by accepting additional *sutras* from great teachers. Over the centuries, Mahayana Buddhism has developed a large spectrum of metaphysical analyses and devotional practices, expanding the Four Noble Truths and Eightfold Way. The three jewels of Buddhism (Buddha, *dharma*, Sangha) were accepted, but were treated in a manner that differed significantly from Theravada Buddhism. This expanded universal message fared well throughout East Asia, permeating philosophy and art.

Today, Mahayana Buddhism prevails in Japan, China, Korea, and Vietnam. Its tolerant spirit has given rise to many new schools and disciplines, and its compromising nature allows it to coexist with other religious systems. Its entry into Tibet in the seventh century C.E. caused it to merge with the shamanist beliefs of the local population. Tantrist Buddhism from India was influential in the founding of a lasting Tibetan Sangha at the end of the eighth century C.E., a Buddhism distinct from other lands. This resulting Tibetan Buddhism is known as Lamaism, because its chief figure is the Dalai Lama, fourteenth in the line of bodhisattvas from the original Sangha. This "living Buddha" of the Tibetans has been in exile in India since the unsuccessful Tibetan National Uprising in 1959. Nevertheless, he continues to be venerated by 6 million Tibetans as a human manifestation of their patron bodhisattva, a lord of mercy and compassion, who will guide them on the path of enlightenment. Their current struggle is only one of many Buddhist struggles with secular authorities around the world.

Buddhism is now virtually extinct in the land of its origin. It may have expanded successfully and even triumphantly throughout other parts of the Orient; but in India it had difficulties, so that in the century after Asoka's death powerful influences against it began to arise. Within a thousand years after Asoka it had vanished in India, in part because Hinduism, from which it had originally sprung, absorbed Buddhism and its distinctive nature; and partly because the armies of Islam invaded India in the twelfth century and destroyed whatever remained of Buddhism. Ironically, the same Tantrist strain of Buddhism that gave rise to the perpetual Sangha of the Dalai Lama in Tibet, also contributed to the absorption of Buddhism by Hinduism in India. The mixture of occult and erotic practices in Tantrist Buddhism permitted the Hindu tradition to incorporate the last vestiges of a separate Buddhist community in India. As Buddhism disappeared from the Indian landscape, its influence and appeal outside India became greater with the passing of the centuries.

ZEN BUDDHISM

A descendant of Mahayana Buddhism is Zen Buddhism, which has become popular in Western countries. Paradoxically, it resembles Theravada Buddhism because of its austerity and its belief that a flash of intuition, occurring during carefully disciplined meditation, brings enlightenment.

Zen Buddhism developed in the latter part of the sixth century C.E., when Bodhidharma came to China, shortly after the conversion of the Emperor Wu Ti to Buddhism. According to a generally accepted legend, the Emperor summoned Bodhidharma from North China to question him about the merit that would come from his donating to Buddhist monks and encouraging the translation of sacred works. Bodhidharma, dour and blunt, answered, "No merit at all." He told the Emperor that good works and wide reading were useless; only through meditation would His Majesty know anything about the reality of Buddha. To prove his point to the skeptical king, Bodhidharma went to Mount Su and, for the next nine years, faced a wall in meditation, maintaining perfect silence.

Although a Chinese Ch'an sect was present in Japan in the seventh century, it gained popularity only during the Kamakura period (1185-1333 C.E.). The Japanese translated *Ch'an* into *Zen*. Zen Buddhists refused to define the Buddha principle and scorned all scriptures; they held an iconoclastic attitude toward life and encouraged complete individualism. Zen insisted that reason must be distrusted, using riddles to go beyond reason to enlightenment: "What is the sound of one hand clapping?"

In its varied kinds of meditation and its several divisions, Zen affected Japanese religion greatly, bringing its influence to bear on Shinto, a religion native to Japan. (Shinto and other Buddhist sects in modern Japan will be discussed in chapter 6.) Zen has had a profound effect on Japanese culture because Zen Buddhism's plain living and rigorous self-discipline in preparation for prolonged meditation and an inward vision appealed greatly to Japanese warriors in the twelfth and subsequent centuries. It encouraged single-minded thought about sacrifice of the self and the devotion to one's native land and to the emperor. Japanese martial arts, including archery and swordsmanship, were cultivated by Zen monks.

Zen made other cultural contributions, however, for it highlighted the importance of intuition, especially in imagining and then designing houses and temples, planning household furnishings and civic buildings, arranging flowers and maintaining a reserved, detached attitude toward life. From the highly stylized Noh drama to ink wash painting, Zen Buddhism is visible in Japanese culture today, even though its adherents are but a small percentage of the population. The relation of the Zen novice to a Zen master, as the master rebukes or rejects him, questions and confuses him, stands over him with a stick he will not hesitate to use, indicates some of the intricacies of Zen. Through its monks, the same Zen heritage that demands such discipline introduced tea and the tea ceremony to Japan.

Due to the efforts of Zen teachers and interpreters such as D. T. Suzuki, Zen Buddhism has been introduced to the West. Thousands of sensitive, knowledgeable intellectuals of the Western world have joined highly cultured intellectuals of the East, to pursue the mental and spiritual self-discipline of Zen Buddhism. They look to it as a way of guidance in a thing-centered, seemingly purposeless world. Books and views, discussions and sermons mean little to Zen monks or their disciples. While books and sermons are concerned with a world of distinctions, Zen Buddhism seeks to bring the novice to the realization that distinctions are only theoretical—Buddha-nature is the universal, all-encompassing harmony. This Buddha-realization of the cosmic harmony leads to Buddha-action or inspiration, the knowledge that Buddha is in everything. Thus involved questions and obscure, puzzling riddles are much more effective in probing for truth, for one's clouded awareness must be cleared and awakened.

The essential principle of Zen Buddhism is apparent in the story of a disciple of Buddha who brought him a golden flower as a gift and asked him to reveal the secret of his outlook. Taking the flower, Buddha held it high and looked at it silently. In this way he indicated that his secret could not be found in words but rather in contemplating the flower in all its beauty and meaning.

THE MIDDLE PATH

Born in India amid the complexity of Hinduism, Buddhism challenged the Indic religious tradition and presented the Middle Path. Today, over 300 million Buddhists in hundreds of theological, philosophical, and social systems seek enlightenment and strive to understand ultimate reality. Mahayana Buddhism easily accommodated to Confucianism and Taoism in China and Shintoism in Japan, historically flourishing in both countries. The next two chapters briefly discuss the ethical and religious heritage of China and Japan, recognizing that Buddhism confronts social changes and intellectual ferment in both countries similar in scope to the challenges Gautama Buddha faced in the sixth century B.C.E.

Perhaps Gautama Buddha's calm counsel will encourage his followers to meet the challenges of the twenty-first century as he did 2500 years ago:

"Follow the Middle Path."

5

CONFUCIANISM AND TAOISM

The Will of Heaven

Confucius and Lao Tsu, contemporaries of the sixth century B.C.E., seem never to have met, save once, if a vague legend is true. But their parallel though differing lines of thought bridged the remote past of China's vast realm into their own present and on into a future of 2500 years more, down to our present day. Their basic traditions, "Confucianism" and "Taoism" as we call them, combined at times with certain aspects of Buddhism; all three, unconsciously and without organized pattern, colored the thought and conduct of countless millions of Chinese across more than a hundred generations. Both Confucius and Lao Tsu would have agreed on one fact: thousands of years from the Chinese past had molded the outlooks of both, individual and unique though each was.

ANCIENT CHINA

Ancient Chinese civilization developed in an immense area of more than 4 million square miles. Separated from other areas by mountains, deserts, high plateaus, and seas, China developed a sense of isolation that led to her great originality. For much of their history, the Chinese believed their territory to be the center of the world. They had little desire to search out other lands and even less proclivity to accept foreign cultures.

Many ancient settlements in China have been uncovered, some dating to 4000 B.C.E. Before 2000 B.C.E., the Yang Shao culture domesticated pigs and dogs for food, engaged in farming, and produced a beautiful red and black pottery. Later, the Lung Shan culture domesticated more species of animals and used the potter's wheel. Techniques were developed that would become hallmarks of Chinese civilization. For example, these ancient Chinese built walls, one of them thirty feet thick and stretching for a mile.

It was on a site called An-yang, however, that the remarkable Shang civilization (c. 1700-1027 B.C.E.) was born; and numerous artifacts and writings date from this period. The Shang written language contained over two thousand words in a highly developed pictographic script. Cities grew, and bronze was used extensively. Some bronze bowls were decorated with dragons, and these became prominent symbols in Chinese culture of Imperial rule and of beneficent as well as terrible justice. Fragments of animal bones and tortoise shells, "oracle bones," have been excavated, numbering in the tens of thousands. Questions to gods, spirits, and ancestors were inscribed on them, and they were then heated in a fire. The resulting cracks were interpreted by shamans.

The Shang city-state was ruled by hereditary kings who were also shamans. Thus, religious rule and political leadership were combined, and the Shang kings mediated between the many gods and the people. Ancestors were venerated early in Chinese history, and one of the deities during the Shang era was Shang Ti, the supreme ancestor. The Shang kings understood Shang Ti as their connection to heaven, their personal link to the gods.

While Shang rulers and aristocrats lived in imposing buildings and rode in horse-drawn chariots, the common people were virtually enslaved. Shang rulers conducted human sacrifices and were famous for their "death pits," in which scores of live servants were buried with their dead masters. Little wonder that when a frontier people conquered the Shang and formed the Chou dynasty (1027-256 B.C.E.), they claimed that the Shang rulers had been replaced because of their cruelty and immoral practices. Chou rulers declared that Shang Ti, the supreme god in a pantheon of gods, had brought down a corrupt Shang administration. The documents of the period refer often to the "Mandate of Heaven," and this rule by divine right differed from some Western concepts in that heaven rewarded virtue. When virtue vanished from a Chinese dynasty, Heaven would confer earthly rule on a lineage that deserved it. "Heaven also had pity on the people of the four quarters," *the Book of Documents* from the Chou dynasty reports, "and looking to it with affection and giving its mandate, it employed the zealous ones [the Chou]."

EARLY BELIEFS

Like almost all religions, early Chinese beliefs memorialized a golden era: earth had been a paradise and people had lived in blissful peace and accord. The earliest traces of Chinese worship reveal ceremonies in honor of the earth and its fertility, heaven and its beneficent rains (the dragon could symbolize water). The rites honored the spirits to be found in the fields, rivers, roads, valleys, and mountains, but guarded also against wild animals and unfriendly spirits in swamps, caves, and stagnant water.

Chinese folk religion began to gravitate toward ancestor worship. Thus could the living honor the entire relationship from which had come both their physical life and spiritual legacies. By the same token the departed, in the link with posterity through sacrifices and prayers, could strengthen and guide the living, enhance their happiness, and bring prosperity. By visits to the graves and by recounting the lives of ancestors, the living might honor the dead and re-establish their sense of continuity with earlier generations.

The ancient Chinese saw order, interdependence, and unity in all the processes of heaven and earth: the stars in their courses and the seasons in their cycles. Humanity was to harmonize its actions with the laws of heaven and earth. Otherwise, heaven would punish the disruptions by sending disasters. Harmony would again prevail only if humans acted in consonance with nature. Such was the Will of Heaven.

Yin and Yang

Although the technical religious use of the interacting forces of *yin* and *yang* occurred during the Han dynasty (206 B.C.E.-220

C.E.), the belief in these balancing forces is deeply rooted in Chinese history.

Yin was the female element in nature. Here was an element measured in its pace, low in key, wet and cold, secretive and mysterious, fecund and brooding. *Yin* was to be found amid quietude, among shadows. *Yin* was the south bank of a river in shadow. It was the north side of a hill in shelter.

Yang, in turn, was considered to be the masculine element. It called forth such adjectives as positive, procreative, warm and dry, active and bright. *Yang* was the south side of a hill, and the north side of a river. Fire and sunlight were *yang.*

Most objects had both *yin* and *yang.* The log in the woodpile was *yin* in appearance but became *yang* when kindled into fire. People, were they men or women, possessed both, though the men more of *yang* and the women more of *yin.* Yet the Chinese thought that good spirits *(shen)* were *yang* in nature, and evil spirits *(kwei)* were *yin.* *Yin* and *yang* were not to be posited as opposites in conflict, although they were the primary categories of all the objects that existed in the world. Rather, they were complementary forces that transcended such dichotomy and required one another to achieve harmonious balance.

When asked why, Chinese philosophers of long ago answered, "Tao." In *tao* (pronounced *"dow"*) reposed the unity of *yin* and *yang,* of heaven and earth. *Tao,* "the way," implied the road or direction they were to follow if they were to fulfill their function in the plan of the universe. When people rebelled against that pattern or were goaded by devilish spirits to recalcitrance, heaven and earth and humankind were not in harmony and the universal well-being of all three was threatened, often shattered.

Chou Dynasty

For the Chou dynasty, harmony was to be shattered. They had set up their capital at Hao, and then began to conquer. They overran most of the North China Plain. Because unification was so difficult, the Chou kings delegated authority to relatives and friends in the hope that filial ties would produce control and harmony. These vassal states, however, grew to be huge bureaucratic domains that were virtually independent, and in 771 B.C.E., with a company of barbarians they captured the capital and killed the Chou king. Part of the royal family escaped to Lo-yang, and continued the dynasty for another five centuries.

Amid such sizable growth and subsequent decimation of its empire, the Chou dynasty carried on the culture of the Shang and added more sophistication. The eight centuries of the Chou dynasty are viewed as China's Classical Age. Commerce flourished, canals were constructed, beautiful silks were woven, copper cash was minted (small round coins with square holes), and chopsticks were invented. In religion, an intricate mythology was developed to explain the birth of the Chou. Ceremonialism abounded, and sacrificial rites and customs were elaborated that endured for millennia. Rural folk religion, divination, and shamanism were widely practiced in the midst of an era of philosophical inquiry. Human life was to be a mirror of the harmony of the cosmos.

Chou society was, however, feudal. An elaborate gradation of classes, ranging from the emperor down to the vassals and the most menial of serfs, lay imbedded in the feudal order continued by the Chou. When rebellion occurred in the eighth century B.C.E. this class structure, once so rigid and prescribed, began to crumble. The aristocrats became poor, and upstarts of lowlier rank clamored for position and privilege. Serfs shook off their fetters and became small landowners; indeed some eventually became men of property. Chou kings became mere puppets, and China was left without a centralized government.

During these five centuries of slow but steady change, of reshuffling and readjusting, the basic schools of thought of the Confucianists and of the Taoists emerged: the Confucianists seem to have been furthered by princes and dukes and to have come from the region of the Yellow River, while the Taoists appear to have included many cynical, disillusioned intellectuals and to have had most of their followers in the area of the Yangtze River. Regional origins and ideas may be debatable, but it is clear that the Confucianists opposed the group called Legalists, who wanted to wipe out the feudal structure. The Confucianists, following the aristocratic Confucianists, sought to restore feudalism, but they wanted a modified, reformed system. In contrast, the Taoists wanted to rid the land and their time of any order that might be highly central-ized. A smaller group, the Mohists, desired a reversion to the by-gone days when they, as farmers and craftsmen, depended on the universal benevolence for their happiness and prosperity.

In such an era of rebuilding and recasting, Confucianism evolved. So powerful was the influence of Confucius himself, so all-pervading were his life and character, so inextricably entwined were his ideas in Chinese social institutions—especially in the fam-ily and the government—that for scores of generations after his death he still shaped the education, the conduct, and the politics of China. These environmental supports fitted with the objective needs of Chinese society for almost 2500 years. The intense oppo-sition of Mao Tse-tung's Red Guards to Confucianism in the twen-tieth century, even to its last vestiges of belief and its final remnants of adherence, reveals in fact the tenacity of Confucianists and af-firms the durable qualities of the faith "Master K'ung" began in the sixth century B.C.E.

CONFUCIUS

Confucius (551-479 B.C.E.), or K'ung Fu-tse as he was called in Chinese, was born in a town called T-sou, in a county named Ch'angping in the province of Lu in the Shantung Peninsula. His ancestors had fled there to a new but poverty-ridden existence as a result of a revolution in the area. After his father's death, Confucius supported his mother; she in turn saw to it that her son had the requisite teaching and tutoring he needed to know ancient China's music, history, and poetry. Trained also to be a sportsman, fisher-man, hunter, and archer, Confucius adhered to the standards of both scholar and gentleman. He endured an unsuccessful mar-riage, which did, however, grant him the boon of a son to continue the ancestral line. The sorrowful occasion of his mother's death plunged him into the traditional twenty-seven months—and even longer—of mourning, and then he became a teacher of the Six Dis-ciplines: poetry, music, history, government, etiquette, and divi-nation (foretelling the future).

Confucius now openly and frankly aspired for higher office in the government so that his views might affect an era so obviously in transition. He rose through the ministries of public works and justice to become the chief justice in his state; but he soon became a victim of intrigues and lost his position and prestige. With several disciples as companions, he began a long period of wandering in search of a new position. Sometimes he met with a friendly, hospitable reception; at other times he encountered contempt and violence, sarcasm and taunts.

Toward the close of his life, in 484 B.C.E., Confucius received an appointment in the government of Duke Ai to a prestigious post that enabled him to spend his remaining years, 484 B.C.E. to 479 B.C.E., in compiling the material we know as the Confucian classics: *The Book of History (Shu-Ching), The Book of Poetry (Shih-Ching), The Book of Rites (Li-Chi), The Book of Changes (I-Ching),* and *The Annals of Spring and Autumn (Ch'un Ch'iu).* The last book was his own writing, while the other four were anthologies of wisdom from pre-Confucian times. A sixth work, the *Book of Music (Yueh-Ching),* though fragmentary, is reputed to have been compiled by him.

Some scholars maintain that Confucius only used these materials and did not even assemble them. He may have edited, changed, and even added to them; but they were, we are told, not his own. It is true that proofs of his authorship and editorial hand are few and, at best, flimsy. Yet this fact remains: he drew the necessary inferences from them and, with some degree of originality, uttered statements that were recorded by his disciples in *The Analects of Confucius (Lun Yü).* "I believe in and have a passion for the ancients," he often said with due deference to the past; and with the honesty of an authentic editor he was accustomed to say, as in the *Analects,* "I am a transmitter and not a creator."

Confucianists of later centuries carried on the traditions through the *Four Books,* of which the *Analects* is closest to Confucius' mind and times; one of the other three was known as *The Great Learning (Ta-Hsueh)* and is attributed to Confucius but was probably prepared by one of his disciples. It appears to have been Tzu Ssu, the grandson of Confucius, who assembled statements about human nature in relation to the universe and its basic moral order in *The Doctrine of the Mean (Chung Yung);* but even this supposition is not verified. A valuable book of the third century B.C.E., *The Book of Mencius*, was a record of the teachings of Mencius, whose philosophic relation to Confucius resembled that of Plato to Socrates. Many additions, offered by later Confucianists and altered by conflicting opinions, brought varying views for almost two thousand years; but certain central ideas of Confucius stood out clearly and forcefully.

The basic concept of Confucianism was *jen*, which is variously translated as benevolence, true manhood, human-heartedness, altruistic steadfastness, uprightness of character; but is probably best rendered as humanity, namely the quality that makes one human and renders one different from animals. When applied to specific human relations *jen*, a general and all-inclusive concept, becomes *te* or "virtues." *Jen* has to do with inner feelings, not the norms of external behavior.

Confucius urged a second and very significant concept upon his corrupt era—and thus upon all succeeding generations as well—namely the necessity of living by *li*. This is translated in a number of ways: "reverence" or "propriety," "the ideal forms of social ceremonies for the proper forms of public conduct," "the courtesy of all social and religious behavior," or "the moral and religious way of life." Through *li*, society would be reordered and kept intact. Thereby, explained Confucius, men would give due and proper reverence to the spirit of the universe, honor the emperor and his advisors, establish proper moral standards for both sexes, as well as for children and parents, and ensure that all would live in harmony and establish the proper social institutions. If *li* prevails, he maintained, all of life from birth to death, from sports to business, from attendance at the emperor's court to diplomatic protocol, will be favorably fashioned and affirmed. *Li* establishes total harmony—in the home, in the village, in the empire—and ensures *tao*, the Will of Heaven, and its cosmic harmony between heaven and earth.

Confucius believed in the social order of his time, wherein the superior and the inferior remained in their accorded places, following the formal and prevalent patterns of politeness and procedure. As in most religions, the Golden Rule was inherent in these admonitions; and, also characteristic in a number of other religions, Confucius defined it negatively. When referring to "reciprocity" *(shu)*, he cautioned: "What you do not want done to yourself, do not do to others."

In *The Doctrine of the Mean*, however, Confucius stated the matter in positive fashion; at least his followers accredit him in *The Conduct of Life* with this more direct way of praising *shu:*

> There are four things in the moral life of man, not one of which I have been able to carry out in my life. To serve my father as I would expect my son to serve me: that I have not been able to do. To serve my sovereign as I would expect a minister under me to serve me: that I have not been able to do. To act towards my elder brother as I would expect my younger brother to act towards me: that I have not been able to do. To be the first to behave towards friends as I would expect them to behave towards me: that I have not been able to do.

To Confucius *shu*, reciprocity, impelled men to seek *li*, the noblest propriety or reverence, by the Ten Proper Attitudes, which result in the Five Relationships: (1) kindness in the father, and filial piety in the son; 2) gentility in the eldest brother, and humility and respect in the younger; (3) righteous behavior in the husband, and obedience in the wife; (4) humane consideration in elders, and deference in juniors; (5) benevolence in rulers, and loyalty in ministers and subjects. Then would harmony prevail among all people and the real character *(jen)* of a person would be revealed. The practice of *jen* and *li* might vary according to social status and human relationships, but one could always rely on *shu*, the unifying principle of reciprocity.

Confucius' ideal was the *chun-tzu*—the superior person—who, by following these injunctions, could achieve the "Five Constant Virtues": self-respect, magnanimity, sincerity, earnestness, and benevolence.

These were the goals for Confucius, too, who performed his own duties with *jen* (the principles of genuine humanity and uprightness), without arrogance, or boasting, but with the assurance of one who knew *li* (the proper attitude) and tried to fulfill *shu* (reciprocity).

As one who had attained the blessed man's "three score years and ten," Confucius was able to say, we are told in the *Analects:* "At fifteen, I had my mind bent on learning. At thirty, I stood firm. At forty, I had no doubts. At fifty, I knew the decree of Heaven.

At sixty, my ear was an obedient organ for the reception of truth. At seventy, I could do what my heart desired without transgressing what was right."

It might appear that Confucius taught essentially ethics and little else. Yet such an assertion would be both inaccurate and inadequate, for at heart he was a man of faith; he was a believer in religious ceremonies and in the reality of religion. Those who rely solely on reason and those who deny the existence of a God claim him as their own. They are not wrong, for Confucius was indeed both a rationalist and a humanist. He used the mind to analyze and appraise religion, to temper enthusiasms, and to restrain acceptance of the improbable or incredible. To Confucius, life's central purpose was to serve humankind. Over and over again he would say: "To devote oneself earnestly to one's duty to humanity and, while respecting the spirits [of the dead], to keep aloof from them, may be called wisdom."

Confucius was vague about his idea of ultimate reality or the supernatural. He talked of a universe that was a unity "under heaven." To Confucius, heaven originated the world and regulated the moral order. Family and society were important links to heaven's unity. Nor did he have anything more than a faint belief in the mystical, that is, the mysteries beyond human comprehension or the experiences by which one intuitively grasps truths beyond human understanding. His stress on ancestors is his only reference to an afterlife. His focus centered rather on issues and individuals having relation to human welfare. As for heaven and its will, he believed and taught that the Will of Heaven was fulfilled when one practiced the moral law. His conviction that his precepts were backed by the very nature of the universe and were in accord with the Will of Heaven made him one of the foremost religious thinkers and writers in all of Asia's recorded history.

After the death of Confucius, divisions in the ranks of his followers caused differing schools of thought to form. His disciples gathered in bands of the faithful and split that faith into various groups. They gathered the sayings and teachings of Confucius into the books listed earlier in this chapter and prepared still more documents that were unfortunately lost and have thus not come down to us through the centuries.

LAO TSU

Among the competing faiths were the powerful Taoists, with ideas contemporary with Confucianism and with equally famous, honorable antecedents. Taoists, who had only disdain for the Confucians, were part of a larger movement known as Taoism (pronounced *"dow-ism"*), the system of thinking and living with the *tao* at its core. The founding spirit of Taoism was the legendary Lao Tsu, born, according to some traditions, at least a half century before Confucius, that is, 604 B.C.E. Other scholars date his birth at 570 B.C.E. The traditional date for the death of Lao Tsu is 520 B.C.E. Despite considerable debate over the dating of this figure (with some experts insisting that he lived two centuries after Confucius), Lao Tsu's importance is firmly rooted in the ideas he represented and the spread of Taoism throughout China.

For many years in the sixth century B.C.E., Lao Tsu is said to have been curator at the imperial archives in Lo-yang, capital city of the state of Ch'u. Doubtful of the need for any kind of government, he resigned. Convinced that the quest for knowledge was futile and only perverted the simple life that men were destined to follow, he decided to go away. Irritated by questions from the curious, angered by the invasion of his privacy by visitors (including, according to one tradition, Confucius himself), "the old man" fled.

The most picturesque of the tales about Lao Tsu describes the black oxen drawing the two-wheeled carriage as he prepared to depart by the western gate, happily leaving behind him the world of noise and anxiety, disease and folly. But Yin-hsi, his friend who guarded the gate, persuaded him that he should record for posterity the philosophy he taught and lived. Lao Tsu consented and stayed on in the gatehouse just long enough to write his *Treatise of the Tao and Its Power (Tao Te Ching)*. The sentences and paragraphs were brief and taut, though many of them were far from clear; but he had fulfilled his promise. Then he went through the gate, out into the western pass, and over the horizon, never to be heard from again.

While these details are not historically verifiable, this much is certain: *Tao Te Ching*, the classic explanation and expression of Taoism, came from a later century, as the internal evidence of language and the references to current events attest. When it was written is unimportant. What it had to say is all important. Taoism now had a Testament, and the leading thinkers of "philosophical" Taoism now had a weapon by which they could struggle against the Confucianists, who had their own canons.

Difficult though the Tao might be to define, Taoists nonetheless did define it as the mystery of the cosmos that, when plumbed, resulted in even more mystery. This was the ultimate reality, the substance, the vital principle. For the Taoist it was important to be in accord with the Tao, the only way to know well-being: harmony and health and abundance. If a person or a nation, a culture or a civilization, rebelled against the course of events and moved in opposition to everlasting Tao, pain and disaster would result.

In the *Tao Te Ching* the Taoist read that if one refrained from interfering in people's lives, succumbing to anger, falling prey to ambition, the results would be not negative but positive. The result of the positive force would be favorable and beneficent. Allowing oneself to be imbued with Tao would result in a long life, free from illness and decay. The central emphasis is on *wu-wei* (active not-doing), the subtle, elastic power by which Tao moves nature.

The same principle for governing one's self was valid in the larger sphere of governing society. The major way to freedom and peace was not to interfere in the lives of the people: "If kings and princes could but hold fast to this principle, all things would work out their own reformation."

The leading light among the Taoists was Chuang-Tzu, who lived in the fourth century B.C.E., about a century after Lao Tsu. With rare wit, apt illustrations, and delightful dialogues, he wrote essays to combat the Confucianism of his time. He progressed beyond the Taoism of the past, however, and wrote of change taking place naturally, all in accord with Tao. He differed from the Confucians by insisting that people could be natural and simple and just, merely by reverting to their basic natures and simple living. He loved nature and thought of it as the chief fount of imagination and inspiration, a reflection of Tao, so awesome and mysterious, yet so lovely and ordered. He inspired the poets and artists of his people to gaze upon nature and interpret it as an outer manifestation, but nonetheless a true mirror of Tao.

Later Taoism thrived on using magic and alchemy to seek the elixir of life in search of immortality. In the second century C.E., Emperor Huan of the second Han dynasty decreed that Lao Tsu be honored by a temple and by official gifts. Five centuries more went by, however, before an emperor made Taoism the official imperial religion.

RIVAL GROUPS

Meanwhile, Buddhism had been introduced into China from India as early as the first century B.C.E. By the period of Emperor Huan, Mahayana Buddhism had firmly entrenched itself and was apparently regarded by most Chinese as a form of Taoist thought. This made Buddhism the first foreign religion to be assimilated into Chinese culture and perhaps the only one incorporated until the twentieth century. The ability of Mahayana Buddhist teachers to adapt Chinese culture and to use Taoist terminology produced a Chinese Buddhism quite unlike any Buddhism in the rest of the world. Chinese Buddhist sects, such as the Ch'an (the Indian *dhyana* and the Japanese Zen) and the Ching-t'u (Pure Land Buddhism, where Amitabha Buddha leads one to a place in a "Western Paradise"), followed masters who had selected "authoritative" Buddhist texts and had chosen special *dharmas* from them appropriate for the group. Meditation was widely practiced in some of these sects, and they believed in a concept of a Chinese Buddhist "heaven." Generally, Southern China accepted some of the diverse philosophical teaching of Mahayana Buddhism, while rural northern groups incorporated the magical worship practices.

Near the end of the Han dynasty (c. 220 C.E.), a dynasty that had made Confucianism the civil service system of its empire, China experienced political turmoil and the disintegration of the Confucian state. During the following four centuries the uncertainty, strife, and hardship among the Chinese populace increased their yearning for a relevant and personal religion. The average man and woman found Confucianism to be too mundane to satisfy religious yearnings, while to the masses, philosophical Taoism had seemed too intellectual and too obscure. Saturated with Chinese culture, Mahayana Buddhism met their needs more adequately, they felt, because of the spiritual help and promise of paradise they received from the Chinese bodhisattvas. Family-oriented China was inundated with monks, nuns, pagodas, statues, and temples. Ironically, by 500 C.E. temples to Confucius were located in every district; and Emperor Wu (reigned 502-549 C.E.), the Confucian founder of the Liang dynasty, converted to Buddhism.

Challenged by Buddhism, Taoism now looked to the past and found strength in becoming an institutionalized religion. The Taoists lifted Lao Tsu to a new level of respect, even of reverence. They gathered their writings into books, built temples, formed orders of disciples, and brought their several spirits and gods into an ordered pantheon. To all of this the people responded; Taoism had a strong counter to the established Confucianism of the past and the Buddhism of much more recent vintage. Confucianism would challenge Buddhism through the teaching of Chu Hsi (1130-1200 C.E.), leader of a neo-Confucian movement and one of the most influential Chinese philosophers in the last millennium.

None of the three religions—Confucianism, Taoism, and Mahayana Buddhism—required exclusive allegiance. Thus every Chinese could be something of all three, depending upon the area of life affected, temperament and mood, success or failure, and preference. Religion with the Chinese is a matter of viewpoint and emphasis, of living one's life. It can shift from day to day, from moment to moment or from activity to activity or inactivity. Such permissiveness in polyreligious views and religious syncretism is somewhat puzzling to our own experience in the West, but underscores the mystery of the *yin-yang* way of thinking of our Oriental neighbor. In recent times, religionists from the East have suggested that Western Christian theologians adopt the *yin-yang* method, a both/and system that would replace the highly categorical either/or system of the Greco-Roman world. In this way, it is said, traditional Christian dogma, such as of the human and divine in Christ, the nonrational Christian mysticism that defies categorization, and the conflict between the body and the spirit, would be better perceived. Through the *yin-yang* way of thinking, it is alleged, Christians would also experience environmental peace with nature, and harmonious coexistence with other religious systems would become a reality for Western Christendom.

Among other rival groups to Confucianism and Taoism, the Mohists were important, but neither in numbers nor in influence could they claim victory. Fired by the thoughts and enthusiasms of Mo-tzu (c. 468-390 B.C.E.), the Mohists struggled against Confucianism, believing that traditional Chinese religions were best for governing. Unknown to most people now and only dimly explained in history, Mo-tzu led his followers in a highly disciplined way and looked to the day when people would be united for the common good in a fellowship of companions. He believed that universal love came from heaven and pleaded for the simple, thrifty life, stripped of all formality and rituals. Opposed by both Taoists and Confucians, the Mohists were foiled in their teaching and living a doctrine of the universal love.

The Legalists, more powerful than the Mohists, were no less articulate in speaking and writing about their concepts. Their school of law believed the crumbling feudalism of their day should be succeeded by a strong, all-inclusive legal system as the basis of a new social order. Confucianism was too elementary. The Taoists had interpreted the Tao too simply. Their own interpretation of the Tao, they maintained, demanded that the prince should control all government. The Legalists actually triumphed briefly over Confucianism in the third century B.C.E.

More than a century after Confucius had died, Mencius (372-289 B.C.E.), a well-known writer of Confucian thinking, came on the scene to share the belief of Confucius in the goodness of human nature and the ability of paternalistic feudalism to elicit that goodness. Coupled with his faith in the essential goodness of human beings was the conviction that environment was responsible for evil and that proper environments would work for good. He followed Confucius in claiming that heaven created the disposition for the good and the creative; he opposed the Taoists by contending that within each person lay a strong inclination to create moral order. He influenced the Chinese for hundreds of years by his insistence on the presence of a vital energy, great and powerful, in each person and in the universe. The Taoists might find this energy in nature outside themselves, but Mencius said it flowed deep within himself and all humans.

A Confucian interpreter ranked on the opposite side was Hsün-tzu (298-238 B.C.E.), who was exposed to many influences, especially from the Taoists and the Legalists. Unlike Mencius he had no illusions about human nature. He focused entirely on its weakness and inherent evil. Believing that humankind was bad by nature, Hsün-tzu went further than Confucius in emphasizing *li*, the proprieties, and in relying on ceremonies and law to control the behavior of the people. He followed the Taoists in looking upon heaven as impersonal and considered *li* to be simply ornaments in civilized life to give proper expression to emotions. Hsün-tzu believed law, restraint, and proper training elicited goodness in a basically evil people.

THE CHINESE REVOLUTION

None of the rival groups would challenge the religious *status quo* or change China as extensively as did the Chinese Revolution of the twentieth century. Mao Tse-tung (1893-1977) who, as a child in southern Hunan province memorized the Confucian classics and whose mother was a devout Buddhist, progressively fell under the spell of socialist and revolutionary writers during his university education. Finally converting to Marxism-Leninism, he helped found the Chinese Communist Party in 1921, led the famous Long March in 1934, and controlled the Chinese Communists by 1935. After World War II, Mao defeated the Nationalist forces of Chiang Kai-shek, establishing the People's Republic of China in 1949 as a Communist nation, and becoming one of the world's most powerful leaders.

Attacking religion as an exploitive force, Mao and his Chinese Communist Party set about eradicating gods and sacrifices, rites and traditions. Missionaries were expelled by 1952, and places of worship were closed or appropriated for state purposes. More severe persecution of Chinese religious worshippers occurred during the Cultural Revolution that was instituted in August 1966 and continued for a decade. So radical was this attempt to create a new people with one Communist will, that in 1982 a chagrined Chinese Communist Party's Central Committee described the effort as an ultra-leftist deviation, stating that the "counter-revolutionary cliques [of Lin Biao and Jiang Qing] willfully exploited these 'leftist' mistakes [of increased religious persecution] and took them to the extreme." After the Great Cultural Revolution ended in 1976, religious freedom was reintroduced in China under a new constitution in 1982.

China's new policy on religion was also spelled out in its Central Committee's Document 19, "Our Party's Basic Policy on Religious Questions during the Period of Socialism." This document is a backhanded compliment to the tenacity of religious practice and practitioners in China. Freedom of religious belief and individual conversion (over age 18) is underscored in Document 19 as a right of the Chinese citizen, and prison sentences are to be imposed upon any official or group found guilty of denying religious freedom according to Penal Code 177. While Communist Party members are not to be affiliated with a religious institution (and a number still thwart religion whenever possible), they are instructed to protect the rights of religious institutions to train religious leaders, publish materials, provide places of worship, and question past injustices for redress.

"True, we communists are atheists, and we advocate and will propagate atheism among the masses of people," Document 19 states. "However, we, at the same time, understand that it is not only ineffective but also very harmful to use simple methods to handle the ideological problems of the people and problems concerning the spiritual world of the people, especially the problems of religious belief." While insisting that proper development of the socialist economy, science, culture, and technology will "gradually eliminate the social and cognitive sources that have given rise to religion and enable it to exist," the Chinese Communist Party acknowledged that this could take a very long time and that "the religious problem" would not be easily solved.

China has officially designated Buddhism, Taoism, Catholicism, Protestantism, and Islam as religious institutions that must be protected in the Communist nation. A great effort has been extended to nationalize a Chinese version of each and to mold them into a "patriotic front." Nevertheless, Document 19 declared that China "must never allow the abolished systems of feudal privilege of religion and religious exploitation and oppression to be restored . . . must in no way allow anybody to use religion to carry out propaganda against Marxism-Leninism-Mao Tse-tung thought." How such statements are interpreted depends on the leadership in power. Currently, China is opening her doors to the West and is seeking international respect. Whether future Communist regimes will deem this a wise policy remains to be seen.

Confucianism is regarded by the Central Committee as one of the "abolished systems of feudal privilege." Yet strains of Confucianism are visible in the culture and traditions of the people of China, a population that comprises one-fifth of the world. The current Communist leadership is portraying Confucius as an important leader who contributed to a concept of mutual respect for everyone. While asking the people to reject the errors Confucius made in his teaching, the Communist Party appears to be acknowledging that the strains of Confucianism still evident in China are more than mere vestiges. Indeed, they are an ineradicable part of China's past and, it would appear, of her future also.

6

SHINTO

The Way of the Gods

The word *Shinto* reflects the religious faith of the Japanese people in their country, its origin and its past, and it bespeaks Japan's special blessedness at the hands of the divinities. In the Japanese language *Shinto* means "the way of the gods" (*Kami-no-michi*, i.e., the way of those "above"), but when translated into Chinese, the words emerge as *"shen-tao"* and refer to Taoism.

SCRIPTURE AND TRADITION

The sacred scriptures and historic sources of Shinto are four in number: two sagas from the eighth century C.E. (*Koji-ki, The Records of Ancient Events,* and *Nihon-gi, The Chronicles of Japan*—from 712 and 720 respectively and considered to be the two chief bodies of scripture), another from the ninth century (*Manyo-shiu, The Collection of Ten Thousand Leaves*), and the fourth from the tenth century (*Yengi-shiki, The Institutes of the Period of Yengi*—from 901 to 923). They tell the story of how these lovely islands became a unique creation of the gods. Here are legends of the land's founding and the national religion's beginnings, prayers for ceremonies and important events, as well as ancient poems and ballads, carefully preserved for the Japanese people.

The tales are fanciful, candid, charming, and fearsome, as we read of two creator deities—Izanagi, meaning the Male-Who-Invites, and Izanami, the Female-Who-Invites—who came down upon the earth after the original chaos had separated into ocean and heaven. At the behest of the other gods, they created the islands and began the generation of all future inhabitants of Japan. Descending from the Floating Bridge of Heaven (i.e., a rainbow), Izanagi thrust his jeweled spear into the salty waters and the thick mud, stirred it, and then withdrew the spear, allowing the brine that dripped from its end to form an island. Izanagi and Izanami stepped down to the islands and were wedded. In due time Izanami gave birth to the eight large islands of Japan.

The two deities then created thirty-five lesser gods. Kagu-Tsuchi, the heat-god, was the last to emerge from the womb. By his searing flames he killed his mother. Izanagi, outraged by the fatality, avenged himself for Izanami's death by cutting Kagu-Tsuchi into countless pieces; but he found that all the bits of Kagu-Tsuchi that his swiftly slashing sword produced themselves became more deities.

On Izanami's death she entered the Land of Yomi, the underworld. Izanagi, in sorrow and despair, followed in the hope he might induce Izanami to return to the world with him. It was too late, however; she could not go back. She was now ugly, for decomposition had set in. She begged him not to gaze upon her, but he took a comb from his hair and, lighting its end, illumined the hideous scene of her body covered with crawling maggots.

Izanami shrieked at Izanagi that he had disgraced her. She dispatched the Ugly Females of Yomi to follow after him. Izanagi fled and evaded the pursuers. Izanami then sent after him eight thunder-gods that had been created in her body's decay and, in addition, ordered 1500 warriors from Yomi to capture him. Izanagi battled them, while Izanami joined in the pursuit. When Izanagi returned to the upper world, he lifted a rock mountain and with it blocked off the passage to the underworld. The two deities, now separated by both the rock and their hatred for each other, angrily said good-bye, hurling curses and epithets at each other through the wall of rock.

Izanagi, polluted and filthy, walked to the ocean's edge to bathe.

He discarded his staff and his wearing apparel, whereupon each of these became a god. As he washed the corruption from his left eye, he created Amaterasu, the sun-goddess, who is the most revered of all Japanese gods. Then, by washing his right eye, he created Tsuki-yomi, the god of the moon; and by washing his nostrils he produced Susa-no-wo, the storm-god.

When, in later years, Amaterasu, the sun-goddess, gazed upon these islands from above, she was so disturbed about their problems, especially their lack of order and unity, that she decided to supplant the then-ruler, son of the storm-god Susa-no-wo. She sent down from heaven her own grandson, Ni-ni-gi, with the command: "This Luxuriant-Reed-Plain-Land-of-Fresh-Rice-Ears is the land which thou shalt rule." Obeying her, Ni-ni-gi ruled on the island of Kyushu, where three generations later in 660 B.C.E. his great-grandson, Jimmu Tenno, became the first human emperor. He set out to conquer the province of Yamoto and establish the capital in the midst of the province of Hondo in the center of Japan's islands. The Japanese people, thinking of their emperor as in direct lineage from Amaterasu, consider themselves and their islands even now, twenty-six centuries later, to have been divine in origin, and thus they reaffirm their belief in Shinto as "the way of the gods."

The major difference between Shinto and other living religions in the world lies in the fact that Shinto's principal deity is feminine and not masculine. Another, though lesser, distinction between Shinto and other faiths is the unbroken lineage of Japan's ruling dynasty which was made possible, the Japanese have always believed, by its divine origins. While Japan's emperor, Hirohito, disavowed his "divinity" in 1946, several months after the surrender of his country in World War II, the outpouring of respect by the entire nation for the dying monarch in the fall of 1988 underscored the emotion surrounding such a religious and national symbol. Undue frivolity was stricken from television programs; weddings and rock concerts were cancelled; government leaders stayed close to home; and local festivals were called off. Some prepared for the multimillion-dollar Shinto ritual that would transform Crown Prince Akihito into the next "divine" emperor. A nation of 125 million mourned the death of their beloved emperor in 1989, and a world marvelled that traditional beliefs, supposedly obsolete in Japan after World War II, ran so deep in the national consciousness.

In its earlier centuries Shinto knew no influences other than those of Japan. Purely Japanese in its inception, it offered its devotees meaning and purpose solely in their loyalty to Japanese customs, reverence for Japanese places, and a love of the land, both in its totality and its smallest plot of ground. Their hills and mountains—such as Mount Fuji—their lakes and rivers, shrines and temples, trees and gardens had all belonged to their ancestors and were loved by them; so do they belong to and are loved by this generation.

Although the Japanese people no longer consider Japan's divine nature to be unique among the nations of the world, it is nevertheless difficult for them to believe that Japan is not specially chosen for blessings. The gods still make their way to those beautiful shores, for to this hour most Japanese call their country "the land of the gods."

The gods had not communicated a written language to the ancient Japanese, and the islands had no national unity at first. Simple shrines separated from areas of human habitation were the common links to nature and the unseen spirits. Today Shinto shrines have a gateway approach (the *torii*), the upper crosspiece of which curves upward at the ends to point toward the heavens. The vista is usually upon tall cryptomeria trees or a waterfall. As in the ancient period, these sites are designed to heighten the worshippers' appreciation and reverence for nature. Shinto festivals, both plentiful and popular, pertain to the cycle of the seasons and the richness of the earth: seedtime and harvest, the full bloom of crops and fruit in fields and orchards, testing the new rice and the first products, the fullness of the moon, and the longest days of sunlight.

The shrine at Ise, dedicated to Amaterasu, is the holiest among all the shrines of Japan. Yet there are many deities almost equal with Amaterasu—not only those already mentioned but many others: the rain-god and the thunder-god, the god of lightning and the god and goddess of wind, a mountain-god and many minor mountain-gods, food and fertility deities, harbor-gods and river-gods, earthquake-gods and volcano-gods—spirits almost without number, or, the Japanese say, 800 myriads of gods and goddesses. These are all called *kami,* meaning "superior" or "above."

NEW TRENDS

In earlier centuries the Japanese celebrated the divine origins of their country and its people by deifying objects of any kind and natural forces of every sort. Shamans, most of them female, existed throughout Japanese history and served to communicate with the enormous spectrum of spirits. Until the fifth century C.E., a seemingly unorganized old Shinto prevailed; but new trends began. In those formative years of Japan, Shinto began to take shape as certain aspects of Chinese civilization attracted Japanese people. They altered their lives completely by learning Chinese skills and adopting more sophisticated ideas, not the least of which were the influences of Confucianism and Taoism.

Hitherto, old Shinto had for the most part been tied to nature worship and an undefined ancestor worship; but now the filial piety of Confucianists led the Japanese to a veneration of ancestors unequaled in any other country or by any other people. The emperor had been honored by the common people's claim of authentic direct descent for him from Amaterasu, the sun-goddess. Now not only the high officials claimed such ancestry from gods and goddesses closely associated with her, but the lowest subjects, too, claimed at least remote connection. The newly acquired magic and mystery of Chinese Taoism also affected Japanese rituals and folk religion.

In the following century, the sixth, an even greater intellectual and spiritual force came to bear upon old Shinto, also by way of China: Buddhism opened a new world to the Japanese. Not only art and literature, medicine and social service were brought to the people, but also the claim on the part of the Buddhists that religious truth as well as the power of determining and asserting it originated not in Japan but rather in China and in India. The common folk proceeded to make Buddhism their own faith because the royal family, followed quickly by the court aristocrats, had done so.

In the eighth century a virtual merging of Shinto and Buddhism occurred. Certain priests of Buddhism claimed they had known visions that proved that Japan's native gods were really buddhas and bodhisattvas who had come into being once again among the islands of Japan. The Japanese called this amalgam of faiths a "two-seated" religion, meaning that their gods had been seated in Japan and abroad, at one and the same time. Such a syncretic religion meant that there was a "twofold way of the gods" *(Ryobu)*; Buddhist gods were "the originals," but Shinto gods were their representation in Japan. Shinto absorbed so many Buddhist customs and decorative motifs that it was referred to as "two-sided Shinto" or "mixed Shinto"; and for at least five centuries Japan was more Buddhist than Shinto, even though the blend appeared on the surface to include both on an equal basis.

From the thirteenth to seventeenth centuries Japanese life was in considerable confusion due in great part to the power of Buddhism, for the emperor found his royal prerogatives challenged by the Buddhist priests and his power over the military *(samurai)* and the nobility greatly diminished. A dozen generations of conflict among the feudal families came to an end around 1600; and the Tokugawas assumed control by establishing a dictator *(shogun)*. The centralized control of this family, known in history as the Tokugawa regime, meant the resurgence of Shinto and its emergence from the Buddhism in which it had been almost submerged. Ryobu Shinto reversed itself; the Buddhist gods became secondary appearances, while the Japanese were the originals. Japan now shut itself off from the world, closed its seaports to foreign vessels, wiped out by ruthless extermination the Christian groups begun with the introduction of Christianity a century earlier, and centered solely on the wisdom of the ancient Japanese. The result was "pure Shinto," a name devised to claim again descent for the emperor from the sun-goddess Amaterasu. This, the scholars of Japan maintained, was "the true ancient Way."

STATE-SUPPORTED SHINTO

Pressure in the 1850s, from North Americans abetted by the Dutch, the French, and the British, finally opened the doors to Japan, first for trade and shipping facilities, then for cultural exchanges. The United States helped in this way to start and then to speed both the modernization and the industrialization of Japan. Oddly enough, the result was to imbed in the Japanese constitution of 1889 the historic concept of the emperor's relation to Amaterasu and to give this religious claim an official sanction by the state. As a consequence, Buddhism was officially superseded; but the average person still thought and worshipped in terms of the two religions virtually in tandem.

Increasingly, however, the Japanese imperial regime continued through the late years of the nineteenth century to strengthen the newly revived national religion. It gave government support to a faith which considered the emperor to be "sacred and inviolable" and revered the empire as having been singled out by the gods, as the imperial proclamation asserted, "to be reigned over and governed by a line of emperors unbroken for ages eternal."

Government-sponsored Shinto had opposition in the opening decades of the twentieth century. Of the opposing elements, the Buddhists were still striving, and protested state support for a rival cult. Another opposing factor was agnosticism, which was based on scientific methods and disciplines and held the view that no demonstrable proof is available to substantiate belief in a God or gods or in a life after death. A parallel, even stronger force was atheism, the rejection of all religious beliefs and a denial of the existence of God or the validity of religious beliefs, attitudes in great measure fostered by the popularity and seeming success of Marxism in the Soviet Union and its attractiveness for certain elements in the revolutionary ferment of nearby China.

During the 1920s and the 1930s, and in 1940-41, just prior to Japan's entry into World War II, the government looked with favor on the efforts of Japanese scholars to reconcile the ancient Shinto with modern science and still retain in the national patriotism the view that their deities (kami) were uniquely their own, whether in the heavens above or the earth beneath, whether in the solitude and beauty of thousands of shrines or in nature itself. Whatever inspired awe and reverence, whether in solemn ceremonies or in impressive landscapes, contained the divine.

Japanese governments from the 1880s down through World War I fostered the state-supported Shinto (Jinja-Shinto), as distinguished from a sectarian Shinto (Kyoha-Shinto). State Shinto was designed to center attention on a national morality, a way of the gods that venerated forefathers and acknowledged its legacy from imperial ancestors. Only through "the sentiment of reverence," the government documents asserted, could people foster "the feeling of respect for ancestors" and establish "the foundations of the national morality."

State shrines, numbering at one time more than 100,000, were considered more as national and patriotic centers than as specifically religious sanctuaries. Yet the line of demarcation was hard to draw. The emperor was accustomed to appear at the Grand Imperial Shrine of Ise when he ascended the throne or when the nation declared war. Usually, through representatives and messengers, the emperor sent both offerings and reports of national significance; in addition, the emperor took part in the ritual of purification (*o-harai*), which absolved the nation's wrongdoings and shortcomings through the intercession of priests at Ise and other state shrines in Japan.

Through the centuries the Japanese paired the way of the gods with the way of their warriors. The military officer caste, the *samurai*, practiced a warrior's code known as *bushido*. For centuries this Way of the Warrior-Knight prevailed in Japan, although as a set of rules it lacked specific stipulations and requirements. *Bushido* was an ideal, a spirit, a mode of military etiquette, a warrior's conduct. Some trace its power to the ethical rigor of Confucianism, and its flawless discipline of the self to Zen Buddhism, but the centuries-old feudalism of Japan had already developed absolute obedience to a superior and a code of honor that must not be altered or compromised. Shinto unified all three of these contributions—and doubtless many more from ancient days. By the fervor of patriotism, Shinto fused them into one, demanding an uncritical loyalty to the emperor primarily, and to the nation and to feudal chieftains secondarily.

The code of *bushido* called for such loyalty, but it also expected gratitude for the gift of life as well as courage in the living of it and, if at all possible, in the giving of it on behalf of a warrior's feudal lord. It elicited unselfishness, especially in the performance of duty; utter truthfulness; politeness, even to an enemy; reticence, particularly in hiding one's emotions; and the primacy of honor, which caused a warrior to prefer death to disgrace and implied unquestioning willingness to commit suicide by the age-old ceremony of *hara-kiri* (self-disembowelment).

The *bushido* code determined the conduct of Japanese soldiers and civilians not only in feudal times but in more recent generations as well. Until 1945, the end of World War II, Shinto priests presided at special rituals before certain altars on a chosen memorial day so that the people might honor the spirits of their hero dead. By such rites the living could invite the souls of these departed soldiers to return for the respect, honor, and gratitude of their kinsfolk and countrymen.

Shinto called for the utmost in patriotism, a nationalism raised to the intensity of religion. This fusion of religion, nationalism, and militarism, sanctioned by the support of the state, led the Japanese people to believe that their destiny was to carry Japanese conquest and power throughout Asia, and eventually the whole world. The surrender of Japan in August 1945 brought an end to that delusion. The new 1947 constitution deprived the emperor of any powers related to government, transferred ruling power and individual rights to the Japanese people, and gave Japanese women the right to vote.

POST-WAR ERA

After the war, state Shinto no longer had government aid or encouragement, for American occupation authorities cancelled such support. The effect, while momentarily disruptive, was eventually healthy. Voluntary support took the place of government subsidy; and a more authentic devotion, uncomplicated by public pressures, developed in its stead. Despite the disestablishment of state Shinto, shrines throughout the land retain the traditional emblems of the emperor's divinity—namely, the mirror, the sword, and the jewel, which hang upon the simple, otherwise unadorned, walls. The mirror symbolizes sincerity, guilelessness, and wisdom; the sword denotes courage; the jewel represents benevolence and generosity. Even the new constitution recognizes in Article I that the emperor remains "the *symbol* of the State and of the unity of the people, deriving his position from the will of the people with whom resides sovereign power."

The practice of Shinto in the home has become stronger in the postwar era. Many homes have their own private shrine *(miya)*, which honors ancestors and has sacred objects on a spirit-shelf *(kami-dana)*. Before this shrine the simplest oblation of the day, an expression of gratitude or an offering of food, is placed, and more elaborate ceremonies celebrating birth and marriage and death are observed. The reverence for nature and the belief in bodily cleanliness remain integral parts of Shinto, but a blind loyalty to the nation and unquestioning obedience to its patriotic demands are no longer expected.

Buddhism, which during the medieval period had established itself as the Japanese religion of family, blended well with Shinto's ancient practice of ancestor worship. Buddhist temple funerals and memorial rites became standard practices in Japan, and, after cremation, the remains of most Japanese are buried on grounds near Buddhist temples. For many Buddhist priests, the funeral rites and care for the graveyards are their most important duties.

Of the Mahayana Buddhist sects that permeate Japan today, Pure Land Buddhism (Ching-t'u) is the most popular. Founded by T'an-luan (476-542) in China, and taught by Honen (1133-1212) and Shinran (1173-1262) in Japan, Pure Land Buddhism emphasized that people could not achieve enlightenment through their own efforts. Instead, Amitabha Buddha, the Buddha of Light, has the saving power and compassion to lead the way to the Western Paradise. By chanting "Homage to Amitabha Buddha" and exhibiting faith, the devotee may be "saved" and prayers will be answered.

Another popular branch of Buddhism in Japan today is the Nichiren sect with its message of the Lotus Sutra. Founded by Nichiren (1222-1282), this sect seeks to reform society through a return to "true Buddhism." By preaching the message of the famous sacred verses of the Lotus Sutra, Nichiren quite rigidly condemned other sects, such as Pure Land. His movement would later be associated with extreme nationalism, but today the lay members chant a salutation to the Lotus Sutra in the belief that this will lead to virtue, buddhahood, and paradise.

In chapter 4, we underscored the importance of Zen Buddhism and its influence on Japan. Approximately 100 million Japanese claim to belong to one of the many Mahayana Buddhist sects. Many a home in this modern nation is graced not only by the spirit-shelf, the *kami-dana*, but also a Buddha-shelf, the *butsu-dana*. Shinto priests are often assigned birth and marriage rites, while Buddhist priests specialize in rites of death, memorial and ancestor veneration. Although Shinto enjoys coexistence with Buddhism, as well as Confucianism, Taoism, and Christianity, it has a basic national flavor and quality that are indigenous to Japan and therefore appeal to the Japanese people, molding many of their habits and coloring their culture.

THE NEW RELIGIONS

During the Tokugawa Period (1600-1867) of military dictatorship, charismatic religious leaders arose who gave rise to a number of *new religions* that personalized religious faith. After World War II and the disestablishment of state Shinto under the new constitution, new religions attempted to fill the void left by the older established traditions. Today, it is estimated that at least 25 percent of Japan's citizens are formal members of a new religion. Ranging from personal faith healing to politicized agendas, the new religions are often mixed with the older traditions in response to the secularism inherent in rapid industrialization and modernization. Needless to say, the laity assumes an important role in each movement.

The Soka Gakkai movement, for example, was founded by a Nichiren Buddhist, Makiguichi (1871-1944), who worked out his ethics on the basis of faith in the Lotus Sutra: beauty, gain, and goodness. Refusing to support the Japanese military effort in World War II, Makiguichi and other leaders were imprisoned. He died in prison for his insistence that the Lotus Sutra should not be compromised, but other leaders carried on his message. With over a million members by the 1960s, Soka Gakkai taught that it was the only true religion and today inspires frequent mass rallies. Its political party, Komeito, founded in 1964, now holds the third largest number of seats in the Diet of Japan.

In contrast to the Buddhist base of the Soka Gakkai movement, Kurozumikyo was founded by a Shinto priest, Kurozumi Munetada (1780-1850). After a bout with tuberculosis, Munetada experienced what he called "Direct Receipt of the Heavenly Mission"—an experience of absolute unity with the one god of the universe. He taught that Amaterasu Omikami was the creator of the universe and the parent of all living beings. Yet Kurozumi Munetada accepted the existence of 8 million *kami* spirits. Heaven and earth, he believed, are one in origin, and all the earth is governed by a single, divine rule. Each living being was a "small soul," a portion of the life soul of the universe. Sickness was merely a lack of harmony with the life soul. Today, with a membership of almost 250,000, the Kurozumikyo movement emphasizes devotion, moral integrity, and faith healing.

Another new religion, Reiyukai Kyodan, the Association of Friends of the Spirits, is entirely a lay movement with no priesthood. Founded after World War I by Kotani Kimi (1901-1977) and Kuba Kakutaro (1892-1944), Reiyukai Kyodan is one of the largest new religions with approximately 3 million adherents. Originally calling for a return to family values and traditional morality, it centered its energies on ancestor worship and faith healing. The Lotus Sutra was adapted to revere ancestors and to "purify the heart." Asserting that "other people are mirrors," members interpret the reaction of others to their teachings as possible messages from the ancestors. Spiritual discipline is believed to be self-cultivated and can lead to the "curing of the heart." The heart-mind that has good *karma* unites the people and society in heavenly harmony; but bad *karma* causes sickness, unhappiness, and misfortune.

While the Western mind emphasizes that "the unexamined life is not worth living," the Japanese stress that "the unlived life is not worth examining." The enjoyment of the world and harmony with the cosmos undergird the new religions as well as the old traditions in Japan. Even in industrial society, the importance of the family and the clan is extended to the corporation, and the desire not to shame or disgrace one's group pervades modern Japanese society. Japanese faiths, old and new, are diverse and legion. The "way of the gods," Shinto, is flanked by a wide variety of religious sects.

The Japanese justify this maze of groups and ideas, this host of deities and practices, by quoting a favorite proverb of their land: "Even though you should worship but one God, yet all the other gods will be pleased."

7

JUDAISM

People of the Covenant

Four thousand years ago, the Hebrew Bible recounts, Abram traveled from the seat of the first Mesopotamian civilization between the Tigris and the Euphrates rivers to a land where a people called Canaanites lived. In the midst of a culture of many gods and sacrificial rites, he forged a covenant with God. The biblical account states:

> Now the Lord said to Abram, Get thee out of thy country, and from thy kindred, and from thy father's house, to the land that I will show thee, and I will make of thee a great nation, and I will bless thee, and make thy name great; and thou shalt be a blessing: and in thee shall all the families of the earth be blessed. (Gen. 12:1-3)

At the age of seventy-five, with his wife Sarah and his nephew Lot, Abram ("exalted father," later to be renamed by God "Abraham," which means "father of many") departed to Canaan.

Childless, Abram asked the Lord who would inherit his estate and carry on his lineage. The "word of the Lord came to him," according to the Torah, promising him a son. Taking Abram outside in a vision, the Lord declared: "Look now toward heaven, and count the stars, if thou be able to number them. . . . So shall thy seed be."

And Abram "believed in the Lord" and the Lord "counted it to him for righteousness" (Gen. 15:6). At the age of ninety-nine, Abram became Abraham, undergoing circumcision as a sign of the covenant between him and God Almighty (El-Shaddai). Genesis 17 states that the Lord appeared to Abram and said to him:

> I am the Almighty God; walk before me, and be perfect. And I will make my covenant between me and thee, and will multiply thee exceedingly. . . . As for me, behold, my covenant is with thee, and thou shalt be a father of many nations. Neither shall thy name any more be called Abram, but thy name shall be Abraham; for a father of many nations have I made thee. And I will make thee exceedingly fruitful, and I will make nations of thee, and kings shall come out of thee. And I will establish my covenant between me and thee and thy seed after thee in their generations for an everlasting covenant, to be a God to thee, and to thy seed after thee. And I will give to thee, and to thy seed after thee, the land in which thou dost sojourn, all the land of Canaan, for an everlasting possession; and I will be their God. And God said to Abraham, Thou shalt keep my covenant therefore, thou, and thy seed after thee in their generations. This is my covenant, which you shall keep, between me and you and thy seed after thee; Every manchild among you shall be circumcised.

This covenant, a solemn and binding agreement with Abraham's One True God, was a promise reaffirmed by God to Abraham's son Isaac and his grandson Jacob.

Abraham's descendants lived in the Levant with their families and flocks and prospered; but when a devastating famine struck, they moved to the border of Egypt. The stories of the succeeding generations—Isaac and Jacob and Joseph—are told in moving fashion in Genesis. Again the Hebrews migrated, this time transferred by the conquering god-king of Egypt, within centuries of Joseph's death to toil as bonded Egyptian slaves.

MOSES

From their midst came Moses, heroic figure of Hebrew destiny. Adopted by the daughter of Pharaoh, he was reared at the imperial court, where he grew to manhood. When he saw an Egyptian beat one of his fellow Hebrews, he killed the Egyptian; then he fled to Midian, where he married and settled. Later the covenant was re-affirmed as described in the Book of Exodus:

> And the angel of the Lord appeared unto him [Moses] in a flame of fire out of the midst of a bush; and he looked, and, behold, the bush burned with fire, and the bush was not consumed. . . . God called unto him out of the midst of the bush, and said: "Moses, Moses." And he said: "Here am I." And He said: "Draw not nigh hither; put off thy shoes from off thy feet, for the place whereon thou standest is holy ground. . . . I am the God of thy father, the God of Abraham, the God of Isaac, and the God of Jacob." (Exod. 3:2-6)

Then Moses asked, "Behold, when I come unto the children of Israel, and shall say unto them: The God of your fathers hath sent me unto you; and they shall say to me: What is His name? what shall I say unto them?"

The answer came: "I AM THAT I AM [*ehyeh asher ehyeh*]. . . . Thus shalt thou say unto the children of Israel: I AM [*ehyeh*, which sounds not unlike Yahweh] hath sent me unto you."

Appointed by Yahweh, Moses accepted his commission to lead the children of Israel out of bondage. The tale, told in dramatic detail in Exodus and Numbers, is one of the most familiar narratives in all literature. The highlight is the confrontation on Mount Sinai, where Yahweh gives Moses two tablets of stone and, in the Ten Commandments inscribed on them, reasserts the covenant:

> "I am the Lord thy God, Who brought thee out of the land of Egypt, out of the house of bondage.

> "Thou shalt have no other gods before Me. Thou shalt not make unto thee a graven image, nor any manner of likeness, of any thing that is in heaven above, or that is in the earth beneath, or that is in the water under the earth; thou shalt not bow down unto them, nor serve them; for I the Lord thy God am a jealous God, visiting the iniquity of the fathers upon the children unto the third and fourth generation of them that hate Me; and showing mercy unto

the thousandth generation of them that love Me and keep My commandments.

"Thou shalt not take the name of the Lord thy God in vain;" for the Lord will not hold him guiltless that taketh His name in vain. "Remember the sabbath day, to keep it holy." Six days shalt thou labor, and do all thy work; but the seventh day is a sabbath unto the Lord thy God, in it thou shalt not do any manner of work, thou, nor thy son, nor thy daughter, nor thy man-servant, nor thy maid-servant, nor thy cattle, nor thy stranger that is within thy gates; for in six days the Lord made heaven and earth, the sea, and all that in them is, and rested on the seventh day; wherefore the Lord blessed the sabbath day, and hallowed it.

"Honor thy father and thy mother, that thy days may be long upon the land which the Lord thy God giveth thee."

"Thou shalt not murder."
"Thou shalt not commit adultery."
"Thou shalt not steal."
"Thou shalt not bear false witness against thy neighbor."
"Thou shalt not covet thy neighbor's house; thou shalt not covet thy neighbor's wife, nor his man-servant, nor his maid-servant, nor his ox, nor his ass, nor anything that is thy neighbor's."

For forty years Moses led his people as they moved on toward their promised land of Canaan, but he died just before the entry into Canaan. His successor, Joshua, led the Hebrews in their battles and finally subjugated the hostile tribes.

FROM MONARCHY TO EXILE

Under Joshua and his successors, the Hebrews changed from a nomadic to an agricultural people. As a group of confederated tribes, each settlement had a history of its own and, sometimes, faced different challenges than the other groups. The Hebrew vision of God was radically different than the polytheistic and pagan world that surrounded them. Constantly forced to resist the fertility worship of the Canaanites and their *baalim*—nature gods and goddesses represented by Baal and the goddess Astarte—some Hebrews lapsed. The Hebrew prophets assumed the difficult task of purifying the worship of one God, Yahweh. The *shofetim* or judges, charismatic leaders such as Deborah and Gideon, from about 1200 to 1000 B.C.E. took command of the tribes during times of danger and led them into battle. Finally, monarchy was established under Saul and subsequently in the united kingdom of Israel under the reigns of David and his son Solomon from 1000 to 922 B.C.E. It was a brief but glorious empire, and Solomon built the first Temple in Jerusalem. The professional Levitical priesthood, its duties meticulously related in the Torah, continued to develop around the spectacular Temple complex.

The brief splendor of the kingdoms of Judah and Israel, united under King David and amply recorded in the Scriptures, soon gave way to division, conquest, and exile. After the death of Solomon, the ten northern tribes seceded, establishing the Kingdom of Israel. The Davidic line retained power in the Kingdom of Judah, a southern kingdom that included the tribal lands of Judah and Benjamin. Bad rulers outnumbered the good, and the moral fiber of the Hebrews waned. In the midst of domestic strife, the children of Abraham encountered the full fury of a growing empire from Abraham's former home. The Assyrian war machine was at the height of its power, and it conquered the northern Kingdom of Israel in 722 B.C.E. Merciless in its policy of torture, murder, and enslavement, the nation of the god Assur was known to devour whole populations, wiping their memory from the face of the earth. So obliterated and scattered was the Kingdom of Israel, that the northern tribes are known as the "ten lost tribes" to this day.

The word *Jew* comes from the Hebrew *Yehudi*, originally referring to members of the tribe of Judah. By the time of King David, it had come to refer to those who dwelt in the area of the Kingdom of Judah. Now, with the Assyrian conquest of the northern kingdom of Israel, the surrounding nations used the word *Yehudi* to designate the religious and national entity of the Hebrews. Thus, the word *Jew* came to signify much more than a specific tribe.

The Hebrew-speaking Jews who remained inhabitants of the land they believed God had given them, however, referred to themselves as "Israelites." *Torah* was the term generally used in ancient Hebrew sources for the whole gamut of Jewish teaching.

The word *Judaism* was a later derivative from the Greek '*Ioudaismos,*' which came to signify the difference between Jewish religion, philosophy, and way of life and the surrounding Greek or Hellenistic culture. "Judaism" has no parallels in the Hebrew or rabbinic literature, although it is popularly used today for the religion of the Jewish people.

In the sixth century B.C.E., the Kingdom of Judah was conquered by the armies of Nebuchadnezzar and his new Babylonian empire. The famed Temple of Solomon was burned to the ground in 586 B.C.E., and thousands of Jews were taken to Babylonia. Others fled to Egypt, founding strong communities there. In the Hebrew Scriptures, one gains a glimpse of the vibrant Jewish community in Babylonia, first under the Babylonians (Chaldeans) and later under the Persians (cf. Esther, Ezra, and Nehemiah). The Jewish captives began to adapt to Babylonian culture, adopting many customs. Some farmed, and others moved into diverse vocations in towns and cities throughout the land.

The Judean exiles may have joined some of the exiles from the Assyrian conquest of Israel a century and a half earlier. This would explain Ezra's mention of the return of descendants of families who lived in northern Israel (Ezra 2). A new Jewish center was developed around Nippur, the second largest city in Babylonia, located on the Kebar River. From there, distinguished leaders from Judah, including religious leaders such as the prophet Ezekiel, led the Jewish people in their traditions. Ezekiel begins his scroll of Scripture by explaining: "In the thirtieth year, in the fourth month on the fifth day, while I was among the exiles by the Kebar River, the heavens were opened and I saw visions of God" (Ezek. 1:1).

THE PROPHETIC TRADITION

Ezekiel was part of a long tradition of Hebrew prophets that included Nathan during the reign of King David, Ahijah in the years of King Solomon, Elijah in the time of King Ahab, and Elijah's successor, Elisha. They felt impelled to speak the truth, bluntly and unequivocally. They fought against polytheism, paganism, and the worship of Baal. During the division of the northern and southern kingdoms and into the exiles, they forged a prophetic tradition that had a lasting impact on Judaism.

Amos, often called the prophet of righteousness, cried out as Yahweh's spokesman: "Let justice well up as waters, and righteousness as a mighty stream" (Amos 5:24). He contrasted their observance with Yahweh's saying, "I hate, I despise your feasts, and I will take no delight in your solemn assemblies."

Hosea, termed by many the prophet of grace, spoke of God's forgiving love:

> I will heal their backsliding,
> I will love them freely;
> For Mine anger is turned away. (Hos. 14:4)

Isaiah announced a divine imperative: "And I heard the voice of the Lord, saying:'Whom shall I send, and who will go for us?' Then I said:'Here am I; send me'" (Isa. 6:8). As a prophet of social justice, he warned of a Day of Doom awaiting the evildoer and the faithless, the exploiters and the heartless: "Woe unto them that join house to house, that lay field to field, till there be no room, and ye be made to dwell alone in the midst of the land! . . . Seek justice, relieve the oppressed, judge the fatherless, plead for the widow" (Isa. 1:17).

The prophet of the exile in Babylon also is remembered from his eloquent writings in chapters 40 to 66 in the biblical book of Isaiah; he described God as the One and Only, for "there is no other":

> Hast thou not known? Hast thou not heard
> That the everlasting God, the Lord,
> The Creator of the ends of the earth,
> Fainteth not, neither is weary? (Isa. 40:28)

He spoke of the coming messiah, "the Suffering Servant of Israel."

Micah, though a spokesman for justice among the people and pleader for peace on earth, inveighed against formalism and ritualism in religion. Much more concerned about social behavior than the methods of worship, he spoke words which, despite worldwide repetition for almost 2700 years that has made them famous and familiar, are never trite or outworn:

> Wherewith shall I come before the Lord,
> And bow myself before God on high?
> Shall I come before Him with burnt-offerings,
> With calves of a year old?

Will the Lord be pleased with thousands of rams,
With ten thousands of rivers of oil?
Shall I give my first-born for my transgression,
The fruit of my body for the sin of my soul?
It hath been told thee, O man, what is good,
And what the Lord doth require of thee:
Only to do justly, and to love mercy, and to walk
    humbly with thy God. (Micah 6:6-8)

Jeremiah, a prophet of both personal religion and social justice, cared less for Jerusalem and the Temple than he did for a renewed covenant with God. In contrast, Ezekiel, a priestly prophet, emphasized purity of worship by evoking visions, enunciating allegories, and presenting a new code of observances for the temple.

These literary prophets had concern for the community and bespoke the dignity of human beings, giving renewed emphasis to the commands in the book of Leviticus: "Thou shalt love thy neighbor as thyself" and "thou shalt be kind to the stranger within thy gates. . . . If a stranger sojourn with thee in your land, ye shall not do him wrong. The stranger that sojourneth with you shall be unto you as the home-born among you, and thou shalt love him as thyself; for ye were strangers in the land of Egypt. . . ."

These stalwarts, holding forth hope for the future and underscoring the unique mission of the people of Israel, called for a return to a purer worship of Yahweh and a more righteous life for both the individual and society. They were emulated by less well known but equally redoubtable men like Habakkuk of 600 B.C.E., who preached that "the just shall live by his faith"; the sensitive, aristocratic Zephaniah of an earlier generation, who was so morally earnest and warned against sin's punishment of the "Day of the Lord"; Jonah who preferred universalism to exclusiveness and preached of God's redemption; Nahum, poet and patriot, who predicted retribution for the evildoer; and Joel, who prophesied—with both vividness and accuracy—that plagues of locusts would bring disaster, but held out against pessimism and shared his high hopes for a better day:

And it shall come to pass afterward,
That I will pour out My spirit upon all flesh:

And your sons and your daughters shall prophesy,
Your old men shall dream dreams,
Your young men shall see visions. (Joel 2:28)

All underscored the need for a proper relationship with Yahweh, God of righteousness and justice. These prophets are extraordinary among religionists of any era; and the predominant prophets among them—Isaiah, Jeremiah, and Ezekiel, Amos, Hosea, and Micah—must be included among the religious geniuses of history.

In addition to the prominent postition given to women such as Eve, Sarah, Rebekah, and Rachel in the Hebrew Bible, a heroic female leadership is also recorded. Miriam, the sister of Aaron and Moses, was a prophetess who with timbrel in hand led the women in singing and dancing after the Exodus from Egypt. She gloried: "Sing ye to the Lord, for He is highly exalted: The horse and his rider hath He thrown into the sea" (Exod. 15:21). Deborah was both a prophetess and a judge of the Hebrews, administering justice in the open air under a palm tree in the hill country. She initiated a war of liberation against Canaanite oppressors of her people. The Song of Deborah in Judges 5 ends: "So perish all Thine enemies, O Lord; But they that love Him be as the sun when he goeth forth in his might." The Hebrew Bible relates, "And the land had rest forty years." Likewise, Huldah was a prophetess consulted by Hilkiah the high priest and other emissaries of Josiah, the King of Judah. She prophesied God's ultimate judgment on the nation because of the people's worship of other gods (cf. 2 Kings 22).

BELIEFS AND TEACHINGS

By the time of the prophets, Jewish beliefs and teachings had crystallized into a more permanent pattern, a set way of life that was different in emphasis from the peoples' cultures and religions in surrounding lands. The Hebrews taught that men and women did not simply reenact a cyclical, divine drama patterned after nature's spring, summer, fall, and winter and orchestrated by thousands of gods and demigods. The Jews perceived history as a linear record of God's unfolding purpose for human beings. God cared and was involved in the affairs of *every* nation and people. The Hebrews interpreted history in moral terms and saw God as judging the nations of the earth. They viewed their history as part of a much larger picture. Ultimately good would triumph over evil, the lion would lie down with the lamb, there would be no more war. God's purposes were being fulfilled progressively. This Jewish perspective would eventually transform the thought of the entire world.

God

The Hebrews held to the unity and eternal spirit of the One True God. God created everything and actively governed the universe. Monotheism was never questioned, and God's existence was taken for granted. "The fool has said in his heart, 'There is no God'" (Psalm 14:1). In every Jewish worship service today, the *Shema* is recited. It literally means "Hear!" (or "Understand!") and is the first word of Deut. 6:4, which the congregation sings in unison: *"Shema Yisrael Adonai Eloheinu Adonai Echad"* ("Hear, O Israel: The Lord our God, the Lord is one").

Whereas the essence of God was hidden and unfathomable, the attributes of God (such as justice, mercy, and wisdom) were visibly active in the universe. Throughout history, the weekly Sabbath observance has symbolized for the Jewish people the truth of God's personal activity in the affairs of humankind. On the seventh day of the week God culminated the work of creation and declared the day blessed and holy (Gen. 2:1-3). The Sabbath also celebrated God as the Redeemer of His people in world history. The day commemorates the Exodus from Egypt, in which God liberated the Hebrew slaves, presented the Torah, and led the covenant people into the Promised Land.

In Judaism, the relationship between God and humans is one of mercy or grace. *Hesed* is the Hebrew word for the undeserved love that God has for creation. Translated *mercy, love, kindness,* as well as *grace, hesed* connotes God's beneficence in the creation of the world, in God's relationship to creatures and in covenant with the Jewish people. Psalm 118:1 calls on the Jewish people to "give thanks to the Lord; for He is good: for His steadfast love *(hesed)* endures forever." Portraying a gracious, forgiving, and just God who is exceptionally kind and compassionately patient, the Hebrew psalmist also declared: "When I said, 'My foot is slipping,' your *hesed*, O Lord, supported me" (Psalm 94:18). As he dedicated the Temple, King Solomon prayed, "O Lord, God of Israel, there is no God like you in heaven above or on earth below—you who keep your covenant of *hesed.*" (1 Kings 8:22-23)

It was God who had established order, meaning, and purpose in the world, and the Hebrews believed that God had created men and women in God's own image. Their's was a caring God, who fellowshiped with creatures and lovingly sustained them. In Jewish thought throughout history, God as Creator is a continuing reality, not merely the initiator of a single act. Men and women are to respond to God's *hesed* with faith that leads to devotion. Underlying all of the commandments is Deut. 6:5, the continuation of the *Shema:* "And thou shalt love the Lord thy God with all thy heart, and with all thy soul, and with all thy might."

The Jewish concept of faith is one of being faithful or holding firm in the faith. Faith is an ongoing process and must mirror God's faithfulness. In Deuteronomy 7 one of the key Hebrew words for faith, *emunah*, is linked to *hesed.* In this chapter, the Israelites were told that they were not chosen to be God's covenant people because of their numbers or strength. Rather, they were chosen because God loved them and because of God's covenant with their forebears. "Know therefore that the Lord thy God, He is God, the faithful God, who keeps His covenant of *hesed* to a thousand generations of those who love Him and keep His commands" (Deut. 7:9).

Torah

In Judaism, one learns God's commands through *Torah*. Often translated as "law," Torah actually is related to the root "to teach" or "teachings." In the most narrow sense, it specifically refers to the first five books of the Bible (Genesis-Deuteronomy), the foundation stones of Jewish tradition. When Joshua was about to enter the Promised Land, the Hebrew Scriptures record, the Lord commanded him: "Be strong and of a good courage: for thou shalt cause this people to inherit the land, which I swore to their fathers to give them. Only be strong and very courageous, and observe to do according to all the Torah, which Moses my servant commanded thee:

turn not from it to the right hand nor to the left, that thou mayst prosper wherever thou goest" (Josh. 1:6-7). When Cyrus the Persian decreed in 538 B.C.E. that the Jewish people could return from their Babylonian Exile and rebuild the Temple, the Hebrew Scriptures relate that they began to rebuild the altar of the God of Israel "to offer burnt offerings upon it, as it is written in the Torah of Moses the man of God" (Ezra 3:2). Ezra himself is described as "a teacher well versed in the *Torah* of Moses" (Ezra 7:6).

Yet the Jewish concept of tradition is that truth is given once and for all. *Torah* is revelation—the revelation of God. As revelation, the word *Torah* describes the Hebrew Bible as a whole. Its teaching rests on God's authority, not only the written words but also the interpretation of those words. In this broader sense, far from being a narrow code of law, Torah is a "way of life"—God's way of life.

Traditionally, the Hebrew Bible is the base of the Jewish tradition that God revealed. Through Torah one comes truly to know God. Torah is inerrant, God's Word to God's children. Even the original words of the Bible (including every letter) were revealed by God. From this basic concept all Jewish discussion and interpretation builds. Throughout Jewish history, the commentaries and codes, the philosophy and the mystical analysis, all attempts at interpretation and discussion in Jewish religious literature form the larger body of Torah or instruction. Because God originally revealed the interpretation of the Scriptures, most discussion is attempting only to rediscover God's original meaning. Nothing is new; God revealed it all at Sinai. Because God's truth is given once and for all, commentary rather than systematic theology is the form in which the Jewish philosophical and theological literature takes shape.

This is where the Jewish concept of oral tradition originates. In Judaism, Torah demands interpretation. The word *Torah* also implies the concept of guidance. In an effort to explain the message of the written Torah, a vast body of Jewish literature arose even before the first century C.E., conveying an oral inheritance that had been passed down through centuries of teaching through memorization. Such deliberations by rabbinic sages continued to expand until the oral tradition was eventually written down to form the Talmud (see below).

The entire Hebrew Bible is often referred to by the acronym

Tanach (from TaNaK, pronounced *tah-nahk*), referring to the three sections of the Hebrew Scriptures: the Pentateuch (*Torah:* Genesis-Deuteronomy); the Prophets (*Nevi'im:* Joshua, Judges, 1 and 2 Samuel, 1 and 2 Kings, Isaiah, Jeremiah, Ezekiel, and the later prophets, Hosea-Malachi); and the Writings (*Ketuvim*), in this order: Psalms, Proverbs, Job, Song of Songs, Ruth, Lamentations, Ecclesiastes, Esther, Daniel, Ezra, Nehemiah, 1 and 2 Chronicles). In ancient times, the later twelve prophets were written on a single scroll, Ezra and Nehemiah were combined, and the books of Samuel, Kings, and Chronicles were undivided.

Although God has revealed a way of life in the Torah, Judaism teaches that men and women have been granted the freedom either to follow or to reject that way. If rejected, God provides the remedy of repentance and offers forgiveness through *hesed*. Men and women actually share the responsibility with God for rectifying a wrong. Redemption (or deliverance) is both personal and national through the covenant, entailing obedience to God's teachings and commandments, that is, following God's way of Torah. Yet a Jew does not *earn* redemption, but is constantly in process, preparing by building faith in God and faithfully discovering opportunities to serve the Lord. *Mitzvot* ("good deeds" or "commandments," both ritual and ethical) are means to further faith, *not* a substitute for faith. God's *hesed* and the believer's turning toward God's Torah way are the ingredients of salvation.

Thus Judaism traditionally has expanded the common concept of "charity" (good deeds above and beyond) to *mitzvot*, good deeds being the *expected* thing to do—the way of the faithful's life. From the prophetic tradition the admonition endures: *zedek zedek tirdof* ("justice, justice pursue"). Through such a way of life and drawing close to God's gracious deliverance, a Jewish person becomes a *ben Olam Haba*, a son of the world to come. In Judaism, the quantity of legal adherences is no substitute for the quality of one's way of life. Non-Jews are also provided the opportunity for salvation by following God's way as instructed in the seven commandments given to Noah (Genesis 9). To Jews the "righteous" from all nations who follow God's way inherit the "world to come." God's *hesed* is available to all humankind. As for the People of the Covenant, it is said that they "must strive to be Torah incarnate."

The Synagogue

A deep sense of loss had engulfed the Jewish people through the destruction of their Temple and deportation to a foreign land. Although the basic beliefs and teachings were firmly established by the time of the Babylonian Exile, Jerusalem remained the center of their thoughts. Psalm 137 reflects their pain:

> By the rivers of Babylon, there we sat down, yea, we wept,
>   when we remembered Zion. . . .
> If I forget thee, O Jerusalem,
>   let my right hand forget her cunning.
> If I do not remember thee,
>   let my tongue cleave to the roof of my mouth,
>   if I do not set Jerusalem above my highest joy.

Judaism adopted Babylonian names for the months of its calendar, which endure to this day, adapted and modified to some of its religious practices. Nevertheless, God and Torah were never abandoned.

To those critics who taunted the Babylonian exiles because they were far from Jerusalem and had no Temple, God told Ezekiel:

> Although I have cast them far off among the nations, and although I have scattered them among the countries, and I have been to them a little sanctuary in the countries where they have come, therefore say, "Thus says the Lord God; Yet will I gather you from the peoples, and assemble you out of the countries where you have been scattered, and I will give you the land of Israel." (Ezek. 11:16-17)

Jewish tradition has maintained that *little sanctuary* is a direct reference to the synagogues of these exiles.

The origins of the synagogue, the Jewish house of assembly, study, and prayer, are shrouded in mystery. Some have suggested that synagogues date back to the time of Moses, and the "meeting places" of Psalm 74:8 have been referred to as synagogues. Certainly in Babylon, synagogue worship seems to be indicated, and when the Second Temple was finally rebuilt by the returning exiles, the synagogue continued as an institution wherever Jews lived—even in Judah where the Temple was being rebuilt. The Talmud ascribes to Ezra and his successors, "the men of the Great

Synagogue," the formulation of the earliest liturgical prayers such as the *Amidah*. By the first century C.E., the synagogue was a well-established institution, giving every indication of centuries of growth as a center of religious and social life of the Jewish community.

The reading of both the Torah and the Prophets was a central element in the synagogue service. The scrolls of Scripture were kept in a receptacle called "the holy ark" *(aron ha-kodesh)* located in the wall facing the Temple Mount. In the center of the synagogue was an elevated platform, the *bema*, upon which stood a reading desk. Worshippers sat around the *bema*. When the rebuilt Temple (the Second Temple) was destroyed by the Romans in 70 C.E., the synagogue emerged as the central institution of Judaism.

Eretz Yisrael

It was Babylonian Jewry, through leaders such as Zerubbabel, Ezra, and Nehemiah, that returned to Israel, rebuilt the walls of Jerusalem, and constructed the Second Temple. This history of returning exiles in the tens of thousands is recorded in the books of Ezra and Nehemiah and indicated the extraordinary faith of the Jewish people. Although adapting well as a minority in a foreign land, they continued to believe in a transcendent and holy God who had selected them as a holy nation and had made a covenant with them. They believed that they would continue to suffer until the world accepted their One True God, but in the meantime they determined to accept the responsibility of the "yoke" of the Lord. The Jewish people did not denounce the countries in which they were exiled, but attempted to better those kingdoms while accepting God as their ultimate leader. They longingly looked toward *Eretz Yisrael*—the Land continued to be their anchor.

The name *Eretz Yisrael* (the Land of Israel) is the Hebrew biblical designation that took on the connotation of the promised land during the Second Temple period. By the first century C.E., it was in widespread usage. Prior to then, no one name in general use denoted the land in its entirety. The Romans recognized this important link between the Jewish people and their land, the Jewish people and their God. When the Jews of *Eretz Yisrael* rebelled against Roman domination and authority, the Romans determined to use the Greek term *Palestine* (derived from ancient Philistia) to replace the province of Judea and the concept of a Jewish land. The Emperor Hadrian after the Second Jewish Revolt (132-135 C.E.) hoped to eradicate both Jewish tradition and Jewish culture (as well as the Jewish God) by calling the area Palestine. The designation was commonly used until 1948 and the founding of the modern state of Israel. Ironically, the Jewish people in *Eretz Yisrael* in the nineteenth and early twentieth centuries were not uncommonly referred to as "Palestinians."

Those Babylonian exiles who returned with Zerubbabel, Ezra, and Nehemiah to rebuild the wall of Jerusalem and the Temple were under constant pressure from the local population to renounce their God and their Torah. The book of Ezra records the political machinations, deception, psychological degradation, and assimilation tactics of the non-Jewish population. Ezra 4:4-5 records: "Then the peoples around them set out to discourage the people of Judah and make them afraid to go on building. They hired counselors to work against them and frustrate their plans during the entire reign of Cyrus king of Persia and down to the reign of Darius king of Persia." The link between the Jewish people and their land would constantly be challenged, yet the centrality of *Eretz Yisrael* to Judaism and the Jewish people would not diminish.

GREEKS AND ROMANS

When Alexander the Great (356-323 B.C.E.) in a meteoric rise conquered the Persian Empire, uniting the cultures of East and West, *Eretz Yisrael* was "liberated" in 332 B.C.E. In reality, Jerusalem and the surrounding area of Judea enjoyed the same rights they had under Persian rule. Alexander's death, however, resulted in a struggle for his throne and, subsequently, the struggle of the Jewish people against the spreading Hellenistic culture. Alexander's vast empire broke into several parts. Judea was caught between the Egyptian Ptolemies (a dynasty founded by Ptolemy Soter, one of Alexander's generals) and the Asian Seleucids (a dynasty founded by Alexander's general Seleucus Nicator). The Seleucids controlled Persia, Babylonia, and Syria, as well as Asia

Minor. The ensuing struggle between the Ptolemies and Seleucids seems senseless in retrospect. Personal ambition and imperial expansion were central motives in their warfare. No matter which dynasty gained the upper hand, the crossroad of the Middle East was caught in the middle, and the people of *Eretz Yisrael* suffered. For two centuries these great empires would battle for dominance of *Eretz Yisrael*.

When Antiochus III, "the Great" (222-187 B.C.E.) captured Judea from the Ptolemies in 198 B.C.E., *Eretz Yisrael* became part of "Greater Syria." His conflict with the growing Roman Empire and his collusion with the Carthaginian general Hannibal led to battle against the Romans at Smyrna in 190 B.C.E. Antiochus III was dealt a costly defeat, and, to pay his debt, he plundered the temples of his kingdom, including the Jewish Temple in Jerusalem. Anti-Semitism increased under his successors.

Antiochus IV (ruled 175-163 B.C.E.), surnamed Epiphanes ("the manifest god"), perpetrated the most horrible Seleucid pogroms against the Jewish people. Humiliated by the Romans, Antiochus Epiphanes intended to wipe Judaism from the face of the earth. His goal was to Hellenize thoroughly the population in Judea. He decreed that the worship of Greek gods and goddesses should replace the worship of one God and that Syrian laws and customs were to be followed. He built Greek temples for pagan gods in *Eretz Yisrael*, constructed race courses and public baths, introduced Greek fashions and sexual orgies, and set his hand-picked Hellenized leader as high priest in Jerusalem. Thousands of Jewish men, women, and children were massacred for opposing their Greek overlords. Others were sold into slavery, many of them small farmers who could not keep up with the ever-increasing taxes. They lost everything.

This was the age of the Maccabees, Mattathias and his heroic Jewish family, who led a fervently religious population to oppose the cruelty and Hellenization of the Seleucids. Their victory in 165 B.C.E. is celebrated in the festival of *Hanukkah*, and the history of the heroic Jewish population who held to Torah at all cost is recorded in the books of 1 and 2 Maccabees. Since Antiochus Epiphanes had polluted the Temple with sacrifices of swine's flesh and proclaimed it a temple of Olympian Zeus, a new altar was built according to the Torah, and 1 Macc. 4:59 records that "Judah and his brothers [the sons of Mattathias] and all the assembly of Israel determined that every year at that season the days of the dedication of the altar should be observed with gladness and joy for eight days, beginning with the twenty-fifth day of the month of Kislev."

Even in Alexandria, the new commercial and cultural center founded by Alexander the Great in Egypt, the Jewish people refused to give up their monotheistic practice for the prevailing Hellenistic culture of many gods and pagan worship. The large Jewish population tended, instead, to adapt and modify the Greek culture. Jewish philosophers sought to prove that the Greeks copied from the Hebrews and that all truth emanates from God. They attempted to show that the One True God was the originator of all things, that Judaism was a kind of philosophy with a spiritual God and a rational ethic. The Hebrew Bible was translated into Greek (the Septuagint), and the writings of the Greek philosophers and poets were carefully studied. Jewish poets, historians, playwrights, and philosophers coupled their perspective of Torah with Hellenistic style. They began a rich tradition of intermediary agent, transmitting the ideas of one culture to another. The greatest among them was Philo of Alexandria (c. 20 B.C.E.-50 C.E.). Completely loyal to the Torah, Philo's ideas are biblical, but his philosophical explanations of those religious ideas are decidedly Greek (relying heavily on Plato).

In contrast to the Jewish population that had spread throughout the Mediterranean world, the Romans were thoroughly imbued with Hellenistic culture as they extended their empire eastward. The Romans needed a foothold in the Middle East as their empire expanded, and they continually cultivated friendship with the Jewish community in *Eretz Yisrael*. In the midst of the growing unrest and civil war of Roman citizens in the Late Republic (133-31 B.C.E.), Jewish loyalty was coveted. The Romans, however, were bound to a policy of conquest and expansion, and they had their eye on Greater Syria. Profiting from a dispute between factions in Judea, the Romans besieged Jerusalem in 63 B.C.E. Taking advantage of the Sabbath rest, the Roman general Pompey (106-48 B.C.E.) stormed the gates. The city was burned, thousands died, and Pompey entered the Holy of Holies in the Temple. The Roman Empire would maintain its firm grip on *Eretz Yisrael* for the next five centuries.

PHARISEES AND TALMUD

Among those who united with Mattathias, his sons, and his friends to fight against Antiochus Epiphanes and the Hellenistic Syrian persecution was a group of Hasideans ("the pious ones"). It appears that the Pharisees were a group that arose from among these "pious ones," combating Hellenization and heresy, holding firm to Torah and tradition. To the Pharisees, God's commands transcended the Temple complex, reaching to the common folk and separating the people of God from heathen nations. They believed that God cared for each individual, and although omnipotent and omniscient, granted every person the free choice to follow God's ways. The Pharisees stressed a resurrection of the dead and rewards and punishments in an afterlife. They looked forward to a messiah, and they refused to restrict the spiritual leadership of *Eretz Yisrael* to a religious aristocracy. The Pharisees emphasized piety and learning, and they were a positive influence on the growth of synagogues throughout the ancient world.

The religious aristocracy with which the Pharisees clashed was a group called the Sadducees. Although both groups upheld the divine origin of the written Torah, the Sadducees claimed that they had descended from the high priest Zadok (cf. 2 Sam. 8:17, 15:24-37; 1 Kings 1:34-39; Ezek. 40:46, 43:19, 44:10-16), and that they alone were qualified to interpret Scripture. Through heredity and genealogical ties, the Sadducees controlled the Temple hierarchy for centuries, becoming a wealthy and powerful class. The Sadducees denied resurrection, the immortality of the soul, rewards and punishments in an afterlife, angels, the messiah, and the ability of the common person to interpret the Torah. In fact, the Sadducees were aloof from the common people and appear to have accommodated those Greeks and Romans who gained ascendancy over the Jewish people. Jewish tradition portrays them as worldly and heretical aristocrats, only interested in maintaining their position of privilege.

When Rome reorganized *Eretz Yisrael* as the province of Judea in 6 C.E., the religious situation of Judaism was complex. Many sects and movements stirred among the Jewish people, and the majority of Jews lived outside *Eretz Yisrael*, scattered in thriving communities throughout the Roman Empire. Even among the Pharisees in Judea, two schools of thought flourished—the school of Hillel and the school of Shammai. The exile in Babylon had not only brought the synagogue into prominence, but it had also brought about the *yeshivah*, or academy. This was a place of study where Jewish sages and their pupils learned Torah.

A native of Babylonia, Hillel was a student in the *yeshivah* there, traveling to Jerusalem at about 40 B.C.E. He appears to have chosen to remain poor during his entire life, and his teachings reflect a keen social justice and love for the poor. Hillel is described as a man of deep humility, whose overriding concern was to bring people closer to Torah. His wisdom and kind spirit were noticed early on in his studies, and he was appointed president (*nasi*) of the Sanhedrin, the supreme Jewish religious and judicial body under the Roman regime. Hillel shared his leadership with Shammai, a teacher whose rigidity contrasted sharply with Hillel's merciful and mild-mannered approach.

Shammai was noted for stringent attitudes and extreme literalism. He insisted on complete separation from Gentiles. When a "heathen" came to Shammai and claimed that he wanted to convert if Shammai could teach him the entire Torah "while standing on one foot," Shammai drove him away. Hillel, however, answered the heathen kindly, stating: "What is hateful to you, do not do unto your neighbor; this is the entire Torah, all the rest is commentary—go and learn it." The heathen converted.

Followers of both men seem to have in their rulings and judgments exaggerated the traits of Hillel and Shammai, and conflicts were rampant in the first century C.E. Concerning the *Shema*, for example, the school of Shammai took the words, "when you lie down and when you rise up" (Deut. 6:7b) with extreme literalism, claiming the *Shema* must be recited in a reclining position in the evening and only while standing in the morning. Hillel's school taught that the passage referred to the times of recitation rather than the posture. It was the school of Hillel within pharisaic Judaism that survived the First and Second Revolts against the Roman Empire and whose interpretations endure to the present day.

The tension between Rome and the people of Judea steadily increased between 6 and 66 C.E. No fewer than fourteen prefects were sent to Judea during that period. Most were inept administrators who made foolish judgments and were cruel. A good example of ineptitude was Pontius Pilate (governed Judea 26-36 C.E.), who among other absurd actions pilfered the Temple treasury to build an aqueduct. When Jewish citizens complained, Pilate had his military units whip them unmercifully so that some citizens died from their wounds. Pilate's reign of terror ended when he attacked a defenseless group of Samaritans. He was then transferred to Vienne in southern France, where he reportedly committed suicide. This internal conflict under the prefects led to increasing calls for armed rebellion. Groups such as the Zealots gained a large following, setting the stage for both the First Jewish Revolt in 66 C.E. and the Second Jewish Revolt in 132 C.E.

With the First Jewish Revolt in Judea and the subsequent destruction of the Temple in Jerusalem in 70 C.E., Jews throughout the Empire were appalled at the ruthless actions of the Emperor Vespasian and his son Titus. Jews at Masada, the last bastion of Judean resistance (fell in 73 C.E.), were pursued with fanatical Roman vengeance, 960 choosing death rather than submitting to pagan Rome. For their part, the Romans gloried in their victory, striking coins with the inscription "Judea Is Captured" and commemorating the events with a triumphal arch (Arch of Titus) in Rome, where Jewish captives were dragged with the Holy Menorah. These events brought forth a new term of forced dispersion into the Jewish vocabulary, *Galut* ("exile"), those driven into the *Diaspora* ("dispersion," all Jewish people residing outside of *Eretz Yisrael*) from unimaginable cruelty.

Emperor Hadrian (ruled 117-138 C.E.) provoked the Second Jewish Revolt in Judea by his decision to establish a Roman colony on the ruins of Jerusalem. Unable to understand a people who refused to accept the "enlightened" Greco-Roman culture and polytheistic religion he valued so highly, Hadrian visited Judea in 130 and 131. Scholars are divided on whether Hadrian's cruel edicts forbidding circumcision and demanding that a temple to Jupiter be built on the Temple Mount in Jerusalem were proclaimed before or after the rebellion. The result, however, was that Hadrian's Roman forces crushed the Jewish rebels led by Simon bar Kokhba in a three-year campaign (132-135 C.E.), and an entire pagan city, Aelia

Capitolina, was built on the ruins of Jerusalem. A temple to Jupiter and Hadrian's statue were constructed on the Temple Mount. A temple to Aphrodite, the goddess of love and beauty, was placed next to the new forum on the west side of the city.

Hadrian declared it a capital offense to study Torah and to practice Judaism. Circumcision was forbidden by reviving an ancient law against "mutilation." A bloody purge of Jewish sages ensued, and the elderly Rabbi Akiva (c. 50-135 C.E.) was martyred. Jews in the area were either enslaved, killed, or forced to flee for their lives. For a time, only Galilee contained a significant Jewish presence in the area. Hadrian's edicts remained in effect until his death in 138 C.E. Gradual improvement in Jewish-Roman relations took place during the long reign of his successor, Antoninus Pius (138-161 C.E.).

Although a Jewish remnant would remain in Judea and Jerusalem for the next eighteen centuries, the Holy Land would be passed among foreign conquerors. Not until 1948 would a Jewish nation again exist in *Eretz Yisrael*. The exiled Jewish community would spread its creativity, discipline, and spiritual depth among other Jews dispersed throughout the Roman Empire. Together they would influence the direction of Western civilization. Stable areas of Jewish scholarship would continue in the *yeshivot* in Babylon and Galilee. Jerusalem, however, would remain a special place in the hearts of Jews everywhere. Although the Temple was gone and pilgrimages and sacrifices no longer could be made, the Babylonian Exile had prepared the Jewish people. The synagogue structure maintained the Sabbaths and the festivals. Judaism was alive, and its people believed that God had indeed provided once again a "little sanctuary" (Ezek. 11:16).

In the pharisaic tradition that became normative Judaism, God is said to have revealed the interpretation of the Torah at Mount Sinai. Torah demands interpretation, and the discussions and insights by Jewish sages attempted to rediscover the original meaning of God's Word—the divine framework that surrounded God's message to humankind.

The vast oral tradition and its decipherment dates back to the time of Ezra. The *Soferim* (a word translated "scribes" but literally meaning "men of the book") began to interpret and supplement the written Torah so that it could apply to life in Judea after the Babylonian Exile. Their clarification and amplification of Scripture to understand its fuller meaning was known as *Midrash*. Ancient biblical precepts and guidelines were applied to new living conditions, and legal conclusions began to build. Once collected, these conclusions began to be taught separately as *halakhah* ("the way one goes"). Oral tradition was not meant to be a scholastic exercise in legalism, but rather was aimed at creating a pious, humble, and righteous life.

The Pharisees who succeeded the Soferim believed that the teachings of Judaism had been communicated in an unbroken chain from generation to generation since Sinai. This chain of tradition was called *Shalshelet Hakabbalah* (*kabbalah* meaning "that which has been received"). The process is described in the Talmud in these words: "Moses received the Torah from Sinai and transmitted it to Joshua, Joshua to the Elders, the Elders to the Prophets. And the Prophets transmitted it to the men of the Great Synagogue."

Hillel contributed to the standardization of the methods and guidelines employed for interpreting Torah and applying Tradition. *Hesed* became the normative principle to be applied by a humble spirit in a faithful relationship to God. The Jewish sages from the period of Hillel to the compilation of the *Mishnah* (see below), a period to approximately 200 C.E., are called *Tannaim*. Johanan ben Zakkai, a disciple of Hillel, was one of those important scholars decades before the destruction of the Temple. He seems to have foreseen the impending crisis for Judaism. He strengthened the pattern of the Tannaim to make the study of Torah the aim of one's life and to spread the knowledge of Torah among the masses. Yet the necessity of humility is found in his warning to his students: "If you have learned much Torah, do not ascribe any merit to yourself, since it was for this that you were created."

Judah ha-Nasi ("Judah the Prince"), a seventh-generation grandson of Hillel, provided the skeletal outline upon which the Talmud is based. Judah was the head of a *yeshivah* at Bet She'arim, three miles west of the modern settlement in lower Galilee on the Nazareth-Haifa road. Well respected as the "holy teacher" and "patriarch" of the day, Judah met with at least one Roman emperor who came to *Eretz Yisrael* and circumspectly forged a policy of nonintervention in Roman affairs.

Like his great-grandfather, Hillel the Elder, Judah devoted himself to the study of Torah and to spreading its precepts.

Judah ha-Nasi's skeletal outline (c. 200 C.E.) of the vast oral tradition is known as the *Mishnah* (derived from *shanah*, "to repeat") and is written entirely in Hebrew. It not only codified the *halakhah* but also recorded the teachings of the Tannaim. So well respected was the Mishnah that it was regarded as authoritative in both *Eretz Yisrael* as well as the academies of Babylonia. A new group of Jewish scholars, known as *Amoraim* ("spokesmen, interpreters"), arose in both *Eretz Yisrael* and Babylonia from approximately 250 to 500 C.E. They provided an extended commentary on the Mishnah, a commentary on the commentary, which became known as the *Gemara* ("completion," "compilation," or "tradition").

Together, the Mishnah and the Gemara are known as the *Talmud* ("study" or "learning"). There are two Talmuds, reflecting the two great centers of Amoraic scholarship. The Jerusalem Talmud (actually collected in academies in Galilee) is the Talmud produced by the Amoraim in *Eretz Yisrael*. Less than one-third the size of the Babylonian Talmud (produced by Amoraim in Babylonia), the Jerusalem Talmud is considered less authoritative than the larger Babylonian Talmud. This is not only because of size but also because the discussions in the Babylonian Talmud are more sophisticated, the writing style more lively, and the development of themes more focused. It also has more extensive "tractates," divisions dealing with a variety of subjects. With the compilation of the Talmud, the basic beliefs and values, customs and ceremonies, forms and character of the living *Torah* were written and established.

Thus, the Talmud includes Torah teachings, legal precedents, guiding principles, and personal accounts spanning a period of nearly one thousand years. The rabbis compared it to a sea in which one must submerge oneself. From Soferim to Pharisees, from Tannaim to Amoraim, the rabbis have derived principles of practice and God's commands for Jewish life in a foreign culture.

FESTIVALS AND TRADITIONS

Judaism is a liturgical religion. It has a prayer book and a fixed liturgy for worship. Although spontaneous prayer and private expressions toward God are never discouraged, the prayer book (known as the *Siddur*, "order") is used in both the synagogue and the home. The basic framework of the *Siddur* dates back to at least the period of the Second Temple and, next to the Hebrew Bible and Talmud, is the most revered book of Judaism. It has never been considered "completed" or "canonized," and the principles of *keva* (fixed times and fixed liturgy) and *kavanah* (inwardness and spontaneity) work freely in its translation and composition. Throughout Jewish history, the principles of *keva* and *kavanah* have operated to produce the Jewish prayer book of today. One generation's spontaneous expressions were compiled to become another generation's fixed liturgical heritage. Specifed prayers and liturgy are used not only during the weekly Sabbath services, but also have traditional significance during the yearly festivals and fasts.

Stirring festivals and fasting times historically have internalized the Jewish experience and dictated an understanding of life itself. Through the yearly cycle, a Jew reflects on past and present dependence upon God as well as on hopes and aspirations for the future. The continual experience of the Jewish peoplehood and the adventure of life itself thus turn mere commemorations into vehicles for witness and mission. The festivals denote obligation to God as well as to one's people.

Pesach or Passover, the festival of freedom, referred to the time of the Exodus, the Hebrews' redemption from Egyptian slavery, and was linked with the coming of springtime; the *Seder*, a ritual meal on the first evening of Passover, centered around eating unleavened bread during the entire week, drinking four cups of wine, and eating bitter herbs and roots and parsley, dipped in salt water, as a reminder of suffering in previous centuries. These reminded the participants of Jewish ordeals in the days of captivity, and at the *Seder*, the *Haggadah*, or "Narration," retold the whole story, with part of it in question-and-answer form. After the singing of Psalms, the repeating of prayers, and relating the story of the Exodus, the door was opened, partly to symbolize that all hungry passersby were to be admitted, partly to show that nothing was concealed and, to refute the hoary charges of ritual murder, to prove that no child had been killed, but mostly to enable the spirit of Elijah, forerunner of the messiah, to come in and drink from the

Elijah Cup, standing ready for him on the *Seder* table during the ceremony.

Fifty days after the *Seder*, Jews observe *Shavuot*, the Feast of Weeks, to give thanks for the Torah that had been given on Mount Sinai in that season of the year and to rejoice over the first fruits of the spring harvest of wheat.

In the early autumn, they celebrate *Rosh Hashanah*, their religious New Year's Day. This day is noted in the Talmud as a "Day of Judgment" and is observed by the blowing of the *shofar*, the ram's horn, which summons the listeners to the synagogue that they may reassess their lives, think about their actions in the past, recall their Creator, and come to God in contrition and repentance.

Dovetailed with this holiday are the subsequent ten days of repentance. At the conclusion comes the observance of *Yom Kippur*, the great Day of Atonement, when the people fast in complete abstinence from all food and drink for twenty-four hours—from just before the previous night's worship service to the following evening when the stars appear. The *Kol Nidre*, the atonement prayer chanted in a traditional melody on the eve of *Yom Kippur*, grants absolution from the sin of unkept vows. Each worshipper is expected to turn away from evil-doing and to atone for the wrongs he or she has done during the past year, promising to fulfill the will of God from this time forward.

Five days later is the observance of the thanksgiving-harvest of *Sukkot*, the Feast of Tabernacles or Booths, when for eight days the participants take their meals in a tabernacle or booth decorated with flowers and fruit and hold in prayer branches of the myrtle, the willow, and the palm along with the citron fruit, all symbols reminiscent of the Land of Israel and its grain and grapes, fruits of the fields and of the vine, and God's providence.

To conclude these holy days comes *Simchat Torah*, the day when Jews rejoice in the Torah. The sacred scrolls of the Pentateuch are taken from the Ark of the synagogue to be carried in solemn, yet joyous, procession through the aisles of the house of worship. The reading of the Pentateuch is ended for the year, for it has been the practice to read a portion every Sabbath in the services; and then the cycle of readings is immediately begun again, to be continued for another year.

In recent decades two ancient festivals of the winter season have become increasingly popular. One is *Hanukkah*, the "Feast of Lights," when, through a period of eight days, candles are lighted each night in synagogue and home—one on the first night alongside a special candle, or oil, reserved to light all others, and additional ones on subsequent nights, until all eight have been lighted to fill the Menorah, the festival candelabrum; these candles recall the recapture of Jerusalem and the rededication of the temple in 165 B.C.E. by Judas Maccabeus. The second feast is *Purim*, the "Feast of Lots," observed in February or March, four weeks before Passover, and associated with the Book of Esther in the Bible, which relates Queen Esther's successful efforts to rescue her fellow Jews from abuse and persecution in Persia. A festive atmosphere with singing and dancing in the homes of the people prevails for the entire day of Purim; gifts are sent to poor people, while members of the family and close friends exchange gifts. Hanukkah and Purim combine the religion of the Jewish people with strong nationalistic overtones, the former with its reference to the Maccabees and the latter with its retelling of the story of Esther.

In more recent generations, departures from strict traditionalism have arisen within Judaism. Conservative Judaism holds many of the basic precepts of its nineteenth-century forebearer, Zacharias Frankel (1801-1875), a scholar and rabbi born in Prague, who was called in 1836 by the government of Saxony to be chief rabbi of Dresden. The Conservatives believe that modern culture necessitates some adaptation and change, the Jewish peoplehood being a living organism that historically responded with creativity to new challenges. Yet such change is to be made with only the greatest reluctance, because Conservative Judaism maintains the validity of the traditional forms and precepts of Judaism. Reform Judaism, the product of nineteenth-century religious liberals from Germany, Great Britain, and the United States, emphasizes that a Jew should be free to exercise his or her individual judgment in choosing the basis of commitment and knowledge. Flexibility of belief and diversity of views remain the group standard of modern Reform Judaism.

THE HOLOCAUST AND ISRAEL

Maimonides (1135-1204), the famed Jewish philosopher, once stated: "If a Jew is murdered for no other reason except that he is a Jew, and, had he not been a Jew, he would have remained alive, then it may truly be said that he sacrificed his life for the holiness of God." *Tisha Be-Av*, the ninth day of Av, is the saddest day on the Jewish calendar and symbolizes the persecution and murder that have plagued the People of the Covenant throughout history.

Traditionally, *Tisha Be-Av* is a fast day for mourning the destruction of the First and Second Temples in Jerusalem. Viewed historically as a time of calamity, it has become the "Friday the 13th" of Jewish life. Not only were the First and Second Temples destroyed during this period, but the children of Israel were forbidden to enter the Promised Land on that date and condemned to wander forty years in the wilderness. In 135 B.C.E., the last bastion of the Second Jewish Revolt against the Romans (Betar) was captured on *Tisha Be-Av*, and in the following year Emperor Hadrian built a pagan temple and a pagan city on the original Temple site. Hadrian renamed Jerusalem *Aelia Capitolina*; called Judea "Palestine"; and, on the ninth of Av, forbade Jews access to or even a look from afar upon the sacred city.

In more modern times, the Christian Crusades destroyed entire Jewish communities on the ninth of Av. On this date in 1290, Jews were expelled from England, and, again on the ninth of Av during the Spanish Inquisition in 1492, Jews were expelled from Spain. Four hundred fifty years later, in 1942, Polish Jews in the Warsaw Ghetto were deported by the Nazis on *Tisha Be-Av* to the Treblinka extermination camp. There more than 800,000 Jewish men, women, and children were slaughtered.

Without an understanding of the Holocaust, one cannot truly comprehend the psyche of the Jewish people today. In the land of the Protestant Reformation, religious institutions were impotent to protect Jewish people. Four thousand years of anti-Semitism and 1900 years of Christian anti-Semitism converged, culminating in the loss in seven Nazi-dominated years, 1939-45, of more Jewish lives than under *all* the anti-Jewish riots, massacres, and pogroms in the preceding thousands of years of Jewish history. Two-thirds of European Jewry (one-third of the world population of Jews) was killed; 1,500,000 were Jewish children, a whole generation lost. Tragically, even conversion to Christianity could not save Jews during the Nazi Holocaust, as racial anti-Semitism had labeled the Covenant People vermin, bacilli, the lowest of creatures. The Nazis were determined to kill all Jews, and they searched out every hovel, even thwarting their own war effort to do so. For those who miraculously escaped the Nazi tentacles, there was no place to go— no country would have them.

Creation of the modern State of Israel from the ashes of the Holocaust has had an incalculable impact on the Jewish people and on Judaism itself. For a religion that proclaimed "Next Year in Jerusalem!" at the end of every Passover meal, reestablishment of a Hebrew-speaking Jewish state, Israel, the third Jewish commonwealth, was the fulfillment of the national hope that had always been present in the prayers of the Jewish people. After the final Roman expulsion, the "Zion" idea had never been divorced from Jewish thinking, and religious Jews dreamed of the ultimate release from their dispersion, a return to the land of promise.

While premodern Zionism emphasized a religious motive and quiet territorial settlement, Dr. Theodor Herzl's publication of *Der Judenstaat* ("the Jewish State") in 1896 gave birth to political Zionism and with it the modern conception of Zionism. A new era of Jewish history unfolded when Herzl, an Austrian Jewish journalist, changed from an advocate of Jewish assimilation to a belief that anti-Semitism was inevitable as long as the majority of Jewish people lived outside their homeland. Ultimately, the horror of the Nazi Holocaust, in which 6 million Jews were exterminated, drew Zionists and non-Zionists together in support of Palestine as a Jewish commonwealth—a haven for the persecuted and homeless. In November 1947, a partition plan creating a Jewish state, endorsed by both the United States and the Soviet Union, was adopted by the General Assembly of the United Nations. The State of Israel was formally recognized on May 14, 1948, when British rule ended.

Today the Jews of Israel are divided on the steps to be taken toward peace and security for their state. Confronting Arab terrorism, Palestinian liberation demands, and internal Israeli dissension, Israel's major parties of centrist Labor and rightist Likkud are too equally balanced to provide a clear mandate for immediate action. The elections of November 1988 proved once again that the more than twenty smaller parties would capitalize on the inability of Labor or Likkud to command a majority, thereby delivering the government to fragile coalitions with parochial concerns. Between the minority of hardliners on the right and on the left, a majority of Israeli Jews hold a kaleidoscope of moderate opinions. This majority is consumed with the daily burden of supporting a family, raising children to be responsible and caring human beings, and providing for their safety. And the mind-set, rugged individualism, and the pride of the Israeli Jew can never be severed from the events and lessons of those four millennia of historical experience, including the sobering losses and hopeful gains of four decades of modern statehood.

THE PEOPLE OF THE COVENANT

Judaism, at this juncture, proves that the Jewish people have survived because of a sense of oneness, an ethnic consciousness, and a religion kept aglow by the heritage of the covenant. Jews have succeeded in reviving their own religion, by recapturing the meaning of that covenant, by reaffirming the meaning of the prophetic faith, by critically appraising the social order, and by refurbishing ethical concepts in spiritual ideals from the past. The leading Jewish communities of today are those of North America, Israel, Great Britain, France, and Argentina. The Jews of the Soviet Union are the second largest Jewish community in the world but, in spite of *Glasnost*, they suffer under severe governmental restrictions against their religion and peoplehood. Nevertheless, they too are taking an active part in changing their society and proclaiming to the world the importance of human rights and freedom of religion.

Something of the lasting strength of this monotheistic faith from ancient Ur of the Chaldees and Mount Sinai is highlighted for our own age. The Jews of the modern world—descendants of the Patri

archs and the Judges, the Prophets and the Talmudists—still repeat their ancient declaration as the People of the Covenant:
"Hear, O Israel: The Lord our God, the Lord is one."

8

CHRISTIANITY

The Greatest of These Is Love

No living religion today focuses so clearly and unequivocally on a single man as does Christianity. In Jesus of Nazareth, as both founder of the faith and the incarnation of God, Christianity centers all its meaning and all its allegiance—on his birth, the words and deeds of his active life, the drama of his death and resurrection.

The Gospels of what Christians have termed the "New Testament" (an addition to the Hebrew *Tanach*, which is referred to as the "Old Testament")—Matthew, Mark, Luke, and John—tell the story of this unique person. The Book of Acts describes the first days of the early Christian movement and its expansion throughout the Mediterranean world. The Epistles convey essential elements of the thought and aspiration of the first generation of Christians.

As we have seen in chapter 7, Judea was the homeland of Jesus' people, the Jews, and was subject to an oppressive Roman rule. The Jews of *Eretz Yisrael* resented and resisted the inept Roman prefects, but their community was splintered into many opposing factions so that they did not present a united front. Conflict between Pharisees, Sadducees, Essenes, Zealots, etc., was intense in an atmosphere of clashing religious ideas and political turmoil. Of the two schools of Pharisaic thought that flourished during the first century C.E., Hillel's appears closer to what we understand of the teaching of Jesus the Jew. Like the Apostle Paul, he definitely was Pharisaic in orientation and had little regard for Sadducean emphases.

BIRTH AND CALL

Jesus was born in Bethlehem, a town in Judea a few miles south of Jerusalem, where his parents, Mary and Joseph, had traveled from their hometown of Nazareth to register in a census decreed by Caesar Augustus. The year was not the first year of what has come to be known as the Christian Era. Rather, it was 6-4 B.C.E. because of the census decree and the fact that Herod the Great, who attempted to kill the child, died in 4 B.C.E. The incorrect date was set many centuries later by a monk who made a miscalculation, and it has affected the calendar year of Western countries to this very day.

Matthew and Luke record that although Mary was pledged to be married to Joseph, she was "found to be with child through the Holy Spirit" before they had had intercourse. God sent the angel Gabriel to Nazareth to explain to Mary that "the power of the Most High" would overshadow her, so the "holy one to be born will be called the Son of God." Traditional Christianity has accepted the intervention of God in the virgin birth of the Son, Jesus. Jesus' use of *Abba* (Father) for God has been held by some to be a unique expression among the Jewish milieu.

As Jesus grew to manhood in Nazareth, a town of Galilee, he followed the family trade of carpentry (a trade that may have been more of a stonemason in the rocky, rugged terrain of Judea). Luke's account of Jesus tells us that, at the age of twelve, Jesus lingered in the temple long after his parents had begun the return journey to Nazareth from Jerusalem, where they had participated in Passover. One learns of his intense religious inquiry and interpretation from an early age. As he sat in the Temple courts "among the teachers, listening to them and asking questions," they were amazed at his understanding and his answers (cf. Luke 2:46-47). His obedience to his parents was overshadowed by his question: "Why were you searching for me? Didn't you know I had to be in my Father's house?"

Jesus had been circumcised into the covenant on the eighth day by his Jewish parents and received thorough religious training in the Nazareth synagogue. He appears to have mastered the written and oral Torah, and his use of parables was in line with rabbinical teaching techniques. Immersed in the festivals and commemorations of the Jewish people, many of his potent statements were made within the context of a holy day celebration. During the festival of *Sukkot*, for example, Jesus made allusion to "streams of living water" and the Spirit of God (John 7:37). Since the festival in the ancient period, including prayers for rain, had spiritual as well as physical connotations, Jesus' declaration in a loud voice had a clear message: "If a man is thirsty, let him come to me and drink. Whoever believes in me, as the Scripture has said, streams of living water will flow from within him." All his days, Jesus had a sage's mind and a poet's sensitivity with a rare gift for putting deep thoughts into simple words and illustrations.

At about the age of thirty, Jesus began his ministry. He left Nazareth and visited John the Baptist, possibly his second cousin (cf. Luke 1). John had been preaching a baptism of repentance for the forgiveness of sins, and crowds from Jerusalem as well as all Judea flocked to hear him, confess their sins, and to be baptized in the Jordan River. He also declared that one would come after him who would baptize them with the Holy Spirit. "Repent," John the Baptist declared, "for the kingdom of heaven is at hand!" While all the people were being baptized, Jesus also asked John to baptize him. According to tradition, John did so only reluctantly, believing that he needed to be baptized by Jesus for Jesus was the greater. Matthew 3:16-17 states:

> As soon as Jesus was baptized, he went up out of the water. At that moment heaven was opened, and he saw the Spirit of God descending like a dove and lighting on him. And a voice from heaven said, "This is my Son, whom I love; with him I am well pleased."

The Gospels also relate that Jesus was "led by the Spirit into the desert to be tempted by the devil." After fasting for forty days and forty nights, Jesus was told by Satan to turn a stone into bread, "if you are the Son of God." Jesus answered with the Torah: "Man does not live on bread alone" (Deut. 8:3). Showing Jesus all the kingdoms of the world, the devil said that he would give him their authority and splendor if Jesus would worship him. Again, Jesus answered with the Torah: "It is written: 'Worship the Lord your God and serve him only'" (Deut. 6:13). Taking Jesus to Jerusalem, the devil had him stand on the highest point of the Temple, saying "If you are the Son of God, throw yourself down from here." Quoting Psalm 91:11-12, Satan reminded Jesus that the angels would protect him. Jesus declared from Deut. 6:16: "Do not put the Lord your God to the test." The devil left him for a time.

EXPANDED MINISTRY

Returning to Galilee in the power of the Holy Spirit, Jesus taught in the synagogues. People were amazed at his teaching, and news spread about him over the whole region of Galilee. Proclaiming the "good news (gospel) of God," Jesus preached: "The time has come, the kingdom of God is near. Repent and believe the good news!" Going to the synagogue in Nazareth on the Sabbath, "as was his custom," he was handed the scroll of the prophet Isaiah as he stood up to read. Unrolling it, he found Isa. 61:1-2, reading:

> The Spirit of the Lord is on me, because he has anointed me to preach good news to the poor. He has sent me to proclaim freedom for the prisoners and recovery of sight for the blind, to release the oppressed, to proclaim the year of the Lord's favor.

Following the traditional Jewish pattern of reading Scripture, Jesus rolled up the scroll and sat down. As all eyes were fixed on him, he said: "Today this scripture is fulfilled in your hearing" (Luke 4:21).

Calling together his twelve disciples, Jesus performed many miracles, healing the sick, the lame, the blind, the mentally disturbed, and the demon-possessed. Many other disciples followed him, and he was thronged by great crowds. His key theme was the nearness of the kingdom of God. By this most of his hearers took him to mean a sudden miraculous transformation of the earth and its inhabitants, liberation from the shackles of the Roman Empire, to be expected in the near future, when men and women would be judged for their thoughts and their acts. He spoke of a loving and forgiving God, who was the Father of all humankind, both the Source and the Ruler of the universe. Complete faith in God meant inner security that would banish anxiety. God was in nature and in history, but also in the human heart. Access to God came through repentance and prayer; repentance would engage the Father's forgiveness, while the prayers would lead to what Paul the Apostle was later to describe as "the peace which passeth all understanding."

Such thoughts were in accord with the centuries-old tradition in the Hebrew faith. This latter-day prophet, however, gave it new force. The content of Jesus' preaching, a love for one's neighbor so all-forgiving and all-inclusive that it reflected God's love for human-kind, was as penetrating as the method of his teaching was effective. His method shone through in the instance of his rebuking the crowd about to stone the woman "taken in adultery, in the very act": "He that is without sin among you, let him first cast a stone at her." And when the men who "heard it, being convicted by their own conscience, went out one by one, beginning at the eldest, even unto the last," Jesus could say to the woman, "Neither do I condemn thee: go and sin no more." It was also to be seen in the prayer he uttered as the Roman soldiers crucified him: "Father, forgive them, for they know not what they do."

He taught his precepts in words spoken privately to the band of a dozen chosen intimates who walked with him from town to town and in sermons to the thousands who gathered to hear him declare such truths as the Beatitudes: "Blessed are the pure in heart: for they shall see God. Blessed are the peacemakers: for they shall be called the children of God. Blessed are the meek: for they shall inherit the earth. Blessed are they that mourn: for they shall be comforted. . . . ." Jesus' teaching in this "Sermon on the Mount" was grounded firmly in Jewish thought and the prophetic tradition. He insisted: "Not everyone who says to me, 'Lord, Lord,' will enter the kingdom of heaven, but only he who does the will of my Father who is in heaven" (Matt. 7:21).

Balanced in his attitude toward women, children, and the outcasts of society, Jesus saw the potential of the individual. His love and compassion have drawn people of all races, religions, and walks of life ever since. The Sermon on the Mount clearly illustrates his attitudes and daily living, where statements on love, compassion, and understanding abound. "You have heard that it was said, 'You shall love your neighbor and hate your enemy,'" he declared, "but

I say unto you, love your enemies, and pray for those who persecute you in order that you may be sons of your Father who is in heaven" (Matt. 5:43-45). No less powerful as a means of teaching were his picturesque stories: the parables of the Good Samaritan, the Lost Coin, the Talents, and many other narratives. He used this Jewish means of teaching very effectively, and the Gospels record: "Without a parable spake he not unto them."

Jesus was a master at illustrating how a proper vertical relationship with God would be evidenced by a loving and compassionate horizontal relationship with human beings. He often alluded to the fact that this relationship extended beyond the barriers of religion and race. Luke 10:25-29 relates:

> And behold, a certain lawyer [an expert in Torah] stood up and put [Jesus] to the test, saying, "Teacher, what shall I do to inherit eternal life?"
>
> And He said to him, "What is written in the Torah? How does it read to you?"
>
> And he answered and said, "You shall love the Lord your God with all your heart, and with all your soul, and with all your strength, and with all your mind: and your neighbor as yourself."
>
> And [Jesus] said to him, "You have answered correctly; Do this, and you will live."
>
> But wishing to justify himself, he said to Jesus, "And who is my neighbor?"

Jesus replied with the story of the Good Samaritan, a story of a man robbed, stripped, and beaten, half-dead on the road from Jerusalem to Jericho. Two important religious leaders passed him by, not stopping to help. However, a religious and racial outcast, a despised Samaritan, came upon the dying man, and "when he saw him, he felt compassion, and came to him, and bandaged up his wounds, pouring oil and wine on them; and he put him on his own beast, and brought him to an inn, and took care of him" (Luke 10:33-34).

"Which of these three do you think proved to be a neighbor to the man who fell into the robbers' hands?" Jesus asked the lawyer who had memorized his Scriptures so well and constantly dealt with the intricacies of rabbinical interpretation.

"The one who showed mercy toward him," answered the lawyer.

Jesus' reply, "Go and do the same [as the Samaritan]," is a contrast to his previous answer, "Do this [the commandments] and you will live" (cf. Luke 10:28, 37). Again, mercy and justice, compassion and love, are stressed by Jesus, not only to one's own, but also to those despised by one's friends, acquaintances, and peer groups.

Jesus not only taught against racism, but also practiced his teaching. In John 4 it is recorded that he entered the culturally forbidden religious and racial ghetto of Samaria. As he listens to the Samaritan woman, draws her into conversation, and ministers to her, one notes a sensitivity that is extraordinary. The men and women of the city asked him to stay on, and he stayed two days. The same sensitivity and compassion are evident in Jesus' total disregard of social class: he loved the rich and he loved the poor. In fact, his love of the despised "tax-gatherers and sinners" brought him grumbles and provoked gossip within his own religious tradition. Jesus' choice of disciples illustrates his love of the lowly and keen perception of human beings. For example, Jesus chose Matthew, from the detested tax-gatherers, rather than a well-versed lawyer.

Such methods and thoughts ran counter to some time-hardened views and practices of the Sadducean hierarchy and to the rigid theology of some Pharisees. A few scholars have suggested that Jesus' chief problems with his Pharisaic cohorts were with the more rancorous members of the school of Shammai (see chapter 7). Whatever the case, the Talmud itself teaches that there were unworthy and hypocritical religious leaders at the time of Jesus. In the recorded disputations, one finds most of the unflattering rhetoric that Jesus used for some hypocritical teachers of his day ("whited sepulchres," etc.) is used by competing schools of Jewish scholars against one another. Jesus was simply using the illustrations and language of his day—a language with which most of his hearers were very familiar.

In fact, the Talmud speaks of seven types of Pharisees, including those who wear their good deeds "so all the world can see and admire them" and those who say, "Wait a bit until I have done the good deed" (it *never* gets done). Only the last two types listed are the "God-fearing Pharisee" (who patterns his life after Job) and the "God-loving Pharisee" (who patterns his life after Abraham as a friend of God who loves his heavenly father). It is an ironic and sad fact of history that with such diversity and complexity in the world of Judaism during Jesus' ministry, the Jewish Jesus' negative comments to a few of the hypocrites of his day have been used in all ages by Christians to stigmatize all Pharisees (and even all Jews). The Pharisees were loved by the common people and known for their sincerity and piety. *Jesus did not hate Pharisees.* He did not attack the basic concepts of Pharisaism, but (like the apostle Paul) was Pharisaic in orientation. Jesus spoke against hypocrisy, wrong interpretations, and excesses. He would no doubt do the very same with "devout" Christian leaders and movements today.

DEATH AND RESURRECTION

Nevertheless, Jesus' words and actions embroiled him in controversy from the very inception of his ministry. When four men brought a paralytic to him, lowering the paralyzed man on a mat through an opening in the roof when they could not get through the crowd, Jesus said to the paralytic: "Son, your sins are forgiven." Some teachers of the Torah were very upset because they thought to themselves, "Why does this fellow talk like that? He's blaspheming! Who can forgive sins but God alone?" Such offense and antagonism at Jesus' teaching, as well as jealousy, escalated for more than two years. For an unknown reason, Judas Iscariot entered at length into negotiations to betray the whereabouts of Jesus on a given day to powerful leaders among his enemies, who were plotting his death.

When Jesus turned toward Jerusalem at the time of the Passover feast, he warned his disciples that death awaited him. They, in turn, tried to dissuade him from his decision to return to the city but to no avail. As he entered the great city, his popularity reached its zenith. The day was traditionally to be commemorated from that time on as Palm Sunday, for the Jewish multitudes are said to have "cut down branches off the trees and strewed them in the way, crying out, 'Hosanna in the highest.'"

The simmering revolt against Jesus started to come to the surface as he went into the Temple "and began to cast out them that sold and bought in the Temple, and overthrew the tables of the moneychangers, and the seats of them that sold doves, and would not suffer that any man should carry any vessels through the Temple. And he taught, saying unto them, "Is it not written, My house shall be called of all nations the house of prayer? But ye have made it a den of thieves."

On a Thursday evening (according to tradition), now observed as "Maundy Thursday," when Jesus celebrated the Passover feast with his disciples in an upper room on Mount Zion, he instituted the rite that has come to be known as the Lord's Supper or Holy Communion. The story, which has been retold across all the centuries, has touching notes of resignation and faith, of bowing before the inevitability of his tragic destiny while yet trusting in the Eternal:

> And as they did eat, Jesus took bread, and blessed, and brake it, and gave to them, and said, "Take, eat; this is my body."
> And he took the cup, and when he had given thanks, he gave it to them: and they all drank of it. And he said unto them, "This is my blood of the new testament, which is shed for many. Verily I say unto you, I will drink no more of the fruit of the vine, until that day that I drink it new in the kingdom of God."
> And when they had sung a hymn, they went out into the Mount of Olives.

Judas, who had earlier left the company in the upper room, then achieved the betrayal he had planned. He came to the garden of Gethsemane and pointed out Jesus to the police sent to apprehend him. Jesus was then taken before an impromptu court drawn from the Sanhedrin, the seventy-one men who composed the highest tribunal for religious and civil decisions among the Jewish people, and there he was sentenced to death for blasphemy. But Jewish courts were not permitted to carry out death sentences. Hence the case was referred to the Roman prefect, Pontius Pilate. Reluctant to enforce a sentence on such dubious grounds, and consumed with hatred for the Jewish religious hierarchy, Pilate sent Jesus on to Herod Antipas, governor of Galilee, who happened to be in the city at the time. Herod refused jurisdiction, however, and returned Jesus to Pilate.

Pilate is said to have announced, "I find in him no fault at all," and to have recommended Jesus' release, for the custom was to free a prisoner at the Passover season. The mob refused Pilate's offer and asked for the release of the robber Barabbas instead.

Hesitantly, Pilate remanded Jesus to the guards for crucifixion, which was the Roman—but never the Jewish—mode of execution. Pilate's motives and desires (in light of his cruelty as prefect of Judea) have been questioned ever since. Some hours later Jesus died, having uttered the plaint, "My God, my God, why hast Thou forsaken me?" and the sigh of resignation, "It is finished."

One of his faithful followers, Joseph of Arimathea, secured permission from Pilate to remove the body. With Nicodemus, another friend who was a Pharisee and a member of the Sanhedrin, he wrapped it in a linen cloth and laid it in a sepulcher that Joseph had originally built to be his own tomb.

On Sunday, the traditional third day of Jesus' death, some of the women who had followed him brought spices they had prepared but discovered the tomb was empty. Suddenly, as they reported later, they saw an angel who told them Jesus had risen from the dead. Jesus appeared to other followers and, finally, to the eleven disciples assembled in the same room. Luke records that Jesus asked them: "Why are you troubled, and why do doubts rise in your minds? Look at my hands and my feet. It is I myself! Touch me and see: a ghost does not have flesh and bones, as you see I have" (Luke 24:38-39). Jesus "opened their minds" to understand the need for his death and resurrection, and he emphasized that they would be his "witnesses." They then watched him ascend into heaven. Luke ends his gospel: "And they stayed continually at the Temple, praising God."

Luke begins his second account, the book of Acts, with the ascension of Jesus (until "a cloud hid him from their sight") and two angels dressed in white explaining to them, "This same Jesus, who has been taken from you into heaven, will come back in the same way you have seen him go into heaven" (Acts 1:11). Thus began this new faith. Christians consider Jesus to have been the long-promised messiah (Christ), the Anointed One, the Son of the Living God. One of the most eloquent spokesmen for the Christian faith summarized their beliefs to the first-century church at Corinth:

Now, brothers, I want to remind you of the gospel [good news] I preached to you, which you received and on which you have taken your stand. By this gospel you are saved, if you hold firmly to the word I preached to you. Otherwise you have believed in vain.

For what I received I passed on to you as of first importance: that Christ died for our sins according to the Scriptures, that he was buried, that he was raised on the third day according to the Scriptures, and that he appeared to Peter, and then to the Twelve. After that, he appeared to more than five hundred of the brothers at the same time, most of whom are still living, though some have fallen asleep. Then he appeared to James, then to all the apostles, and last of all he appeared to me also, as to one abnormally born. (1 Cor. 15:1-8)

"For I am the least of the apostles and do not even deserve to be called an apostle," the writer confessed, "because I persecuted the church of God."

SPREAD OF CHRISTIANITY

The writer of these words was Paul or Saul of Tarsus, a tentmaker from Asia Minor and a rabbinical scholar, who started the spread of the new religion out into the non-Jewish Mediterranean world. Paul claimed to be thoroughly trained under Gamaliel, who was possibly the grandson of Hillel and who is thought to have been the same Gamaliel who in Acts chapter 5 persuaded the "jealous" Sadducean high priest and the Sanhedrin not to kill Peter and the apostles. Paul is indicative of a radical group within the mediating school of Hillel. As an ardent Pharisee with all the reverence for the Torah that this status entailed, he had witnessed and approved of the stoning to death of Stephen, the first Christian martyr, and with the permission of the high priest in Jerusalem he had pursued to Damascus the followers of Christ. On that journey, as told in the Book of Acts in the New Testament, he experienced the conversion he never tired of telling about in his later ministry as the foremost Christian missionary. He had been struck blind, felled to the ground, and suffused with a blinding light. Then he heard the voice of Jesus: "Saul, Saul, why persecutest thou me?"

From that time on Saul's—or Paul's—life was completely altered, and he soon became a leader among the followers of the risen Christ. The persecutor of the new religion had now become its foremost advocate to the world. During his missionary journeys throughout the Roman Empire, he made many converts of all social classes. In important centers he organized assemblies of faith, or "churches," as congregations of Christians came to be called. Scarcely a Christian congregation arose, however, in an area where a synagogue had not preceded it. Thus it was in areas prepared by Judaism that the Christian message flourished.

Acts 15 records that a Jerusalem Council of Jewish believers debated around 50 C.E. whether Gentile converts to Christianity should be circumcised according to the Torah. They were asking: "Should the Gentiles become Jewish *before* they become Christians?" Paul, fresh from a missionary journey through Cyprus and Asia Minor, brought the question to the apostles and elders who believed in Jesus. Only after great debate and a spirited speech by Peter (who had debated on the other side a few years earlier) did James the Just, the presiding elder of their congregation, express his judgment, that they "not trouble those who are turning to God from among the Gentiles [that is, not trouble them to become Jewish first], but that we write to them that they abstain from things contaminated by idols and from fornication and from what is strangled and from blood" (Acts 15:19-20).

The suggestions were very Jewish-oriented, and historical records reveal very *Jewish* followers of Jesus. Little wonder that the Romans for much of the first century C.E. considered Christianity a sect of Judaism. Recent scholarship has convincingly maintained what some scholars of the past had asserted, that is, that the apostles continued their own Jewish identity and practices and probably encouraged other Jewish believers to do so as well. Paul himself appears to have remained an observant Jew his whole life, although he was instrumental in creating a Gentile church that was separated from Jewish observances. While the social ethics of Paul in his epistles are grounded in the Torah, he believed the Christian doctrines he propounded were revealed to him by God, inspired by the Holy Spirit. He preached of the centrality of "Christ Jesus," whose Spirit within a human heart would cleanse from sin and give a righteousness beyond any that could come merely through obedience to commandments. Although the Torah and the Prophets attested to such righteousness, Paul declared:

> This righteousness from God comes through faith in Jesus Christ to all who believe. There is no difference, for all have sinned and fall short of the glory of God, and are justified freely by his grace through the redemption that came by Christ Jesus. God presented him as a sacrifice of atonement, through faith in his blood. (Rom. 3:22-25)

Later in his letter to the Romans, Paul insists that the Gentiles "have been grafted in among the others [the Jews]," receiving salvation. The "Apostle to the Gentiles" also stressed, in spite of intense doctrinal discussion, that "three remain: faith, hope and love. *But the greatest of these is love*" (1 Cor. 13:13).

In his powerful, at times poetic, and always fervent letters to his churches, Paul outlined the new faith with a passion and a directness few Christians have been able to match in the centuries since. Despite the disparity of interpretations given to Paul's ideas they, along with the teachings of Jesus as recorded in the Gospels, have been the major source of Christian thought. Roman Catholic theology traces its norm to him, and Protestants also consider Paul the fount of their thought. The Orthodox church has held him in high regard through centuries of growth. Indeed, his major contribution was the welding together of the many divergent elements of the Christian movement in its earliest years. Paul wrote:

> . . .there is neither Jew nor Greek, there is neither bond nor free, there is neither male nor female; for ye are all one in Christ Jesus. . . . I, therefore, the prisoner of the Lord, beseech you that ye walk worthy of the vocation wherewith ye are called, with all lowliness and meekness, with long-suffering, forbearing one another in love; endeavoring to keep the unity of the Spirit in the bond of peace. There is one body, and one Spirit, even as ye are called in one hope of your calling; one Lord, one faith, one baptism, one God and Father of all, who is above all, and through all, and in you all.

The new faith had become a universal religion, reaching out with its message of salvation to all of the known world.

Christianity spread rapidly across the Roman Empire. During the first century it was confined mainly to the eastern half of the Roman Empire, an urban movement pushing from city to city. Often the Jewish communities received the first message of the missionaries. Other interpreters of Christianity went elsewhere, northeast into the regions around the Tigris and Euphrates rivers, southward to Ethiopia, and eastward to India, though none surpassed the impact of Paul. By 150 C.E., Christianity was active in the rural areas of Asia Minor, rapidly expanding to the Gentile population of the entire empire. By the time of the codification of the Mishnah in 200 C.E. (see chapter 7), Christians could be found in all parts of the Roman Empire, and, although Christianity was an illegal religion according to Roman law, it constituted approximately 10 percent of the empire's population of 75 million. This is the same percentage the Jewish community had constituted a century and a half before.

Violence toward Christians until approximately 250 C.E. was more the result of mob action than the definite policy of the Roman government. Although Christianity was unlawful, government officials did not seek to expose or persecute Christians unless a disturbance had been raised and names of Christians came to the fore. Yet sporadic persecution under an emperor or governor who wanted to use Christians as scapegoats appeared from time to time. Nero (emperor from 54 to 68 C.E.) is an example of such an emperor. The same phenomenon was occurring to the other monotheistic religion of the empire: the "legal" Jewish religion. Emperor Hadrian persecuted both Jews and Christians during his reign. But this was *not* the normal, "official" policy of the Roman state.

CHRISTIAN ANTI-SEMITISM

Development of Christian anti-Semitism was gradual. Relations between Jews and Christians had begun to deteriorate even during the first century. Mutual opposition arose as the Christian church became more gentile and more Roman. Mainstream Judaism had refused under threat of persecution to worship a Roman emperor who claimed to be "god," and it refused to accept mainstream Christianity's claim that Jesus was God. To become a Christian increasingly meant that a Jewish person would have to apostatize from Judaism. A climate of hostility arose.

The Roman wars against the Jews not only destroyed the Temple and ravaged Jerusalem but also resulted in Jerusalem's relinquishing her position as a center of Christian faith in the Roman world. Gentiles of the empire had long disdained Judaism and Jewish nationalism. Now, theological and political power moved from Jewish Christian leaders in Jerusalem to centers of Gentile Christian leadership in Alexandria, Rome, and Antioch. The Gentile Christians interpreted the destruction of the Temple and Jerusalem as a sign that God had abandoned Judaism, that God had provided the Gentiles freedom to develop their own Christian theology in a setting independent from Jerusalem's influence.

Yet the Gentile Christian church found itself in an ambivalent position in regard to the Jewish faith. It realized that Christianity was not a "new" religion and grudgingly accepted its Jewish foundation. Christianity had much in common with Judaism, that is, the God of Abraham, Isaac, and Jacob; a stand against relativism in morals and ethics; the wisdom and proclamation of the prophets; the Torah precept of loving God with all one's being and loving neighbor as oneself; the hatred of war, the spirit of peace, and the hope for the future; the imperishable nature of the human soul; rewards and punishments.

Undergirding all of this was the church's firm belief that the Jewish Scriptures were *her* Scriptures—the Scriptures used by Jesus, Paul, and the disciples. Early church Fathers quoted from the Jewish Scriptures and even defended themselves to the Romans from the Jewish Scriptures. Had the Jewish people at this point disappeared from history, annihilated by the Romans, Christians very possibly would have memorialized them as preparers of God's kingdom. Because Judaism instead remained a vibrant, dedicated Torah faith, which drew converts and was firm in its witness to the one true God, the climate of hostility grew worse.

The Jewish Scriptures being used by the Gentile church required a drastic reinterpretation because, according to those Scriptures, the Jewish people are the chosen people with an immense responsibility to the world. The Gentile church attempted to reconcile this difficulty by reinterpreting those Scriptures to state that the Christian church is the true Israel, the "new" Israel—not just grafted in as Paul stated in Rom. 11:17, but totally *replacing* the Jewish people. According to Tertullian (c. 150-220), for example, the Jewish people no longer had any witness or truth. Their only reason to exist was to testify to the misery and degradation that befell a people rejected by God. The curses of the Bible were ascribed to the Jews; the blessings of the Bible to the Christians. This triumphalism, the attitude of celebrating a victory over an "enemy," has fanned the flames of religious anti-Semitism ever since.

Church Fathers, such as Justin Martyr, Irenaeus, Hippolytus of Rome, Origen, Cyprian, Tertullian, Hilary of Poitiers, Ambrose of Milan and Chrysostom, were men of piety, noted for moral excellence in other areas of the Christian life. When it came to the Jewish people, however, they laid a foundation and conveyed a message that Adolf Hitler would exploit. They declared that the Jews were no longer God's chosen people and that the church had inherited the covenant promises of God—the church was God's chosen people. They insisted that the Jews were "Christ killers." They believed that the Jewish people deserved persecution and the loss of their land. In 300 C.E. a Christian council in Spain forbade eating with Jews on penalty of excommunication from the church.

CHRISTIAN ROME

As a wall of intolerance was being built against the Jewish community, early church Fathers were pleading for religious toleration from the Roman government. They assured the Roman emperors that like their Lord, Jesus Christ, they did not seek earthly power and had no intention of ever wielding such power. They said that they lived in two worlds, but heaven was their true home. They expected Jesus to return at any time to fetch them away from the wickedness that encompassed the world system, and these brave church Fathers reminded the Romans that God would judge them if they did not show tolerance to Christians. The pagan Roman Empire, however, was so "religious" that it actually considered the Christians to be "atheists."

The second-century *Letter to Diognetus* included an entire section that described Christians and their relationship to the world. Explaining that "Christians cannot be distinguished from the rest of the human race by country or language or customs," the Christian writer bemoaned the fact that they were treated as "aliens" because of their religion. He clarified to the Romans that Christians "obey the established laws, but in their own lives they go far beyond what the laws require" in love, purity, and piety. "To put it simply," the writer suggested, "what the soul is in the body, that the Christians are in the world."

Although the Romans would not accept the legality of the Christian religion, they rarely enforced the anti-Christian laws that were prevalent throughout the empire. Thus, no one was more surprised than the growing Christian community when Emperor Decius (249-251) declared that all subjects of the Roman Empire were required to present certificates that stated that they "have always sacrificed to the gods" and to prove loyalty by a current sacrifice in the presence of a royal official. Christians were caught in the dilemma of obeying God rather than men, and the first general persecution of Christians throughout the empire had begun. For the next six decades, persecution of Christians was the policy of the Roman state.

While a number of Christians lapsed, it was said that during this period there were times that the prisons were so crowded with Christians that there was not enough room for criminals. Emperor Valerian (253-259) also directed the persecution at the heads of the churches—the bishops—in an effort to destroy institutional Christianity. Many of them died, others lapsed. At the turn of the fourth century, Christians were ordered once again to sacrifice to pagan idols or die. It appeared that the 300s would be a century of persecution for Christians.

Such was not to be the case. A young commander in charge of his deceased father's troops would claim that he had asked the Christian god to help him defeat Maxentius at the decisive battle of Rome's Milvian Bridge in 312. In a last-minute decision prompted by a celestial vision, Constantine adopted Christian insignia for his army. He won the battle to claim the West and within twelve years was sole ruler of the entire Roman Empire. Questions concerning the legitimacy of his conversion and his reasons for becoming a "Christian" emperor have consumed scholars ever since.

Although Constantine himself remains an enigma, the impact of his rule on both the status and the attitude of the church is clearly observable. With a "Christian" in control, early Christian attitudes toward the state were being reevaluated. The mission of the church to draw the individual to "kingdom with God" changed swiftly to a new idea: conversion of the state. With a Christian state and a Christian leader, church leaders felt confident that God would be glorified and that Christ's kingdom would have dominion over the earth. In the Edict of Milan (313), Christianity became a legal religion (after being illegal for two and one-half centuries!). In the year 380, Christian emperor Theodosius I declared Christianity the "exclusive" religion of the Roman state. A "Christian" empire had been realized, but nearly at the cost of Christianity itself.

Certainly, leaders of the church were in part the victims of circumstances. Their succumbing to the lure of state favors and power, however, is instructive. Constantine showered Christian leaders with "presents." Imperial funds were sent to subsidize churches in the provinces. Clergy and churches were exempted from taxation, and secular power was given to the bishops to judge Christians. The Lateran palace in Rome was given to the Roman bishop and court ceremonies were instituted. The Christian church was legally allowed to have property willed to her and her holdings increased dramatically. It was becoming socially acceptable to be a Christian, and "converts" overwhelmed the fragile institution. In spite of her wealth, the church could not adequately teach them all. To accommodate to Roman "customs," the church adopted trappings of paganism (after rationalizing that it had properly "christianized" them).

One has to understand Roman religion to perceive clearly how easily Constantine and those emperors who succeeded him could accept a one-religion empire. As with many ancient societies, Rome had merged the religious with the secular. There was no political rule without religious rule, and religion was considered a "department" of the state. Sacrifices were conducted by state officials at state expense. The emperor was the *pontifex maximus*, the high priest of the Roman religious system, whose divine status was de-

clared in the provinces to encourage loyalty. He was to be worshipped in conjunction with the goddess of Rome. Sun worship was
very important in state worship, and the sun was considered an
important deity. December 25 was the annual birthday of the sun,
and pagan celebrations were plentiful. Sunday was the day of the
week devoted to the sun. After his Milvian Bridge triumph,
Constantine continued to lead this pagan system, nominating pagan priests and gaining the reputation as the restorer of old Roman
traditions. The Christian god could be accepted as long as the pagan traditions and duties of the royal office were not neglected.

Christianity would soon permeate the royal household as well as
the aristocracy in Rome. Constantius II (ruled 337-361),
Constantine's son and successor, tried to suppress paganism by law
and replace it with his brand of Christianity (he was an amateur
theologian who decided for himself what was "Christian" dogma).
Often neglecting to consult the bishops of the church, he attempted
to make himself the *pontifex maximus* of Christianity.

In spite of the intervention of the Christian Roman emperors,
the churches of the fourth century had time, money, and freedom
to pursue theological debate and to develop Christian doctrine.
This was the age of intense scrutiny of the biblical passages that
resulted in commentaries and canon lists of the books of the New
Testament. This was the age of Eusebius (c. 260-340), Bishop of
Caesarea, learned writer of *Church History* and provider of a canon
list approved by the Eastern churches. This was the age of
Athanasius of Alexandria (d. 373), a theologian and churchman who
was convinced totally that Jesus was very God and that the incarnation was the heart of Christianity. His Easter Letter of 367 designated the twenty-seven books of the New Testament for the first
time in a complete listing.

It was also the period of Augustine (354-430), Bishop of Hippo,
whose stunning conversion to Christianity is recorded in the classic
introspective memoir, *The Confessions*. North African in background and baptized by the famed Ambrose of Milan in 387,
Augustine would set the stage for the Western church in his explanations of the Trinity, his sense of the immediate presence of God,
his conviction that Christ dwelt within him, and his belief in original sin. Doctrinal controversy shaped his life: his six treatises

against the Donatists made him think through the sacraments and the political order, his fourteen treatises against Manichaeism to contemplate reality and evil and to reject Gnostic beliefs, and his fourteen treatises against Pelagianism to hone his views on sin, predestination, and free will. His outstanding work, *The City of God*, was written to defend Christianity against the charge that it was responsible for the successive setbacks the Roman Empire had experienced under the impact of mass invasions by barbarians from the north. In this vast book Augustine drew a sharp distinction between such earthly cities as Babylon and Rome on the one hand and, on the other hand, the City of God, serving as a standard of judgment and an ideal.

Antony (c. 356), the traditional founder of monasticism in the East, lived in the century of Constantine; John Chrysostom (c. 345-407), the "golden-tongued" Bishop of Constantinople in the East, delivered polished oratory to crowds of congregants during the period; and Jerome (340-420), a supporter of monasticism and one of the ablest scholars in the Western church, completed the Latin *Vulgate* translation of the Bible, traveling to Bethlehem to translate the Old Testament from the Hebrew Scriptures with the aid of Jewish friends. This was a time of dignity and pride for the Imperial church, but it also magnified the diverse theological beliefs that inundated the Christian community.

Early in the fourth century this diversity was exemplified by a local dispute that broke out among the churches of Alexandria, soon consuming the energies of the Christian empire. Alexander (d. 328), Bishop of Alexandria, preached that Jesus Christ was eternal, uncreated, always co-existing with God the Father. One of his most popular priests, Arius, took issue with him. Arius believed that the Son was a created being, created out of nothing, first-born of all creatures and the agent in creating the world. The Eastern church had been imbued with a more philosophical, speculative theology; and Monarchians, a unity-of-God movement, felt that an emphasis on Jesus Christ as very God threatened pure monotheism. The Western church through the work of Tertullian (c. 150-220), the "Father of Latin Theology," and others had reached practical unanimity on the unity of substance between the Son and the Father. Bishop Alexander called a synod in Alexandria in 320 that excommunicated Arius and castigated those who would support him. The controversy spread throughout the Eastern church, and Constantine finally called the Council of Nicea in 325 to restore unity.

What was evident was that even the creeds of the local churches of the East were unclear as to the Son's relationship with the Father. When Eusebius of Caesarea offered the creed of his church as a compromise, for example, it contained statements that Jesus was "firstborn of all creation," "begotten of the Father before all ages." After rejecting Arianism and unable to find New Testament passages that clearly delineated the sharing of substance, the Council of Nicea added key credal phrases with reference to Christ ("begotten, not made," "of one substance with the Father") and rejected the phrases "there was when he was not" and "he was made of things that were not." That Constantine forced the bishops to come to a unified position underscores the role of the Emperor in dictating church policy.

Some later emperors would lean toward the Arian position (Athanasius, who became the great defender of the Nicene position was banished five times from his bishopric in Alexandria, depending on the emperor's theological persuasion and social predilection). Constantine would be baptized just before his death by an *Arian* bishop. Through further ecumenical councils and amenable emperors, the traditional position on shared substance of the Father and the Son presented at Nicea and upheld by the Western church became a standard of orthodoxy in both the Roman Catholic and Orthodox churches.

During the Council of Constantinople I (381) under Emperor Theodosius I, the church and the empire once again returned to the traditional views held at the Council of Nicea. This council not only reaffirmed that Jesus Christ is divine, co-eternal with the Father, but also declared that Jesus is human in body, soul, and spirit. From this time forward, the disputes would center more on the relationship of the human to the divine in Christ, although Arian groups would be present in all centuries of church history (including today).

Theodosius I in 380 delivered an edict that Christianity was the "exclusive" religion of the Roman Empire and that any who would hold to any other form of worship would suffer punishment from the Roman state. In 395 he divided the empire between his two sons, and it was never governed as a single unit again. When the Roman Empire "fell," it did not have far to go. Split into the Eastern and Western empires, only the Western part succumbed to the barbarian onslaught. The Eastern Empire survived as the Byzantine Empire, continuing the relationship between church and state established in the fourth century.

From the capital of Constantinople, Byzantine emperors such as Justinian (ruled 527-565) continued to regard the church as a department of the state. The Justinian code (the codification of all Roman law, in final form 534) was an amalgam of Roman law and Christian faith, beginning with a section on the Trinity and including rules governing qualifications of Christian bishops. It also penalized religious dissenters. Justinian ordered the school of philosophy closed at Athens in 529 because he deemed it pagan, and the code stated that any Christian who lapsed into paganism would be beheaded. Penalties were ascribed to Jews, Samaritans, and nonorthodox Christians. Justinian even went so far as to declare that the Christian emperor had the right to settle disputes concerning Christian doctrine. The Eastern Orthodox church would develop in a milieu of oriental "Christian" despotism.

Nevertheless, the church had passed so quickly from "illegal religion" to "privileged patronage" during Constantine's reign, that Eastern Christianity never developed a policy on the emperor's position in Christendom. Although concepts of the "divine right" to rule permeated the theological structure, strong church leaders affected imperial policy, and strong emperors determined and enforced theological dogma. The mingling of politics and religion combines with the ever-changing human drama to caution one against simplistic generalization as to whether state was over church or church over state. To the oriental mind, the question would have been superfluous.

In contrast, the Bishop of Rome in the West gained added prestige, because the Western part of the Roman Empire had crumbled under the barbarian onslaught (476 C.E. is the traditional date given for the "fall" of the Roman Empire). This respected bishop was not under the thumb of an emperor and, fortunately, gained the respect and allegiance of converted barbarians. The Roman church provided continuity with the past and, for many centuries, was looked upon as the sole guardian of civilization and order in the West. It maintained an independence of moral and secular authority that eluded the Orthodox churches.

MAJOR TRADITIONS

While other books in this ecumenical, interreligious series survey in depth some of the major Christian traditions, and other books in the Suggested Reading provide additional detail, Christian traditions and individual beliefs are diverse and far-reaching. A brief summary of the three major traditions should give some indication of how quickly Christians debated and divided.

The Orthodox

The Eastern churches finally separated from the Western Roman Catholic Church in 1054, but rancor and division between them had escalated for many centuries. The Orthodox church believes that it has kept the traditional faith of the early Christian church. It has identified itself with the first seven ecumenical councils of the church, believing that the ancient Fathers expressed the faith of the early church in those gatherings of bishops. Although vibrant theologies and formulations have taken place in Orthodoxy since those councils (the seventh being Nicea II in 787), no new genuine ecumenical gathering can exist in the estimation of Orthodox bishops until the Roman bishop "admits his error" and returns to the fold. That is because the true church, the "one, holy, catholic, and apostolic" body of Christian believers, comprises those in fellowship with the historic patriarchates of Jerusalem, Antioch, Alexandria, Constantinople, and Rome (now Moscow, since Rome defected). Rome's place, however, is still reserved, and if it returns, it will assume once again a vital part of the pentarchy. Orthodoxy rejects Rome's claim that its pontiff is the unique successor to Peter, teaching that all traditionally faithful bishops are successors to Peter.

While the Orthodox church believes in transubstantiation, that is, that the bread and wine in the Eucharist become the literal body and blood of Jesus Christ, the asking of God to send his Holy Spirit to create the change (in contrast to the Roman Catholic priest's declaration) is the crucial part of the liturgy. While Orthodoxy holds to the same seven sacraments as Roman Catholicism, it is not as dogmatic on the number seven as is its Catholic counterpart. Chrismation (same as the Catholic confirmation) takes place immediately after baptism, and the Orthodox baptize by triple immersion, in the name of the Father, Son, and Holy Spirit. The beginning of spiritual life takes place in baptism and is repaired by penance.

When the Roman church added the word *filioque* ("and from the Son") to the Nicene Creed, a creed that stated that the Holy Spirit proceeds "from the Father," the Bishop of Constantinople declared the decision "heretical" in 867 C.E., affirming that the Spirit could only proceed "from the Father *through* [not *and from*] the Son." Again, the thought of tampering with such an important creed, council, and tradition from the church fathers disturbed the Eastern church then (and Orthodoxy today) as much as the theological argument that the Roman Catholics were in the *filioque* tampering with the integrity of the Trinity (by the presupposition of *two* originating principles within the Godhead).

The Orthodox tradition is more mystical and philosophical in that it emphasizes that finite humans can comprehend little of an infinite God. Spiritual experience linked to traditional beliefs of the ancient church are thus more efficacious than the rational, logical, scientific study of theology. Illumination and inner vision are intrinsically linked to ancient Christian tradition and liturgy in a symphony of "Orthodox spirituality."

With the rise of Islam, the Byzantine Empire gradually shrank in size. Orthodox missionaries moved north and west, converting the Slavic peoples and making great inroads into Russia. When Constantinople finally fell to the Ottoman Turks in 1453, becoming Istanbul, Russia had been Orthodox for four centuries. Russia thought of itself as the "Third Rome" (just as Constantinople had been the "Second Rome") and felt impelled by God to uphold the banner of Orthodoxy. This led to an inevitable friction between the Greek Orthodox and the Russian Orthodox churches.

Protestantism would gain an insight into the Eastern origins of the church from its contact with Orthodoxy. The Orthodox church also allows its clergy, up to the rank of bishop, to marry, and Protestantism, too, would oppose the Catholic emphasis on celibacy. The Orthodox churches also insist on being a family of self-governing churches held together by a bond of unity in the faith—a concept not totally foreign to Protestant ecclesiology. There are approximately 180 million Orthodox Christian believers in the world today, in diverse national settings and heritages, some struggling with political regimes as in the days of old.

Roman Catholics

The Roman Catholic church now approaches one billion adherents (counting every baptized infant, child, woman, and man, as the church does). Its heritage of tradition overshadows modern developments, serving as a "living" frame of reference. It has been said that Roman Catholics are at home in history, and their traditional theology holds that only through the Roman Catholic church have the message and work of Jesus Christ and the apostles been accurately represented. The Catholic church is viewed as a divine institution. Christ conferred primacy on Peter and on his successors, the Popes. Had not Christ given "the keys of the kingdom of heaven" to Peter in Matt. 16:19, explaining "whatever you bind on earth will be bound in heaven, and whatever you loose on earth will be loosed in heaven"? Had not Christ told the disciples in Luke 22:29: "And I confer on you a kingdom, just as my Father conferred one on me"? With the deep respect for both the church at Rome and the Bishop of Rome by the ancient world, and the independence and development of the papacy in the face of barbarian onslaught, the belief in such a continuum seems inevitable.

Traditionally, the Roman Catholic church has identified itself with the kingdom of God and believed that salvation of humankind was only through identification with its church. Vatican Council I (1869-1870) went so far as to declare that the Pope was immune from error, binding the whole church in the areas of faith and morals when he spoke *ex cathedra*, from the chair of Peter. Vatican Council II (1962-1965) was called by Pope John XXIII to bring the Roman Catholic church "up to date," the assembled Roman Catholic bishops from around the world agreeing that their church was the instrument by which God calls and moves the world *toward* the kingdom. Nevertheless, one of the most distinctive characteristics of Roman Catholic theology has been its ecclesiology, its doctrine of the church, and through the seven sacraments of the church an exchange between the divine and the human takes place.

During the Protestant reform movement in the sixteenth century, the Catholic reform movement in the final decrees of the Council of Trent (1545-1563) viewed the seven sacraments (Baptism, Confirmation, Penance, Orders, Matrimony, the Sacrament of the Ill or Dying, and the Eucharist) as causes of grace. This built upon the medieval scholastic theology that there was a "chain of grace" from God, through Christ, through Christ's merits, in the sacramental activity of the priest, and ultimately, to the Catholic congregant. Post-Vatican II sacramental theology increasingly has emphasized their function as "signs of faith," repudiating any type of natural magic in the outward phenomena.

The Eucharist, the central act of Roman Catholic worship, continues to be a partaking of the literal body and blood of Jesus Christ, the transubstantiation taking place as Jesus' words are uttered: "This is my body; this is my blood. . . . " To the modern Catholic, the Eucharist represents Christ's sacrificial death and signifies that Roman Catholics trust the meaning of their lives to Jesus Christ, in the midst of the turmoil of earthly troubles and universal tremors. As a believing community, the Roman Catholic church is convinced that God is faithful to the church and to God's people. Though today racked within by fundamentalist movements to the right and liberation movements to the left, this tradition is convinced that the mystery and majesty of God have been known throughout history and may be found in the structure, sacraments, and liturgy of the Roman Catholic church.

Protestants

All of the early Protestant reformers were Roman Catholics. They grew up within the confines of the mother church, some ordained as priests, as in the case of Martin Luther (1483-1546). Luther is viewed as *the* reformer of the sixteenth-century Protestant revolt, in spite of the many luminaries to which Protestant groups trace their heritage. Protestants have much more in common with the Western church than with the East. Protestant reformers were profoundly indebted to the formulations of Augustine. Concepts such as prayer, meditation, fasting, discipline, fellowship, and the importance of communion among Protestants are rooted in the history of the Roman Catholic church. Theological debates in Protestantism reach back into a rich heritage of theological and philosophical discussion of the Bible and tradition, which permeated the Western ecclesiastical milieu. Protestant liturgy and polity are so entrenched in Catholicism that Protestant groups that deviated from the traditional norm have from time to time accused their brethren of being "tainted with popery."

The seeds of the Protestant Reformation had long been sown and soon would break forth in revolt. As early as the end of the twelfth and the beginning of the thirteenth centuries, dissent and discontent were apparent in the Waldenses and Albigenses in northern Italy and southern France. The latter were named after the town of Albi, center of their efforts to return to a purer religion, and the former named for the founder of the movement, Peter Waldo (c. 1140-1218), a wealthy merchant who gave away all he had and assumed a life of poverty. The Waldenses started a trend toward reform in organized religion by insisting that all Christian believers had the right to preach.

Almost two centuries later the call for reform was heard in England from John Wycliffe (c. 1330-1384). He denounced taxation by the popes and questioned the power or the right of a priest to alter the wine and the bread of the communion service so as to make them the blood and the body of Christ; he translated the Bible into the English language, so that the common people might hear at first hand and read with their own eyes the words that "brought down the mighty from their seats and exalted those of low degree."

In Bohemia (now part of Czechoslovakia) Jan Hus (c. 1372-1415) followed in Wycliffe's train. Devoted to a practical reform of the papacy and clergy, Hus incited the people to rebel against the authority of the church, while not opposing the theology of the Eucharist or the doctrine of indulgences. In 1415 he was burned at the stake by order of the Council of Constance.

A great many other men sounded the cry for reform, but Martin Luther of Germany and John Calvin of France, later of Switzerland, remained as the two chief figures of the movement that further split Christendom. Each would have denied any accusation that he had created a fissure but would have stoutly maintained that he sought to restore to the church the purity and the integrity that the Roman Catholics had already destroyed. After all, the primary Latin meaning of the word *protestant* was "a bearer of witness on behalf of something."

The Reformation spread then to France and the Netherlands, to Scotland and to England and brought about profound changes in each of these lands as opposing points of view, Roman Catholic versus Protestant, cast them into turmoil. The most vexing problem on both sides was to fulfill the time-honored imperative: "rightly to divide the Word of truth."

In similar fashion the Protestant radicals, composed of Anabaptists on the one hand and Unitarians on another, nonconformists in one direction and Puritans, Congregationalists, Baptists, and Quakers in still other directions, all reflected something of the yearning for freedom in the faith of Protestantism. Before the Pilgrims set out from Leyden on the *Mayflower* to sail the Atlantic to the New World in 1620, their spiritual leader, John Robinson, had predicted: "God hath yet more truth to emerge from his Holy Word." Each of the new sects, or "denominations," attested to the creative power that bursts forth from a religion grounded upon a personal allegiance—in this case to Jesus Christ—and no longer restrained by either pontiffs or kings.

There were dangers in such absence of external authority; for many the blessings of freedom soon became a bane. The age-old battle between freedom and order was repeatedly and painfully re-enacted. Abuses and violence continued among Protestants as they had among Roman Catholics. Yet Protestantism affirms and testifies to certain principles and concepts that have strengthened the movement over the years, even as its diverse interpretations periodically breathe a fresh spirit of renewal into the movement. Traditional emphases on individual conscience and freedom of religion, grace and faith, the authority of the Bible, and the priesthood of all believers, may at times have been neglected; but they have impressively contributed to the dynamism of the Protestant faith. Today, nearly 300 million Protestants in 8200 denominations in 212 countries attempt to define their modern meaning in terms of their historical meaning.

CHRISTIANITY TODAY

With its 1.5 billion diverse adherents, Christianity is the largest religion in the world. What the Romans considered a tiny sect of Judaism has spread around the globe through its missionary enterprises, charitable institutions, hospitals, schools, colleges, publishing houses, and periodicals. The massive size of the Christian enterprise and the wide geographical spread of its many sects, denominations, and traditions make it impossible to generalize on what the "Christian church" is doing or what direction it is taking. For example, pentecostal and charismatic movements that grew so rapidly among Protestants have diffused worldwide—making inroads into Roman Catholic and Orthodox congregants. At the center of the Christian tradition is God in Jesus Christ illustrating divine power through the Christian's life on earth and promising a better life in heaven.

A greater awareness of Christianity's debt to Judaism, its mother faith, has now begun to prevail among Christians, as well as a sense of contrition for what Christians have done (sins of commission) in persecuting the Jewish people, and have not done (sins of omission) in failing to combat anti-Semitism—most notably in remaining silent during the annihilation of such a large percentage of European Jewry during the Nazi period. Here is a "new" dimension of Christian thinking and doing, coming full circle to Jesus' affirmation of the Torah to love God with all of one's heart and to love one's neighbor as oneself. Living his life on earth, Jesus Christ showed the Christian believer that this could be done. The Apostle Paul capsulized that life and that teaching by emphasizing:
"The greatest of these is love."

9

ISLAM

And Muhammad Is His Prophet

Islam, preceded by two other religions of monotheism, Judaism and Christianity, originated in the seventh century C.E. and is therefore the youngest among the universal religions of human-kind. Its chief spokesman and interpreter was Muhammad, known as the Prophet, or one who "speaks for God." He chose the name *Islam* because in the Arabic language it implied "submission to or achieving peace with Allah, the One God," a major motif in the new faith he taught and followed. Muslims are those who submit to God.

Muhammad, one of the most dramatic figures in history, was born, according to tradition, in 570 C.E. in Mecca, in the Arabian Peninsula (now Saudi Arabia). Orphaned six years after his birth, he was raised by his grandfather, Abd-al- Muttalib, and his uncle, Abu Talib. Both men were leaders of the Quraysh tribe, trustees of the religious sites in Mecca, which was already a holy city because of the huge Black Stone (what appears to be a meteorite) and the cube-shaped shrine of Kaaba built around it. An abundance of idols and the Sacred Well of Zamzam drew many Arab pilgrims to the area.

Aroused by the religious fervor of the region, Muhammad was at the same time detached from its intense excitement and frenetic observances. He became even more removed from these ancient customs and rites and critical of them when he began to travel along the Red Sea and to learn about other religions. During his youth and young manhood he accompanied caravans from Southern Arabia to the present-day borders of Jordan. The travels were of real significance for him, in part because he seems to have encountered Jewish scholars and Christian monks, whom he heard expound their faiths before crowds at fairs, and in part because, at the age of twenty-four, he became the business manager of a wealthy widow named Khadijah, at least fifteen years his senior. He married her when he was twenty-five, and they appear to have had a very happy marriage.

Khadijah helped him through many of his religious conflicts, and in the atmosphere of leisure and comfort her wealth provided, he was encouraged to meditate about his thoughts and visions. During Khadijah's lifetime Muhammad, who sanctioned polygyny, did not allow himself any other wife; only after her death did he marry again, including among his several wives a Jewish girl, a Coptic Christian, and the former wife of an adopted son. Islamic scholars point out that he did this out of compassion, because these women were destined for a harsh existence.

THE VISION

At the age of forty, Muhammad began to be seized by the conviction that he had been chosen by God to be the prophet of true religion among the Arabs. Islam teaches that Abraham's pure monotheistic faith had been taught to the Arabs but had been lost by the time of Muhammad. For days Muhammad remained alone in a cave on Mount Hira, a short distance north of the city of Mecca. Suddenly, his later recollections recorded, the archangel Gabriel came to him in a vision as a messenger of God and told him to preach. Variously translated as "Cry out" or "Recite" or "Read," the words "Speak out" came to Muhammad's consciousness: Speak out in the name of the Lord who created. . . . Speak out. . .for the Lord is the most Beneficent and has taught the use of the pen.

Here in 610 C.E. began the Koran (meaning "recitation" or "the Word") or Qur'an, a spelling that resembles more closely the correct pronunciation. From that time on, Muhammad's revelations were recorded and then collected in this sacred book of the Muslims, for them the Word of God, which in its authoritative Arabic version has a haunting charm, a lyric beauty, and rhythmic flow of almost hypnotic power.

Though reassured by his devoted Khadijah and by her cousin, a blind old man, who was quite possibly a Christian, Muhammad went through months of anguish and self-doubt. But recurrences of his visions and revelations convinced him that he was indeed "the Prophet of Allah, the One and Only God." The utterances Allah impelled him to reveal were, he believed, even more important than those given to Jews and Christians, for they were meant primarily for Arabians and were the final revelation from God.

THE HEGIRA

In Mecca, center of the Quraysh tribe and site of the Kaaba idol worship, Muhammad's hearers were not impressed. They resented his preachments against the 354 idols (one for every day of their lunar year) and his inveighing against the superstitious practices of the time. To their resentment they added resistance; around the year 620 his plight was at its worst. Moreover, his wife Khadijah had died; and shortly thereafter occurred the death of his uncle Abu Talib, a strong and loyal ally.

Yet within two years Muhammad's fortunes began to improve. He found friends and supporters in nearby Medina, the prosperous oasis then still known as Yathrib. Populated by Christians and Jews as well as idolatrous Arab tribes, Yathrib's majority of allies made Muhammad their newly chosen overlord. In 622, Muhammad swiftly migrated there from Mecca in the famous flight known thereafter as the *Hegira* (or *Hijra*, from the root word for "emigration"). Muslims date the first year of their calendar from this event.

Muhammad built the first mosque in Yathrib and established the customs of holding a weekly "Sabbath" service on Friday noon, facing Mecca for prayer, and giving alms to the poor. Now Yathrib officially became Medina—that is, *Madinat an nabi*, "the City of the Prophet," and it served as the base for Muhammad's campaign against Mecca. When the local Jewish community in Medina refused to accept Muhammad's interpretation, he and his allies drove them out of Medina, reportedly killing some and selling others into slavery. Disrupting the trade routes to Mecca, Muhammad finally conquered Mecca in January of 630. The Prophet of Allah had become the foremost man in Arabia.

Two years later—in 632—Muhammad was dead. By that time, however, his power had been firmly established. He had united the tribes of Arabia under a regime that acknowledged the Will of Allah as the one and only God, and he had established the brotherhood of all Muslims. For two years all Arabia was in revolt, but by 634 the opponents of Islam were gone; for all had been put to the sword. Reluctant converts, recalcitrant and refractory, were thought to be better dead, especially the two aspiring prophets, Tallah and Musaylimah. Muhammad's closest companion and disciple, Abu Bakr, became the Caliph—"successor"—as political and religious leader of Islam. During the two years of rule before his death Abu Bakr led the crusade as Islam moved swiftly to secure more converts and conquer additional territory.

SPREAD OF ISLAM

First in his lifetime and then after his death by the power of his followers, Muhammad had united the Bedouins, nomadic desert tribes in Arabia. They were now welded into an invincible military unit, which moved into the more prosperous lands of the Middle East and to the West across North Africa. Opposing tribal chieftains either came to terms with Muhammad's followers or perished as the Muslim armies moved into the Levant, conquered Damascus in 635, and then, a century later, took over Spain in the West. By this time the armies of Islam had built an empire from northern Spain to India, engulfing much of the Byzantine and Persian empires. The concept of *jihad* (holy war), with eternal rewards as well as temporal plunder in fighting for Allah, spurred the Muslims to victory. Some Jews, Samaritans, and nonorthodox Christians welcomed the Muslims, because the Byzantines had leveled such cruel punishments through their "Christian" constitution.

In the following centuries there developed an intellectual ferment that was to have far-reaching effect: the great philosophical achievement of Islam. The Central Asian-Arab Avicenna (980-

1037) and the Spanish-Arab Averroes (1126-1198) and other Muslim scholars helped to perpetuate Greek thought in Europe and preserve the works of such philosophers as Plato and Aristotle, as well as make substantial original contributions of their own. Without this Islamic contribution, the thinkers of the Middle Ages might have been deprived of the writings of the Greeks. Aided by a number of Jewish scholars, Muslim intellectuals sometimes translated the Greek works into Syriac, Aramaic, or Hebrew, and then rendered them into Arabic; in some instances neither the Greek nor the Arabic versions are extant and only the Hebrew renditions are available. The Western world is deeply indebted to those Muslim intellectuals and philosophers for this legacy.

In 762 the Caliph al-Mansur founded Baghdad in the area of modern Iraq. It soon became the center of the Muslim world. Under the leadership of the famed Caliph Harun al-Rashid (c. 763-809), this "abode of peace" at the "crossroads of the world," became known in both East and West as one of the greatest of cities. A patron of learning and the arts, he loved to travel in disguise to learn the thoughts and conditions of his people. As a commercial center and a scholars' abode, Baghdad experienced varying fortunes; despite a steady decline it remained the strong core of Islam until the Mongol invasion in the mid-thirteenth century. Then the Arab-dominated Muslim world lost both power and unity, giving way to the Ottoman Turks, the Persians, and the Mogul emperors of India.

The Ottoman Empire gradually took possession of the area, captured Constantinople in 1453 (it became Istanbul), and controlled the strategic Bosphorus. Under the impulse of Islam the Turks invaded Europe as far as the city of Vienna where, in the decisive battle of 1683, they were defeated. Had the Turks won, all of Europe might have become Muslim. The Turks then withdrew into their Middle Eastern empire, which remained comparatively intact until World War I. In 1917-18 the Allies, mostly under British leadership, destroyed its power and divided the Middle East into smaller states destined in the following years to become independent according to "self-determination" under the aegis of mandates granted by the League of Nations. The secular Republic of Turkey was organized in 1923, and Turkey became the first Muslim state to separate the powers of Islam and the state.

The power of Islam was not stayed, however, by the rise of the secular government in Turkey or by the decline of its authority in such lands as Egypt, for today an estimated 850 million people accept its tenets. Islam is a leading religion in Asia, including not only Pakistan and Malaya, but also parts of Indonesia, the Philippines, Iran, Afghanistan, and Iraq, the Arab states, and portions of the Soviet Union and India. Apart from its large numbers of followers in Asia, the Middle and Near East, and Africa, Islam has a sizable foothold in such European areas as Albania, parts of the Crimea, and the former state of Bosnia, now part of Yugoslavia.

BELIEFS AND TRADITIONS

What was and is this faith, which blazed with such fire, spread with such speed, conquered with remarkable success, and still elicits a loyalty of such fervor and fidelity? In contrast to the diverse, often bizarre religious practices of the Arabian world into which Muhammad was born 1400 years ago, an explicit, forthright set of beliefs and practices emerged in the first decade of this new religion. With singularly little change, these basic beliefs have remained constant in the modern period.

Muhammad's teachings were the basic foundation for his followers' beliefs. Explained with simplicity, though not always with clarity, they were outlined in the Koran (Qur'an). In accordance with the meaning of Islam—namely, the way of submission—the Muslim was expected to believe without question or argument. By so doing one guaranteed salvation in this world and in the next.

God

God the Creator and Judge came first, last, and always. Allah is all-powerful and all-knowing, all-merciful and all-compassionate. He was—and is—supreme. He is One.

Muslims differ from Christians in their concept of God because trinitarian formulas of "God the Father, God the Son, and God the Holy Ghost" are, in the Muslim's view, polytheistic. A Muslim calls God "Father," and thinks of God as "love," attributes that overshadow those of might and majesty. Allah, say the prayers of Muslims and the verses of the Koran, is both the Lord of the Day of Judgment and the maker of the universe, the ruler of the world and the lord of all life. God's creative presence is viewed in nature by those who are wise. A Muslim will repeat the ninety-nine beautiful names of God and, when asked if there is a one hundredth, answers, "Only the camel knows it and that secret gives the camel his dignity." When a Muslim counts the beads of his prayer necklace, he tells them one by one on three sets of 33 each; he construes the total of 99 to comprise the human lexicon of names for the Almighty. In its uncompromising monotheism, with its simple enthusiastic love of God and submission to God's will, Islam finds its strength.

Angels

Muslims believe that Allah created angels from light. Through angels is revealed Allah's will, as in the instance of the leading angel, Gabriel, who, as an emissary of God's revelations, brought the Koran to Muhammad. Similarly Azrael is the Angel of Death, and Asrafel will blow the trumpet when the Judgment Day is at hand. Allah, as portrayed by Muhammad, occupies a throne of eminence in the seventh heaven; he has about Him a host of angels who wait upon Him and do His bidding. Among these are Nakir and Munkar, entrusted with the task of subjecting every dead person in his grave to an examination. Preparations for these tests have been made by the recording angels, two of whom are assigned to each person and charged with listing deeds, both good and evil. All the angels, born of light, are capable of reason and decision. In this world of spirits there are *genii* or *jinn* (*jinnis*). Often they are of good intentions; but for the most part they are troublemakers and evildoers.

Satan, a variation on *Shaytan* of the Zoroastrians and called *Iblis* (in contracted form from the word *Diabolos*), the fallen angel, became the Devil when evicted from the Garden of Eden; he had failed to obey God's command to show respect to Adam, God's first prophet. His task is to tempt people and to impede the purposes of Allah. The Devil is doomed to failure, however, for not only does Allah know all, but he wills everything, including the most nefarious machinations and devious maneuvers of the Devil. Ultimately the victory belongs to Allah, not the Devil.

Koran (Qur'an)

As Muhammad is the messenger of Allah and angels are the doers of His will, so the Koran is His means of revelation. Revealed and written in Arabic, the Koran is God's revelation to Muhammad, and to this day remains the authoritative word of God. According to tradition, the Prophet's followers memorized all of the revelations and wrote them down. The established orthodox text was collected during the rule of Caliph Othman (644-656). Its 114 *suras* (chapters of main divisions) were organized by length, rather than chronologically, longest sura to the shortest. The longest contains 287 verses, the shortest sura, the last, contains three verses.

Originally written without vowel indicators, even variant Arabic readings are authoritative, the object of devotion for all Muslims everywhere. The Koran cancels and replaces all previous revelations, among which Muslims number the respected but rejected Torah and Christian Testaments. Allah explained through the Koran that the original revelations by the prophets to Jews and Christians were accurate, but were corrupted as texts and were misconstrued by followers of these religions. Only the Koran is genuine and holy; it is Truth absolute. Though apparently derived in considerable part from both Jewish and Christian sources, the Koran is to the Muslim the unalloyed Word of Allah.

The *Hadith*, sayings of the Prophet or teachings conveyed by Muhammad to his followers in his own words, also have been collected. Muslims point out that when one compares these human words to the lofty divine revelation of the Koran there is no comparison. Nevertheless, the Hadith became the primary source of Islamic law and tradition. Because the Islamic state is to be a theocracy (God-rule), divine law is needed in all areas of life. Through many generations of Islamic scholars the *Shari-ah* ("the way" or "a constitution") was developed, a complex code of law affecting all aspects of life, yet firmly grounded in the divine revelation of the Koran. It is the backbone of the *Ummah*, the community of Muslims worldwide, and is interpreted by scholars called *Ulema*.

Prophets

Muslims believe that Allah has revealed Himself in a progressive succession through His prophets. The first of all prophets was Adam, the father of humankind, who was created from mud; the last was Muhammad. The prophets held to the truth, were sincere and faithful, conveyed their messages fully without fail, and were highly intelligent. They are portrayed as the best of men. Although people may not heed such prophets, God forgives them and continues to send new prophets of whom Muhammad is the culmination, the final revelation. If humankind fails to heed the revelation of Islam, the end of the world is soon at hand.

God has sent six great prophets who are given the honorific title *Ulu-l-'azm* (people of determination and perseverance), each of whom has a special relationship to Allah: Adam, "The Father of Man"; Noah, "The Preacher"; Abraham, "The Chosen"; Moses, "The Friend of God"; Jesus, "The Spirit of God"; and Muhammad, "The Apostle." Each of the six is thus related in specially chosen titles to Allah; but Muhammad himself is given the center of the stage and scores of honoring names describe him: "Peace of the World"; "Seal of the Prophets"; "Glory of the Ages," etc.

Although many prophets have come from Allah to the human race (a Muslim is not required to determine their number), twenty-five are mentioned in the Koran. Nineteen of these are from the Torah: Adam, Noah, Enoch, Abraham, Ishmael, Isaac, Jacob, David, Solomon, Job, Joseph, Moses, Aaron, Elijah, Elisha, Jonah, Lot, Ezekiel, and Zechariah. John (the Baptist) and Jesus are listed from the Gospels.

Tradition holds that Muhammad existed before the world was created and not only was he without sin (despite his prayers that his own sins be forgiven); but he could perform all manner of miracles. To the Muslim, however, Muhammad is not a mediator or Anointed One as the messiah is in Christian tradition. Being called a "Mohammedan" is an offense to a Muslim. Rather, Muhammad was the Appointed One, chosen by Allah to wash away heresies, ban false teachings, and repair and complete former revelations. Doctrines stemming from former prophets were revived and purified, completed and perfected. Muhammad was indeed Allah's final revelation, the "seal of the prophets."

Predestination and Afterlife

Central to a Muslim's faith is the belief that every occurrence in life, whether good or bad, has been determined long in advance by the immutable order of Allah. Many a Muslim thinker contends that Allah is the author of evil, too, and that humans have no free will. Muslims therefore tend to face life with an innate fatalism; and when burdened by poverty, scourged by illness, oppressed by tyrannies, or hobbled by circumstance, they often accept their "fate."

The submission concept in the Muslim's faith stems from a belief in the judgment day. Of this signal and awesome event Muhammad preached often, and on it he centered much of his teaching. Both in the Koran and in later writings of Islam, the last day, the day of reckoning, is the focal point. Muslims are warned that their wrongdoings will be balanced against good and meritorious deeds. The descriptive warnings of the last judgment tell of the soul's crossing a vast bridge that is as sharp as a sword, as thin as a hair, and as long as a caravan's journey. The evildoer is destined to fall into hell-fire beneath, but the good and righteous will quickly move into a very sensuous paradise. The Koran and subsequent Islamic writings describe in picturesque, persuasive detail the celestial gardens of the afterlife, which will abound with succulent fruits, rivers of rare wine, and lovely women, all in stark contrast to the fiery torments of hell.

FIVE PILLARS

To avoid the fires of hell and be eligible for paradise, the Muslim accepts five religious duties, the Pillars of Islam, which are inescapable obligations: (1) repetition of his witness to Allah; (2) recital of specific prayers; (3) observance of Ramadan, the lunar month of fasting; (4) distribution of alms; and (5) the pilgrimage to Mecca.

Shahadah, the Declaration of Faith

The good Muslim repeats the basic creed of Islam ("There is no God but Allah, and Muhammad is His Prophet") all life long, from infancy till death. The dying Muslim seeks to utter these as final words before expiring; and the bereaved whisper them into the ears after the Muslim has drawn the last breath. These eleven words, taken from two separate parts of the Koran, have elicited a single-mindedness and determination rarely paralleled in any other religion. Although the believer recites them by rote several times daily and a hundred thousandfold more times during a long life, the true Muslim is expected to have at least one sublime occasion during a lifetime when the believer utters them with complete understanding and wholehearted acceptance.

Salat, Prayer

Five times a day the Muslim prays—at the rising of the sun, at noonday, in the middle of the afternoon, as twilight merges into night, and after dark. No matter where one is, whether on desert sands or country road or city street, at workbench or study table, the Muslim washes the hands, face, and feet with water (if water is unavailable, then with "clean" sand), faces Mecca, spreads a prayer rug, removes the shoes, and covers the head. Then begin the prayers according to a specified, traditional formula: first in a standing position holding extended hands beside the head, then crouching to a semiseated position on one's haunches, finally prostrating oneself so that knees and toes are on the floor or ground while hands are spread and head is touching a prayer stone, made of baked earth from one of the holy places of Islam and carried everywhere.

Although the five prayers to be said are different in various parts of the Islamic world, they are all repeated in response to the call for prayer cried out from the minaret by a *muezzin.* (Many mosques today use tapes or records amplified through loudspeakers.) Vast numbers of Muslims move to the mosque on Friday noonday as though drawn by a magnet to hear the stated prayers, ponder readings from the Koran, listen to a sermon, and join in uttering the words of their most familiar prayer, the opening lines of the Koran:

In the name of Allah, the merciful, the compassionate.
Praise be to Allah, the Lord of the Worlds,

The merciful, the compassionate, the ruler of the
    Judgment Day!
Thee we serve and Thee we ask for aid,
Guide us in the right path,
The path of those to whom Thou art gracious;
Not of those with whom Thou art wroth;
Nor of those who err.

Only men are required to pray at the mosque on Friday noons, but
if household duties permit, women are encouraged to attend
as well.

Siyam, Fasting

Ramadan, the ninth month of the Muslim lunar year, requires
fasting during the day and permits food only in the hours from dusk
till dawn. It commemorates the period during which Muhammad
received his first prophetic call. The familiar method of determining when the fast should begin is to discern at dawn the difference
between a white thread and a black thread when held at arm's
length; and to terminate the fast at the end of the day one should no
longer be able to distinguish the white thread from the black. A
cannon is fired to denote the end of the day and the beginning of
drinking and eating. There is no set date for Ramadan because the
lunar year is shorter than the solar year, and its ninth month therefore occurs in different seasons through the years. The sick and
physically weak are exempted from the fast, but it is to be a time of
spiritual reflection, self-discipline, identification with the poor, and
obedience to God.

Zakat, Poor-due

Muhammad not only encouraged gifts of alms to the poor but
practiced almsgiving himself. His followers consider the giving of
legal alms as meritorious and distribute them at the end of a journey, the birth of a child, a marriage within the family circle, the
occurrence of good fortune, or the observance of a holiday. In countries where Islam is the state religion, the state collects offerings of
cattle, grain, fruit, etc. Alms are also assessed on savings. The
almsgiving, usually known as *Zakat* or *Zakah,* is for the most part a

voluntary matter now; but social pressure, plus a conviction of its basic merit, is a potent force for continuance of the custom. Centuries ago, when Islam was young, almsgiving to beggars and slaves, strangers and debtors, institutions and charities, was considered "a loan to Allah." The proceeds were assigned to various deserving individuals and institutions by the religious officials who had placed these gifts in a general purse. In our time these donations, still widely expected and still generously given, are, however, voluntary in nature. The Koran and Hadith also stress other acts of charity to strengthen ties of love and brotherhood among Muslims.

Hajj, Pilgrimage

The last Pillar of Islam, and one of the most prestigious, is the pilgrimage to Mecca expected of every Muslim who is financially and physically able to make the journey. At least once in a Muslim's life this *hajj* (pilgrimage) must be taken—but only during the first to twelfth days of the last month in the lunar year, when, during the seventh to the tenth days, ceremonies in Mecca are observed. Some privileged Muslims, such as the King of Saudi Arabia and his retinue of wives and concubines and relatives, visit Mecca each year, but most consider themselves blessed of Allah if they can make a single pilgrimage during a lifetime.

In Mecca a pilgrim meets fellow Muslims from all over the world, reaffirming Muhammad's preachments about the brotherhood of believers in Allah. The pilgrim practices the usual ablutions, puts on the required two seamless tunics, accepts neither food nor drink during the daytime, refrains from sexual relations, and promises not to harm any living thing.

First the pilgrim goes to the Great Mosque and in its court kisses the Black Stone of the Kaaba, the small stone structure containing this sacred meteorite, which is thought to have been given to Abraham by the angel Gabriel. With thousands of others the pilgrim encircles the Kaaba seven times, three times rapidly and four slowly. The Muslim repeats the special prayers, visits the Place of Abraham, and then goes to the Sacred Well to drink the waters. One may now consider oneself greatly blessed.

Next comes the so-called Lesser Pilgrimage: seven times the pilgrim runs between the hills of Safa and Marwa, recalling Hagar in search of water for her infant child Ishmael. Then the pilgrim pays a visit to Arafat, embarking on the Greater Pilgrimage by foot and devoting hours to meditation on the open plain. By nightfall the Muslim has returned with the shouting, clamoring multitudes of pilgrims to Minah, where pilgrims throw the traditional seven pebbles at three pillars of masonry, called the "First," the "Middle Pillar," and the "Great Devil." The pilgrim offers the animal sacrifice on the feast day, shares it with rich and poor alike, and, with the other pilgrims, visits Muhammad's grave in Medina. After three days of feasting, the weary traveler comes back to Mecca and once again encircles the Kaaba. From now on this pilgrim may carry a special title, *Haj*; for the rest of days this Muslim is distinguished for having made the pilgrimage to Mecca.

THE SUFIS

Such a religion, simple and direct though it may be, has always been in danger, because of its formal nature and rigid requirements, of jeopardizing its spiritual assets. Political, economic, and military success tempted Muslims of the medieval period to worldliness and arrogance. To offset such dangers the Sufi movements arose, in part in the eighth century but most powerfully at the end of the eleventh and beginning of the twelfth centuries. Led by the great theologian of Persia, "the Saint Augustine of Islam," Abu-Hamid Muhammad al-Ghazzali (1058-1111), this mystical movement expressed in lyric fashion the union of the soul with God.

The name *Sufi* derived from "wool-wearers," the name given to these men who wore robes made of rough coarse wool. Sufism was not merely literary in nature but also philosophical, for it emphasized both asceticism and quietism. Some Sufis were virtually atheists as they absorbed ideas and influences from Buddhism; a number, in fact, advocated self-destruction. Their beliefs in extreme forms were pantheistic and opposed a basic concept of Islam: a centered idea of one God. The Sufis were intent, however, on achieving union with God in this present life rather than in an afterlife. By the twelfth century the Sufis had their own monasticism, requiring celibacy and meditational discipline. They created rituals of their own, leaning more toward the influencing faiths of Hinduism, Buddhism, Neo-Platonism, and Christianity than toward Islam.

From the Sufis came the dervishes, who might be called the monks of Islam. Many different orders of dervishes sprang up, some of them resembling the friars of Christianity but lacking their vows and avoiding the organization of monasteries. Their mystical beliefs found expression in the practices of whirling and howling by dervishes who considered themselves to be special beneficiaries of the favor of Allah. One of the most gifted of the Persian poets of Islam was Jalal-ud-Din Rumi of the thirteenth century, a dervish who wrote of the ineffable oneness a mystic feels with God.

SECTS

While there is an essential unity to Islam, Muslims are divided into two major sects: Shi'ites and Sunnites. Behind their differences—and linking them with the Sufis and other minor sects—is, first of all, the Koran; then the Five Pillars of Islam, most notably the five-times-a-day prayers and the Mecca pilgrimage; and, lastly, the festivals in the Muslim year, such as the end of the feast of Ramadan, the Great Feast near the close of the pilgrimage to Mecca, the New Year's festival, the Prophet's birthday, and the Prophet's night journey.

The difference between Shi'ites and Sunnites exposes, however, a basic cleavage that occurred in Islam's first centuries in disputes about the caliphate and successors to Muhammad. Political leadership was tenuous in the early years following Abu Bakr. Although he died a natural death, all early successors to Abu Bakr were murdered, and there was disagreement over the succession process. Muhammad's cousin and son-in-law, Ali, finally was made the fourth caliph in 656, but he struggled for power with Muawiya, leader of a stronghold in Syria. Ali's legitimacy to be caliph was questioned, and he was killed in 661. The caliphate passed to the Umayyid dynasty and successors unrelated by blood to Muhammad. The followers of Ali, however, claimed that the successors to Muhammad should be relatives and part of Muhammad's lineage. They came to be known as Shia Ali ("the party of Ali") and finally as Shi'ites. Ali's youngest son, Husain, challenged the Umayyid Caliphate in 680, but he was defeated in battle and executed. The Shi'ites lived on, having the descendants of Muhammad serve as *imams* ("leaders") for many years. In 1502, the Shi'ites became the established religious hierarchy in Persia (modern Iran). They compose approximately 14 percent of all Muslims in the world and have a strong presence in Iraq, as well as a minority status in India, the Middle East, and East Africa.

The Sunnites, usually described as being the more traditional, defend the *Sunna* (the traditional practice of Muhammad)—the basic fundamentals of historic Islamic practice. Variations in reporting these fundamental traditions, however, have caused bitter clashes among Sunni Muslims throughout history. Sunnites generally reject the Shi'ite assertions about Muhammad and Ali, particularly the assertions that Ali had powers akin to Muhammad's. Sunnites also question the Shi'ite assertion that a *mahdi* ("guided one") will come in the future, a figure that will lead the world into justice. Bitter persecution afflicted the Shi'ites; often the group went underground and resorted to violent resistance. Yet nationalism, political dissension, economic squabbles, and tribal group loyalty appear to divide the people of Islam more today than the division into Sunnites and Shi'ites (although religious radicalism persists to this very day). This is indicative of the power of the Islamic creed to meliorate and unify the most diverse of adherents.

BAHAIS

From Persia emerged the Bahai movement, which is to be traced mostly to the Shi'ites but is now cut off from Islam and considers itself wholly independent. More than a century ago, Mirza ali Muhammad named himself Bab-ud-Din, "Gate of the Faith," and gathered many followers who called themselves Babis after him. Like a John the Baptist, he called his work a preparation for one greater than himself. Executed in 1850 for his heretical statements—primarily that his own writings exceeded the Koran in beauty and authority—and because he demanded vast reforms, he was replaced by one of his followers, who adopted the name Baha'u'llah ("the glory of God"). Some years later Baha'u'llah proclaimed himself the religious figure of whom Bab-ud-Din had fore-told. His followers, now known as Bahais, followed him into exile after his flight from Baghdad; and the Turks then put him in the Acre prison for life. From there, however, his writings went into many lands and exerted wide influence because of their aim of in-clusiveness, a kind of liberal universalism, and the call to all reli-gions to unite. Each religion, the Bahais maintain, has some truth, and all religious leaders witness to truth, especially to the brother-hood of all beneath One God. Today Bahais have a magnificent gold-domed temple and archives in their Persian gardens on the slopes of Mount Carmel in Haifa, Israel; and in Wilmette, Illinois, on the shore of Lake Michigan, they have built an impressive and lovely temple.

THE MESSAGE OF THE PROPHET

Islam as a whole undergoes vast changes in these times, some of them reviving the faith, others reforming its practices. As in many of the living faiths today, fundamentalist movements are crying to be heard, in the midst of liberalizing and westernizing influences. They capture the daily news, affecting global politics and religious perceptions. This will certainly continue, for in traditional Islam there is no distinction between religion and state, between sacred and secular. Because Islam was born as a religious and political rev-olution, Muslim revolutionaries today look to Muhammad and his exploits as their pattern; the Koran, Hadith, and Shari-ah as their guide. Their disillusionment with imported remedies in law, gov-ernment, and culture from the West has led them to attempt to abrogate all the modernized legal codes and social norms. In to-day's world we are witnessing Islam's soul-searching as it confronts modernity and evaluates contemporary systems.

To many outsiders, Islam seems remote and detached, obsolete and irrelevant. But to millions of Muslims, the message of the Prophet is as relevant and dynamic as if it had been uttered this very year. The basic tenets of Islam have been and are being re-stated in the light of modern ideas and practices, especially by the growing Muslim communities in Western countries. Satellite com-munication and computer technology have brought East and West into constant interaction in spite of their differences. Cultures at times clash, but they also reconsider one another in the process. Certainly Islam's growth in numbers and influence demands a knowledge of its precepts and an honest appraisal of its concerns.

At the heart of Islam is the tie to the Judeo-Christian tradition. As Jews and Christians echo the familiar verse of Psalm 111, "The fear of the Lord is the beginning of wisdom," so Muslims repeat the lines from the Koran:

"The head of wisdom is the fear of Allah."

10

CONCLUSION

We Are the Heirs

As hundreds of generations passed by, many religions came into being and grew to power. Sometimes they shrank into obscurity, then loomed large again on the stage of history. Some of them have never been practiced again. Through the centuries, as countless millions of men and women lived and died, none of them—kings and chieftains, rich or poor—lasted so long in the memories of humankind or influenced minds and hearts so profoundly as enlightened teachers such as Mahavira, Gautama Buddha, Confucius, Lao Tsu, Socrates and Plato and Aristotle, the Hebrew prophets and Jesus, and Muhammad. They led in the quest for meaning, the search for balance within and assurance without.

In contrast, our study of world religions has revealed that religion could also be used by demagogues and god-kings, oppressors and charlatans, the greedy and the egocentric. Religion could be used to enslave and to inflict pain to maim and to kill, to terrify and to impoverish. The study of humankind's quest for faith and meaning teaches us the value of faith but also alerts us to the dangers of a lack of balance in any religious enterprise—the menace of those who have lost sight of the love, justice, mercy, compassion, kindness, humility of spirit, respect for human life, and dignity taught by the major religious traditions in our modern world.

QUASI-RELIGIONS

In spite of the lessons to be learned from the past, our modern world of automobiles and space shuttles, credit cards and money machines, scientific technology and medical research, has presented new challenges to the quest for meaning and the value of faith.

The established religions of our time have faced a challenge and a threat in the rise of what have been popularly called "quasi-religions." These substitute religions surged to new levels of strength in the late nineteenth century and in the twentieth century. One striking example was—and is—nationalism, always a focal point of human allegiance. For other individuals a devotion to science or democracy, humanity or art became a substitute for formal religion, an alternative to the traditional religions of previous centuries.

The belief in the all-sufficient efficacy of technology is one such "faith," and for many millions of people throughout the world the natural sciences are the sole answer to the age-old question, "What is truth?" To these devotees of technology, the physical sciences contain all there is to know of reality. Life and the universe are explained on that mechanical level. The abstract sciences and the concrete sciences (physical and biological) are for them both the source of explanation and the object of devotion.

Some individuals of these modern times, finding it impossible to believe in a God and preferring to place their belief solely in humanity and its highest attributes, look to the scientific method for their explanation of life; they consider this to be enough, an adequate means by which they can create for themselves satisfactory lives. There are millions, perhaps even tens of millions, who consider Protagoras' dictum, "Man is the measure of all things," to be sufficient explanation of their faith. To them the beliefs and practices of the religions surveyed in this book may be of interest but, so far as they are concerned, not of any real use in the world of today. They consider religion outmoded and look upon conventional religious terms and ideas as expressions of wishful thinking devoid of any reality and validity. To these "humanists" a devotion to social values, to purely human objectives, is enough of a religion. The critic of humanism, on the other hand, contends that such a faith is illusory, for science, ethics, and social values are not enough. A transcendent criterion is lacking and there are no passionate convictions. It is another "quasi-faith."

Most striking of the substitutes for religion have been the doctrines of communism and fascism. In each there were and are many of the characteristics of religious movements through the centuries. Each had a yearning for the messianic and so were susceptible to the manipulation of such messiah-like dictators as Lenin, Stalin, Hitler, and Mussolini. Each movement had a reverence for its basic writings and elevated them into "sacred" scriptures (*Das Kapital, Mein Kampf*, etc.). Commissars and *Gauleiters*, no matter how cruel—and indeed perhaps because of their cruelty—formed virtually a priesthood. The rulers and the ruled observed sacred days such as May Day or *Partei Tag* and revered the word of the Leader—the utterances of Red China's Mao Tse-tung, for instance. The political philosophy of the Marxists (called "dialectical materialism") explained the inexorable, inevitable process of the evolution of humankind from the primitive communism of earliest times to the perfect society of the future when "the dictatorship of the proletariat" would cause the state to "wither away." It anticipated a kind of "kingdom of God" with justice and equality in a classless society ("from each according to his abilities, to each according to his needs"). The theory is appealing, but in its political and economic manifestations, whether in the Soviet Union and its satellite neighbors or in China, Marxism in practice has often substituted greater injustices for the injustice it claimed to be supplanting.

Karl Marx said that religion was "the opiate of the people"; yet the faith of his followers echoes the Hebrew prophets and the early Christians in damning the acquisitive urge and inveighing against accumulation of property. Communists may deny that their beliefs constitute a religion, but denial does not gainsay the fact that their political credo is for them the "center of history." They claim to be atheists but nevertheless accord to certain ideals and objectives the kind of worship and devotion usually reserved for religion. For many moderns communism seems to provide a substitute for a more formal, long-established faith; and Marxism affords a seductive philosophy in giving contemporary history both dynamism and drama. The dynamic and dramatic appear in abundance in annals of the past and are strikingly evident in the history of religions, yet they often seem lacking in religious institutions and movements today. Communism offers an attractive substitute for people too unsophisticated to perceive that its present-day outlook and achievements are misleading.

From the ferment of ideas and events in the last half of the nineteenth century and the opening decades of the twentieth century, the movement known as existentialism emerged, part of it a nontheistic, avowedly atheistic school of thought (from Friedrich Nietzsche to Jean-Paul Sartre) and the other part theistic (from Søren Kierkegaard to Paul Tillich). Although existentialism became something of a fad, it has played a very important role in creating much that is valid and significant in the literature, art, and thought since World War II.

Primarily concerned with the mood of the modern world and with the terrible choices thrust upon all who share human existence today, existentialism puts forth the demand that one be human, not mechanized, not enamored of "progress" and its spurious objectives, not dehumanized or compartmentalized, not unrelated to the truth humans try to grasp, not entranced by objectivity or ensnared by rationalism.

The attractiveness of existentialism, the sheer magnetism of its ideas, the power of the movement—whether with an idea of God or without one—derive from its stress on the centrality of human beings, their aloneness, their reluctant but inevitable commitments, their inescapable freedom as contrasted to their limitations and finiteness. Existentialism, whether anti-theistic or theistic, lays emphasis on sincerity and inwardness, on intuition and involvement. It seeks to protect the individual and creativity in the midst of a society that generates pressures that inhibit and destroy.

From the existentialist movement came much of the impetus for the "death of God" movement. When Nietzsche declared almost a century ago that "God is dead," he was sounding a dirge and celebrating funeral rites at the grave of a conception of God that he had learned in childhood and rejected in adulthood. He was anticipating the "death" of many lesser gods, both false and real, which two World Wars and the threat of a third were ultimately to destroy.

This kind of "deicide," this wholesale destruction of inadequate, specious ideas of God, is wholesome, decidedly salutary.

It is this same drive for honesty in thought, for authenticity in commitment, for integrity of the harassed individual that had given such momentum to the "death of God" movement of the 1960s. If to Nietzsche the God of the *bourgeoisie* in Germany in particular and Europe in general was dead, so for many in our day the God of the middle class of America in particular and of Western civilization in general is dead, dead beyond recall. In ancient days the most meaningful message in religion came from those who first destroyed the idols. No less in our day do people try to discern truth in the midst of illusion and idolatry, such as the vain hope that science will be our salvation, or a belief in the false god of "progress." Only by rejecting such delusions can humankind move on toward a more valid, more vital, meaningful concept of God.

The unmistakable impact of existentialism and the all-pervasive influence of the "death of God" movement have an added importance in the light of the spiritual problems in the last decade of the twentieth century, when decisions more difficult than humans had ever imagined face this generation. All living religions today—not just Judaism and Christianity, as many Westerners mistakenly think—are affected by problems of unprecedented complexity.

The vast changes in the world in recent decades and the extraordinary difficulties faced by 4 billion people, with their myriad tongues and cultures, have caused some people to plead for a single world religion as a necessary condition for the establishment of peace and equity among nations. There will, however, never be a world religion in which all people and cultures share a core of basic beliefs, simple as such a solution seems and attractive though it may appear. There are, nevertheless, points of contact between the major world religions today—points of contact with our global neighbor.

GOLDEN RULES

The affinity among religions is not apparent in creeds and ceremonies, but it is clearly reflected in the area of ethics—that is, on the level of one's relationship to one's neighbor. Note the striking parallels among all faiths with their versions of the Golden Rule.

The Hindu reads in the *Mahabharata:* "This is the true rule of life and the sum of duty: do nothing unto others which might cause you pain if it were done to you. Guard and do by the things of others as they do by their own."

The Buddhist finds counsel in the *Udana-Varga:* "Do not hurt others in any way that you would find hurtful. Seek for others the happiness you desire for yourself."

Confucius, as reported in the *Analects*, asked: "Is there one word of counsel by which one should act throughout his whole life?" He then answered: "It is indeed loving-kindness; do not unto others what you would not have them do unto you."

The Taoists, the *T'ai Shang Kan Ying P'ien* relates, must consider their neighbor's gain as their own and their neighbor's loss as their own.

Judaism has cherished Hillel's response, recorded in the Talmud: "What is hateful to you, do not to your fellowman. That is the entire Torah; all the rest is Commentary."

The Zoroastrian follows the words of the *Dadistan-i-dinik:* "Only that nature can be considered good which refuses to do unto another what is not good for itself. Do as you would be done by."

The Christian recalls the words of Jesus in his Sermon on the Mount of the Gospel According to Matthew: "All things whatsoever ye would that men should do to you, do ye even so to them."

The Muslim knows from the *Sunna* that no one is a believer until he desires for his brother that which he desires for himself: "Let none of you treat his brother in a way he himself would not like to be treated."

The inhabitants of Greece and the Hellenic world taught: "Do not that to a neighbor which you shall take ill from him."

The Stoic of ancient Rome held that "the law imprinted on the hearts of all men is to love the members of society as themselves."

Each of these ten renditions of the Golden Rule points to a concern for others, a consideration for another's needs. Two of these faiths, Judaism and Christianity, have suggested that to make the Golden Rule of real significance one should "do unto others *more* than one expects from another." One should give of one's self in love and in service without expectation of reward. That noble goal is seldom achieved, however, for among most people, no matter what their faith, self-interest is too often the rule rather than the exception.

In sharp distinction to these parallels of the Golden Rule are the startling, often harsh contrasts among religions that no sentimental appeals to common humanity can resolve. Virtually every faith vies with every other for supremacy. Some religions lay claim to being the sole revelation of God and to being, therefore, superior to all other faiths. Religion often becomes a divisive factor, leading to hatred and conflict instead of mutuality and harmony.

INTER-RELIGIOUS ENCOUNTER

While we are scholars who have worked to break down the walls that separate communities of faith, we firmly believe that there are fences of tradition and fences of religious teaching that are necessary for living, that are necessary for our particular peoplehood, that characterize our individuality and human spirit. Inter-religious encounter is an encounter between *religious* persons, each having a particular religious experience, a particular insight into the mysteries of God, ultimate reality, and the world about them. Some fences are necessary for the life of faith.

Nevertheless, gates—gates in those fences—are imperative for movement, for interaction, for access. We *do not* have to break down all of the fences of tradition that separate the religions of the world, but we *do* need to build more gates!

No faith can be indifferent to its own claims, but it can learn to understand, respect, and even appreciate the viewpoints of others. Inter-religious encounter should not direct itself to the goal of impersonal, diluting, melting pot unity. Rather, its practical aim should be understanding, mutual enrichment, and initial consideration of unique traditions. Through inter-religious encounter one should not be required to surrender one's basic theological convictions; but one will learn that our religious heritages have some things in common, and mutual global concerns compel us to work together.

When we learn about other faiths, it helps us to define our own identity. We actually learn much about our own beliefs and practices when we consider the faith claims of another tradition.

Through a broadened awareness of the faith and values of others, we are able to move from *self*-reference to *cross*-reference.

A new spirit animates religious dialogue today. Philosophers and priests, teachers and writers, monks and savants are in closer touch with one another, sharing their insights with colleagues of other lands and faiths. The novel aspect of this interaction of faiths in our day is that the interchange is so fruitful. At no time in previous centuries have religious faiths been so near each other as radio, television, instant worldwide communication by satellite, and the wide circulation of printed matter have brought them. Most of the inhabitants of the world are more aware of other lands and other faiths than their parents and grandparents were; inevitably they are also becoming aware that other religions have parallels to their own, as well as valued differences in both belief and practice. Such an awareness will grow, not diminish, in coming years; and in this respect the hundreds of millions who adhere to the major religions cannot help but be influenced toward a greater mutual respect.

Socrates left a priceless legacy in his declaration: "I am neither Athenian nor Greek but a citizen of the world." He presaged the world of twenty-five centuries later in which, whether we are Americans or Europeans, Asians or Africans, we are the heirs to the spiritual treasures of every age and every land.

SUGGESTED READING

General Texts

Carmody, Denise Lardner. *Women and World Religions.* Nashville: Abingdon, 1979.

Carmody, Denise Lardner, and John Tully Carmody. *Ways to the Center: An Introduction to World Religions.* 2nd ed. Belmont, Calif.: Wadsworth Publishing Company, 1984.

Eliade, Mircea. *From Primitives to Zen: A Thematic Sourcebook in the History of Religions.* New York: Harper & Row, 1978.

Ellwood, Robert S., Jr. *Many Peoples, Many Faiths: An Introduction to the Religious Life of Humankind.* Englewood Cliffs, N.J.: Prentice-Hall Inc., 1987.

Hopfe, Lewis M. *Religions of the World.* 4th ed. New York: Macmillan Publishing Company, 1987.

Müller, F. Max. *The Sacred Books of the East Series.* 50 vol. Oxford, England: Clarendon Press, 1895.

Smart, Ninian, and Richard D. Hecht, eds. *Sacred Texts of the World: A Universal Anthology.* New York: Crossroad, 1982.

Ancient Traditions

Coles, Robert. *Children of Crisis.* Vol. 4: *Eskimos, Chicanos, Indians.* Boston: Little, Brown, 1977.

Gill, Sam D. *Beyond the "Primitive": The Religions of Nonliterate Peoples.* Englewood Cliffs, N.J.: Prentice-Hall, 1982.

Grant, Michael. *History of Rome.* New York: Charles Scribner's, 1978.

Harner, Michael. *The Way of the Shaman.* New York: Bantam, 1982.

Pritchard, James B. *Ancient Near East: An Anthology of Texts and Pictures,* vol. 1. Princeton, N.J.: Princeton University Press, 1958;

A New Anthology of Texts and Pictures, vol. 2. Princeton, N.J.: Princeton University Press, 1973.

Ray, Benjamin C. *African Religions: Symbol, Ritual, and Community*. Englewood Cliffs, N.J.: Prentice-Hall, 1976.

Ruffle, John. *The Egyptians*. Ithaca, N.Y.: Cornell University Press, 1977.

Hinduism

Hawley, John Stratton, ed. *The Divine Consort*. Berkeley: University of California Press, 1982.

Hindu Tradition. Religion in Human Culture series. Niles, Ill.: Argus Communications, 1978.

Hopkins, Thomas J. *The Hindu Religious Tradition*. Encino, Calif.: Dickenson Publishing Company, 1971.

Johar, Surinder Singh. *The Sikh Gurus and Their Shrines*. Delhi, India: Vivek Publishing Company, 1976.

O'Flaherty, Wendy P., trans. *Hindu Myths: A Sourcebook*. Baltimore: Penguin Books, 1975.

Organ, Troy Wilson. *Hinduism: Its Historical Development*. Hauppauge, N.Y.: Barron's Educational Series, 1974.

Jainism

Gopalan, S. *Outlines of Jainism*. New York: Halsted Press, 1973.

Jaini, Padmanabh S. *The Jaina Path of Purification*. Berkeley, Calif.: University of California Press, 1979.

Buddhism

Bharati, Agehananda. *The Tantric Tradition*. Garden City, N.Y.: Doubleday, 1970.

Buddhist Tradition. Religion in Human Culture series. Niles, Ill.: Argus Communications, 1978.

De Bary, William T., ed. *The Buddhist Tradition: In India, China, and Japan*. New York: Vintage Books, 1972.

Dumoulin, Heinrich. *Buddhism in the Modern World*. New York: Macmillan Publishing Company, Inc., 1976.

Henry, Patrick G., and Donald K. Swearer. *For the Sake of the World: The Spirit of Buddhist and Christian Monasticism*. Minneapolis: Fortress Press, 1989.

Hoover, Thomas. *Zen Culture*. New York: Random House, 1977.

Rinpoche, Tulku Thondup. *Buddhist Civilization in Tibet*. New York & London: Routledge & Kegan Paul, 1987.

Robinson, Richard H., and Willard L. Johnson. *The Buddhist Religion*. 3rd ed. Belmont, Calif.: Wadsworth Publishing Company, 1982.

Confucianism and Taoism

Bahm, Archie J. *The Heart of Confucius*. New York: Harper & Row, 1971.

Bush, Richard C. *Religion in China*. Niles, Ill.: Argus, 1977.

Merton, Thomas. *The Way of Chuang Tzu*. New York: New Directions, 1969.

Rawson, Philip, and Lazsio Legeza. *Tao: The Eastern Philosophy of Time and Change*. New York: Avon Books, 1973.

Saso, Michael R. *The Teachings of the Taoist Master Chuang*. New Haven, Conn.: Yale University Press, 1977.

Thompson, Laurence G. *The Chinese Religion: An Introduction*. 3rd ed. Belmont, Calif.: Wadsworth Publishing Company, 1979.

Shinto

Hardacre, Helen. *Kurozumikyo and the New Religions of Japan*. Princeton, N.J.: Princeton University Press, 1986.

Kageyama, Haruki. *The Arts of Shinto*. New York & Tokyo: John Weatherhill, 1973.

Leggett, Trevor. *Zen and the Ways*. London & Boston: Routledge & Kegan Paul Ltd., 1978.

Ono, Sokyo. *Shinto: The Kami Way*. Rutland, Vt.: Charles E. Tuttle, 1967.

Judaism

Eban, Abba. *Heritage: Civilization and the Jews*. New York: Summit, 1984.

Eckstein, Yechiel. *What Christians Should Know about Jews and Judaism*. Waco, Texas: Word, 1984.

Flannery, Edward H. *The Anguish of the Jews: Twenty-Three Centuries of Antisemitism*. Revised and Updated. New York: Paulist Press, 1985.

Greenstein, Howard R. *Judaism: An Eternal Covenant*. Philadelphia: Fortress Press, 1983.

Holtz, Barry W., ed. *Back to the Sources: Reading the Classic Jewish Texts*. New York: Summit, 1984.

Neusner, Jacob. *Foundations of Judaism.* Philadelphia: Fortress Press, 1989.

Rausch, David A. *Building Bridges: Understanding Jews and Judaism.* Chicago: Moody Press, 1988.

Christianity

Frend, W.H.C. *The Rise of Christianity.* Philadelphia: Fortress Press, 1984.

Gonzalez, Justo L. *The Story of Christianity.* 2 vols. San Francisco: Harper & Row, 1984.

Happel, Stephen, and David Tracy. *A Catholic Vision.* Philadelphia: Fortress Press, 1984.

Meeks, Wayne A. *The First Urban Christians: The Social World of the Apostle Paul.* New Haven, Conn.: Yale University Press, 1983.

Rausch, David A., and Carl Hermann Voss. *Protestantism—Its Modern Meaning.* Philadelphia: Fortress Press, 1987.

Schmemann, Alexander. *The Historical Road of Eastern Orthodoxy.* Crestwood, N.Y.: St. Vladimir's Seminary Press, 1977.

Ware, Timothy. *The Orthodox Church.* Baltimore: Penguin Books, 1963.

Islam

Abdalati, Hammudah. *Islam in Focus.* Indianapolis, Ind.: American Trust Publications, 1975.

Cragg, Kenneth. *The House of Islam.* 2nd ed. Encino, Calif.: Dickenson, 1975.

Denny, Frederick M. *An Introduction to Islam.* New York: Macmillan, 1985.

Donohue, John J., and John L. Esposito, eds. *Islam in Transition.* New York: Oxford University Press, 1982.

Esslemont, J. E. *Bahaullah and the New Era.* Wilmette, Ill.: Baha'i Books, 1976.

Islamic Tradition. Religion in Human Culture series. Niles, Ill.: Argus, 1978.

Maududi, Abdul Ala. *The Meaning of the Qur'an.* Lahore, West Pakistan: Islamic Publications Ltd., 1971.

Rauf, Muhammad Abdul. *Islam Creed and Worship.* Washington, D.C.: The Islamic Center, 1974.

Trimingham, J. Spencer. *The Sufi Orders in Islam.* London & New York: Oxford University Press, 1971.

INDEX